TREMAINE BAKER
GARETH EVERS &
RICHARD BROCK

TARGETED TEACHING

STRATEGIES FOR SECONDARY TEACHING

$SAGE | Learning Matters

Learning Matters
An imprint of SAGE Publications Ltd
1 Oliver's Yard
55 City Road
London EC1Y 1SP

SAGE Publications Inc.
2455 Teller Road
Thousand Oaks, California 91320

SAGE Publications India Pvt Ltd
B 1/I 1 Mohan Cooperative Industrial Area
Mathura Road
New Delhi 110 044

SAGE Asia-Pacific Pte Ltd
3 Church Street
#10-04 Samsung Hub
Singapore 049483

Editor: Amy Thornton
Production editor: Chris Marke
Marketing manager: Dilhara Attygalle
Cover design: Wendy Scott
Typeset by: C&M Digitals (P) Ltd, Chennai, India
Printed and bound by
CPI Group (UK) Ltd, Croydon, CR0 4YY

Library of Congress Number: 2016954955

British Library Cataloguing in Publication Data

A catalogue record for this book is available from the
British Library

ISBN 978-1-4739-7303-9 (pbk)
ISBN 978-1-4739-7302-2

At SAGE we take sustainability seriously. Most of our products are printed in the UK using FSC papers and boards.
When we print overseas we ensure sustainable papers are used as measured by the PREPS grading system.
We undertake an annual audit to monitor our sustainability.

Contents

About the Authors

Tremaine Baker

Tremaine Baker is a Senior Lecturer (Practice) in Secondary Teacher Education at Middlesex University, having previously been a teacher in a mainstream secondary school since September 2002. During this time he led a series of whole-school initiatives and supported the development of educational excellence across Essex in his roles as an Advanced Skills Teacher and a Specialist Leader of Education. Central to this was the provision of teacher training and the development of a blended learning approach to initial teacher education which utilised online training modules and open-source learning platforms, alongside the traditional and personal support given to support School Direct trainees on employment-based teacher training routes.

Gareth Evers

Gareth Evers is Programme Leader for Secondary English PGCE and Professional Studies at Middlesex University. Prior to this, he was a Professional Coordinating Mentor at a North London comprehensive school. As a teacher, he has taught English for twelve years. These diverse and challenging experiences have provided him with the knowledge of what makes an effective mentor and, more importantly for the future of the profession, how trainees can develop into effective classroom teachers.

Richard Brock

Richard Brock is a Ph.D. student at the University of Cambridge. Prior to this, he taught secondary physics at a comprehensive school in Essex. He acted as an associate tutor on a school-based M.Ed. course certified by Middlesex University. He has published research on the role of insight and intuition in science education and on students' perceptions of the boundaries between the science and RE classrooms.

Introduction

Learning to teach is a lot like learning to drive

When you sit in a car ready to drive for the very first time, it can be overwhelming if you have had no previous experience. Sure, you've been in cars before, but you may not have been solely responsible for manoeuvring the vehicle, or steering it in the right direction. What to do first? Check the mirrors? But which one first? Seatbelt on? Waggle the gearstick manically like you've seen people do but you're not sure why? And you haven't even started the engine yet.

When you actually begin to drive, you've got other things to consider and lots of things to think about at the same time. Don't give it too much gas. Get the biting point. Check your mirrors. Make sure you don't take out that grandma trying to navigate the pelican crossing with her heavy shopping. Turn the wheel. Don't forget to breathe. Failing to do any one of these things could result in a potential disaster.

It's the same with teaching. When you're planning a lesson for the first time, it can be overwhelming if you've had no previous experience. Sure, you've experienced school before and seen what lessons look like, but you haven't been solely responsible for manoeuvring the learning of a lesson, or steering students in the right direction to ensure they make progress. When you are actually in the classroom, you've got a whole host of other things to consider. Show visible confidence and presence. Challenge the able. Support the weaker students. Make sure you keep your eyes out for the boy in the corner who is about to throw a paper aeroplane across the room. Use a mini-plenary effectively to gauge pupil progress. Don't forget to breathe. Failing to do any one of these things could result in a potential disaster.

Like learning to drive, this possibly overwhelming sensation is – you'll be pleased to know –ephemeral; it will become easier even though it seems daunting in those initial months or even before you start. How can you be expected to do all that in one lesson? How can you consider so many different things at the same time? It's not possible. Consider the driving metaphor (if you've never learnt to drive, consider anything that you have learnt from scratch since you left school). You may have had no clue before you started, but I can guarantee that if you have driven for a length of time, there are occasions when you drive home and forget that you have driven at all. How did you negotiate the roundabout at the top of your road? How did you operate the pedals? How did you know to slow down for the speed camera on the A34? You have become so confident in your driving that you are totally unaware of the actions which you need to drive.

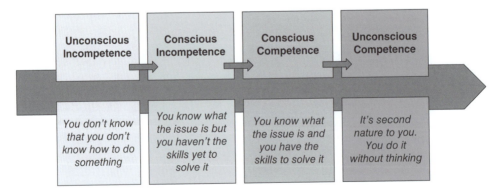

Figure 0.1 Unconscious competence

Driving home on autopilot is a form of *unconscious competence*, in which you drive well without any thought of what you are doing (see Figure 0.1, above). Ultimately, you should aim to become *unconsciously competent* in your teaching. At the moment of reading this book, your teaching might be *unconsciously incompetent*. You don't know what the problem is and you wouldn't know how to fix it even if you did. Embrace your vulnerability – this is a necessary stage in starting to learn a new skill. You are going to learn so much, so quickly. Whether you begin your training year having just completed your degree or are switching from a different profession, the challenges are the same. You are coming from something you have doubtlessly become *unconsciously competent* and successful at to a profession in which you find yourself *unconsciously incompetent* and facing a range of new challenges. It might feel as if you are starting from the bottom again. Embrace your vulnerability. That is probably why you became a teacher in the first place: you wanted to think; to be challenged; not to ghost through your job. The beauty of teaching – and it is a thing of beauty – is that no two days are the same. You can't coast. There will always be a new challenge. Embrace this as part of the best job in the world.

Therefore, you need to appreciate that you can't be Lewis Hamilton straight away. It will take time before you can plan a lesson which is pupil-centred, purposeful and caters for all learners regardless of their background with your eyes closed. It will take time before you can deliver a lesson in which you implicitly differentiate the questions you ask without a second thought. It will take time before you can sense the boy folding his paper aeroplane before he launches it across the room. Be patient – don't worry, it was like this for all of us at the start of our teaching practice.

This book is designed to give you a range of strategies, grounded in research and honed by experienced classroom practitioners, to help you on your learning journey to becoming an *unconsciously competent* teacher. At the moment, you might not know how to ensure there is a formal start to your lesson, how to tier learning outcomes, or how to ensure students with Special Educational Needs are supported. By using the targets and the strategies in this book you should move towards becoming a *consciously competent* teacher: more able to diagnose areas for development in your own teaching practice and more knowledgeable of strategies to resolve these issues. Over time, you will find that the process of diagnosing a problem and identifying strategies to overcome it will become second nature – you will have become an *unconsciously competent* teacher.

You will be surprised how quickly you move through the gears.

Marginal gains

Keeping to the subject of road transportation, Dave Brailsford's idea of the aggregation of 'marginal gains' (Slater, 2012) which contributed to the success of British cycling, argues that if you improve every area by just 1 per cent, then those small gains would add up to remarkable improvement. For example, encouraging riders to regularly use anti-bacterial hand gel minimised the risk of illness, which might have affected their performance. The same principle of 'marginal gains' can be applied to education. Like cycling, teaching has hundreds of different variables, which affect performance. Though each of the strategies in this book might only make a marginal difference in your classroom, the cumulative effect could be remarkable.

Quick click

Zoe Elder outlines how the theory of Marginal Learning Gains can be applied to education in the website below.

https://marginallearninggains.com/

How the book works

Everyone has an opinion on teaching. Everyone has an idea about how it should be done – about what works and what doesn't. Even the authors of this book don't agree on every point, but that difference of opinion should be warmly embraced, not eschewed. As a trainee teacher, this lack of certainty can be difficult to deal with, especially as you sometimes want that definitive solution – that absolute answer – that strategy to solve the problem once and for all. You might be told by one school that you have to use group work as this engenders best learning; another school might say that group work is futile and leads to disengagement. You might firmly believe in the idea of mixed ability classrooms; yet there are many teachers who believe that this approach harms the progress of the highly able. Some think that classrooms should be set up in rows with all students facing the front; others favour a café-style layout in which pupils are gathered around tables.

How can we reach a definitive answer? Put simply, we can't – not definitively. Teaching is a complex and messy process as learners are individual and human. It is unlikely there are any magic bullets in teaching. Few strategies will work in all classrooms, for all learners, at all times.

This book was devised, through working with many trainees and experienced teachers, to help you find your own path through this uncertainty. Rather than feeling frustrated by the multitude of opinions from experienced colleagues, or by contradictory research findings, we believe that there are diverse ways of dealing with the same timeless issues that arise in your training year. Some of the strategies will work; some will not.

We recommend an attitude of open-minded, reflective experimentation: when you try a strategy and it doesn't work, diagnose the possible reasons. Did you deploy the strategy effectively? Does it need to be adapted or be given more time for students to become familiar with the new approach? Might it work with a different class?

There are rarely definitive answers in teaching. Experienced teachers develop a wealth of strategies that they are constantly adapting and trying out with their classes, some of which succeed while others 'fail'. But failing is okay too – even experienced teachers find a 'tried and tested' strategy fails sometimes, and are constantly trying out and adapting strategies to suit the needs of their students. It's what we do after the failure that makes the difference: CS Lewis is purported to have said that failure is needed on the road to achievement. And he sold millions of books about magical wardrobes and talking lions, for crying out loud.

Teaching involves a continuous process of trying out ideas, getting feedback from your practice and adapting approaches.

Features of the book

This book is structured around common targets, which you may well be set during your teacher training year, and are grouped under the following sections.

- Lesson planning.

- Behaviour management.

- Pace.

- Teaching and modelling.

- Questioning.

- Assessment.

- Feedback.

- Differentiation.

The book's format is designed to mirror that of a dialogue between mentor and trainee. In your training year, regardless of the type of training course you are taking, you will be set targets; these form the basis of *Targeted Teaching*. For example, you might be set the target: 'Use questions to encourage higher-order thinking in students'. If you turn to the appropriate chapter, you will find a range of different strategies you can try out.

The targets have been compiled through consideration of the most typical targets set for trainee teachers. The book is designed for you to read as a starting point into your year but works just as effectively if you dip in and out where you need assistance and guidance. It does not replace your relationship with your mentor but should enhance and supplement it.

Each chapter begins with links to the current Teachers' Standards which were rolled out in 2012. Ultimately, these are what your teaching practice will be measured against and, although teaching is far more than a series of individual 'Standards', it is important that you keep them in mind across your training year.

Following the Teachers' Standards box, you will find an introduction to the pedagogy and research which underpins the theme of the chapter. This section summarises the major theoretical ideas, research and common practical issues facing trainees in developing their practice in this area. Although we recommend that you read this section first, to give you a deeper understanding, we recognise that your training year is very busy and you might choose to skip straight to the targets and strategies section. A thorough understanding of not just 'what works' but also 'why it works' will make you a better teacher.

Within this section there are a number of helpful features to further support you, including the following.

- Quick Click boxes giving you links to online resources or reading.

- Key Learning point boxes summarising the essential ideas for you to consider in developing your practice.

- Scenario boxes providing an illustration of a concept in a classroom situation.

Each chapter then has a range of targets, which are divided into 'quick wins' and 'slow burners'.

Quick wins

The quick wins are strategies you can apply with minimal effort and minimal extra preparation. They are there to be attempted, honed and reflected on. Some might work perfectly; others might need adapting to suit your individual circumstances; and a few might not apply at all. Although you might think particular strategies are ridiculously obvious, we all forget at times to do basic things: smile; praise rather than reprimand; move around the classroom. As highlighted above, Brailsford's 'aggregation of marginal gains' can have a large impact. A tweak here and a tweak there could make a significant difference.

Consider this simple scenario: the start of a trainee teacher's first ever lesson. He or she is standing behind the desk, arms folded, eyebrows knitted together in worry as the students trickle in. There is nothing on the board. As there is no direction, students come in, look at the teacher and sit where they want. The teacher doesn't say anything and the volume steadily increases as they wait for all the chairs to be filled. When they eventually try to establish quiet, there is too much noise and their voice is drowned out.

In this scenario – which I have observed on countless occasions in the early parts of teacher training – there are quick wins to help. You will want to adopt and cultivate your own style – of course you will – but there are some strategies you will need to employ before you can find your own distinct voice in the classroom.

Consider: what quick wins would you suggest to the trainee teacher?

Here are two quick wins that could help in this scenario.

	Quick win 1	Quick win 2
Strategy	Be by the door as students enter (see Chapter 2).	Smile genuinely at students (see Chapter 2).
Rationale	You can greet and deal with any behavioural issues at the door. As the class swells, move into the classroom so students know who is in charge. This also gives you presence.	Make it clear to the students that you want to be there and you care.

Just implementing these two quick wins will improve the start of the lesson. It won't miraculously make it perfect, but the lesson should be more positive and purposeful. It will ensure that students know that the trainee is in charge, that they mean business and that they want to be there. Once the trainee has successfully begun to apply these strategies, they could add other quick wins to further improve the start of the lesson (see Quick wins 3 and 4).

These four simple strategies that anyone can utilise will make a massive difference to the creation of a calm classroom environment primed for learning. In the Pace, Lesson planning and Behaviour management chapters, there are additional strategies for honing the start of your lessons.

	Quick win 3	Quick win 4
Strategy	Make sure students 'get in and get on' with a do now task (see Chapter 1).	*Give timed reminders* about when the lesson is formally going to start in an authoritative and confident manner, reminding the students of the expectations (see Chapter 3).
Rationale	This gives the students an instantaneous focus and will avoid the dreaded dead time. A sharp start to the lesson will leave no time for students to become distracted.	This gives the students a realistic time frame to get out their equipment, to prepare for the lesson and to begin an extended starter. It also amplifies your presence and the expectations of the students.

Slow burners

Slow burners are strategies that are conceptually more challenging and might take longer to embed in your teaching practice.

Let's take the example of developing a rapport with the students you teach. There is no quick win for rapport and there are different schools of thought about how best to build these relations. A minority of teachers might not even think it's important that you create a rapport with students as long as students get the work done and get good grades. We believe that developing a rapport with students is a natural feature of an effective classroom as well as featuring prominently within Teachers' Standards 1 and 7.

Personal relationships can be changeable. They can end suddenly and without any palpable warning. They can be volatile. They can be one-sided. They require effort to maintain. In the classroom, relationships can have a powerful impact on learning. They can make students want to do things they wouldn't ordinarily want to do. They can give them motivation. They can give them purpose.

Therefore, consider how you can maintain good relationships with your pupils. They are fundamentally born out of trust, which does not occur overnight or simply through quick wins. Trust grows when you believe in someone. That takes time. It takes understanding and empathy. It takes patience. There's no simple or quick win to building these relationships.

When we talk about *building* rapport, the clue is in the progressive verb tense – *building* – implying the process is ongoing and takes time. There are many things that help you to develop a rapport with your classes: nurture, understanding, encouragement, resilience, self-awareness. None are quick wins, and you will need to keep working on them throughout your training year and across your whole teaching career. As with all relationships, you cannot expect your rapport with classes to be constant over time. At times you might experience a breaking down of relationships – accidentally or purposefully. They are complex things and can ebb and flow.

In my NQT year, I was given a Year 10 group with some of the more troublesome characters in the school (I wasn't told this explicitly; it was the knowing smile and the shake of the head as they read out the class list). Ross was the most difficult boy in school. Nathan couldn't sit still and drew Y fronts on other students' pencil cases in Tippex. Vera swore like Joe Pesci from *Goodfellas*.

But in the first month it had gone well. I heard only positives about me from the class. I was a good teacher. I wasn't like other teachers. I was 'all right'. I had built an instant rapport with some of the more difficult students. Easy. Target achieved. Standards satisfied with room to spare. They said this class was hard.

Of course, the honeymoon ended as quickly as it had begun. On Thursdays, I had the Year 10s after lunch. I didn't lock the door over lunch as I trusted them to look after the room – after all, it was raining outside and I didn't want them to get wet. Lunch finished and I went to my classroom. Before I even crossed the threshold into the room, I could hear the sounds of debauchery, mayhem and furious energy. On arrival, I was greeted with chairs stacked fifteen high, teetering with uncertainty, pressed against the window; the blackboard had been repeatedly stapled (yes, I started teaching in the world of chalk). My Macbeth wall display had been viciously ripped down – Lady Macbeth's face was contorted with anguish, her nose, penis enhanced; my desk was covered in litter, including a half-eaten sandwich which smelt like a rotting carcass. I went ballistic, demanding to know why they had done this to *me*. They openly laughed at me. They refused to tidy up blaming others for the mess. Two girls, who clearly had no part in any of it, cleaned it up. For that lesson, I sat at my desk, confused, upset and disgusted at their actions. How could they do this to *me*? They said I was 'all right'.

Roll on to the end of Year 11. It was our final lesson together and a lot had happened in the time between the devastation of my classroom and the end of the students' GCSEs. I had learnt the hard way: relationships are not decided in the first months of knowing students. I had learnt that they only thought I was an 'all right' teacher because I had let them get away with things that others had not. After that lesson, I went back to the core principles of my training year: clear expectations, rules and routines; firm boundaries; and lessons that considered all learners. I also locked my classroom door over lunch even if it was blowing a monsoon outside.

On our final day together, they had clubbed together and bought me five goldfish as they knew the only pet I had ever had was a stone with fake eyes on it called Roadrunner. In my oversized leaving card, some apologised for their behaviour at the start. Some said, 'You're all right'. This time I didn't mind, because I knew they meant it for the right reasons. They thought I was 'all right' because I worked hard on ensuring that learning was paramount and, ultimately, even though they said I had changed in the remainder of year 10, they realised why. The validation that, even though I felt I was being cruel, or strict, or not the teacher I wanted to be, the boundaries I had set up benefited the students and thus led to effective relationships. We had enjoyed our time together in Year 11 as it was framed in an environment conducive to learning.

This story illustrates that some aspects of teaching can require an extended period of work and this is what the slow burner section is designed to support you with. They are about imbedding strategies into your teaching practice so you can become a better teacher and an *unconsciously competent* teacher.

Finally, you will find a further reading section at the end of each chapter. We have purposefully recommended books which give you both further practical guidance as well as insight into theory and pedagogy.

Final thought

You may begin your training year with the assumption that there is a single correct approach to teaching that will work with all classes and at all times. However, you will soon find that there is no single best approach. This book presents a more pragmatic model of teaching. Expert teachers are not effective because they stick to a 'magic formula' but because they possess a range of strategies that can be applied in different contexts, and understand both 'what works' and 'why it works'. You should be prepared to experiment with the suggested strategies, to adapt them and to continually reflect on their impact in your classroom.

For the strategies in this book, be open-minded. Be ready to give them a go. Be ready to discuss them with a colleague or your mentor. But be ready to question them. Fortunately or unfortunately, despite what some might suggest, there are very few absolutes in teaching – which is both an exciting and a terrifying prospect. However, we hope this book will help you navigate the difficult and rewarding path that is learning to teach.

References

Slater, M (2012) *Olympics cycling: Marginal gains underpin Team GB dominance*. Retrieved from: **www.bbc.co.uk/sport/olympics/19174302**

1
Lesson Planning

Teachers' Standard 4 – Plan and teach well-structured lessons

This section aims to support you in establishing strategies to plan lessons that encourage learning. However, the overarching nature of planning does mean that targets can overlap with other standards, such as those relevant to the following.

- Planning for progress (TS2).
- Developing your subject knowledge for teaching (TS3).
- Planning for differentiation (TS5), assessment (TS6), or behaviour (TS7).

Introduction

Planning a lesson is rather like planning a journey, which starts by establishing where you want to go. Invariably, there will be a number of routes you could take to arrive at your final destination and there are a range of different modes of transport to help you get there. Sometimes you might take the shortest route, at other times you might choose a more leisurely route allowing your passengers to soak up the countryside. Alternatively, you might take a detour to a place of significant interest, allowing the lesson to drift into unplanned but fascinating territory. Essentially, your aim is to always ensure that passengers arrive at their final destination but, given the range of options available, you need to know your passengers very well and work on planning the best route for them, so you don't lose any on the way.

Seen in this way, planning is fundamental to all aspects of teaching, learning and assessment. This might seem daunting, and will no doubt raise a number of questions: How will I know what to teach my students? What are the best activities to support learning? How can I ensure that all students are suitably challenged and supported in the lesson? However, lesson planning is the means by which you will be able to address these questions, and thereby allay any fears you may have. Time spent on planning (though quite substantial in the first few months of your training year) is time well spent in the long term. Proper classroom planning will act as a tool to help you organise yourself, plan for the unexpected and ensure that your lessons are clearly focused on learning.

You will find that planning is a constantly evolving process and, although it is cognitively challenging, by beginning in a very structured way you will soon develop the confidence and ability to deal with the more complex aspects of lesson planning. The quick wins below will help you on this journey and support you in beginning to develop your practice, and the slow burners will allow you to become an expert practitioner who uses planning to support all aspect of teaching, learning and assessment in your classroom.

Targets

What targets does this chapter cover?

- Plan lessons with a clear learning aim.
- Order and structure your planned learning activities more effectively, to ensure there is a clear sequence and flow to the lesson.
- Widen the range of teaching strategies and resources you use to support learners.
- Expand the range of approaches you use for starters and plenaries to ensure lessons begin and end effectively.
- Ensure you appropriately plan the timing of activities to maximise learning.
- Plan appropriate homework activities, which are designed to sustain learners' progress and consolidate their learning.
- Develop your longer-term planning to ensure progress and learning over time.

Issues in planning

I will always remember my earliest attempts at planning. As a trainee teacher I would spend hours trying to think through the lesson plan and searching for exciting and engaging activities. I would look on enviously at my fellow trainees, who all seemed to have a creative knack (which I lacked) for designing exciting lessons with ease. For me, the important shift was to move my focus away from myself as the teacher and on to the students and their learning; I began to think of 'they' rather than 'I' when planning lessons. Indeed, since then, I have observed countless lessons where the teacher puts on a great show; where there is a lively buzz around the classroom; where students are busy completing worksheets or undertaking tasks which the trainee has clearly spent hours designing. Yet, on reflection, I am unable to pinpoint the concrete learning which has taken place as a result of the lesson. By concrete learning I mean the learning that is planned, so that students are able to walk out of a lesson knowing or being able to do something new; what Trevor Wright (2010, p13) refers to as a *small, valuable, solid object*. Instead, the trainee has become so focused on keeping students busy and putting on a show for the observer, by trying to cram in evidence for all the standards in one lesson, that they miss the point: *planning is first and foremost about helping students to learn, not about you as the teacher.*

— Key learning point

When planning lessons, ensure you are focused on the students and their learning, rather than on your own actions and behaviour. Although it might help you to consider your own role in the class-room, this should always be secondary to two key questions.

1. What are the students going to do?

2. How will this support their learning?

For many of you who are just starting out on your journey into teaching, the easiest starting point is to focus on the objectives of the lesson. For each and every activity in the lesson you should be clear on why you are doing it, and how it will develop student learning, with regard to the objective.

In the examples below, a video clip is introduced in very different ways. In itself, a video is an effective way to introduce new concepts, reinforce existing learning or just re-engage and motivate students. However, too often I see lessons where the trainee has not really considered the purpose of showing the clip, or clearly articulated this to students, as with Scenario A. The outcome: students see a nice video clip, but an opportunity is missed to support concrete learning. In contrast, the teacher in Scenario B has been clear to clarify what is expected from students and the purpose of the activity.

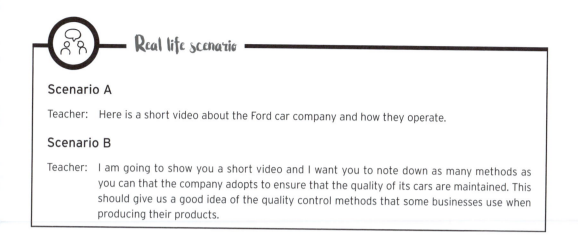

Real life scenario

Scenario A

Teacher: Here is a short video about the Ford car company and how they operate.

Scenario B

Teacher: I am going to show you a short video and I want you to note down as many methods as you can that the company adopts to ensure that the quality of its cars are maintained. This should give us a good idea of the quality control methods that some businesses use when producing their products.

Planning therefore enables you to consider and share with students the purpose of an activity and how it will help their learning, relevant to the objectives. It will also help you to weigh up alternative activities or resources to meet a learning objective. I often ask trainees, 'Why did you choose to do that activity, and what was the purpose?', or the more loaded question, 'What would have been a better activity for that objective?' In planning, you should be prepared to answer these questions yourself, because a key part of your early development is to acquire a pedagogical rationale for the routes you take when planning a lesson.

Planning, in its simplest sense, can be broken down into four stages (Butt, 2008; John, 1995) which begins with the purpose of the lesson, in setting out clear learning objectives (see Figure 1.1).

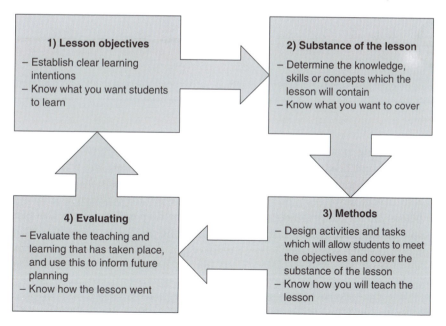

Figure 1.1   You should be aware of the four key stages and the cyclical process of planning (based on John, 2006, p486)

In planning your learning journey, there are many pro-forma lesson plans which are available to you. Pro-formas will help provide a clear rational-linear framework for planning lessons (Tyler, 1950), either through your training institute or on the Internet. Carefully completing these in the early stages of your planning will undoubtedly give you support, and provide a crutch to help you to take the first few steps in mastering the basics of lesson planning. However, like all crutches, you will soon need to put these aside and try to walk on your own. This does not mean binning the pro-forma or disregarding planning altogether. Instead, once you have got to grips with the simplicity of planning lessons around a clear learning objective, it will allow you to engage with the more intellectually and creatively challenging aspects of planning, which considers deeper aspects of subject pedagogy.

Therefore, while it is important not to overly complicate things in the early stages of your teaching career, it is also important not to underestimate the conceptual complexity of planning. Some of you may regard planning as a mere procedural process, which is focused on the organisation of teaching, and the management of learning in a classroom (Rusznyak and Walton, 2011). Indeed, you might see planning as a laborious and long-winded practice in which you are asked to meticulously record the context to the lesson, assessment opportunities, the needs of students in your class, or behavioural issues, to name but a few. However, it is important for you to understand that planning, at least in your early years of teaching, is a combination of both practicalities, in organising the logistics of the lesson, and pedagogy, in deciding how best to teach the subject matter of the lesson. This will help you to see it as a pedagogical construction, which emphasises not just 'what students are going to do' but also 'why they are going to do it'.

Key learning point

You should be clear that it is the process of planning, rather than the plan itself, which is important.

It is rather like learning to swim. Being pushed off the 4m board and expecting you to confidently swim, or even keep your head above water, is unlikely to work. Instead, you will need to start with a range of floating aids, and expert guidance, in helping you to negotiate the paddling pool. While this might restrict your movement and freedom, it will give you the confidence to hone your planning skills before you are ready to take the plunge into the deep end, free from arm bands. While this is possibly an oversimplification of the initial planning process, in presenting planning as a technical process in which you merely follow a series of concrete stages to develop your planning, it will help you avoid the danger of jumping straight into the deep end, even if you have dipped your toe in the water before.

However, there are some critics of the more traditional, rational-linear model for planning who argue that planning should move beyond seeing teaching as a craft, and a set of skills to be learned through observation and replication (John, 2006; Rusznyak and Walton, 2011). They argue that trainees should be supported in engaging with the multifaceted nature of planning, which involves complex pedagogical choices to suit different learners in different contexts. Yet, for all this academic argument about the different models for planning, there is a degree of agreement among educationalists. In the earliest phases of your teaching, it is accepted that you will need more concrete and routine models for planning. However, this does point towards the importance of your recognition that planning is far from a simple process, and although the early days of your training may be dominated by a more rational-linear approach to planning, which appears highly structured and formulaic, you should look to develop an understanding of the complexities of this process.

Therefore, you should first look to master the skills of 'surface planning' by gaining a secure contextual knowledge of the class you are teaching, including behavioural issues or the special educational needs of students in your class. Yet in the long run you should also look to immerse yourself in 'deeper planning', which is underpinned by your developing theoretical knowledge. This will include your developing knowledge of pedagogy, differentiation, assessment or progress in your subject. It is this 'deeper planning', which comes from a more tacit knowledge of ideas and concepts about teaching and learning (Schön, 1983), which is far more difficult to develop and will therefore take you longer to master (see Chapter 4).

Especially important is the development of what Shulman (1986) termed your 'pedagogical content knowledge', which combines both your subject and content knowledge on what is to be taught with the pedagogical knowledge of how it is best taught, to support students' learning for understanding (Berry et al., 2008). Indeed, it is the tripartite development of teaching skills, pedagogy and subject knowledge (see Figure 1.2) which will best support you in developing your planning in the long term, because *mere content knowledge is likely to be as useless pedagogically as content-free skill* (Shulman, 1986, p8).

Although these are important concepts in planning, which will take you some time to get to grips with, there are still changes to your practice which will support you immediately. Indeed, in my experience, trainees who struggle with initial planning largely fall into one of two camps.

In one camp, you have 'the perfectionists' who are overly meticulous in their planning, spending hours rejigging plans and developing resources and activities for their lessons. I always encourage 'perfectionists' to plan more smartly, using some of the strategies outlined below, for a more manageable process. If this is you, avoid trying to constantly reinvent the wheel for every lesson you teach, or perpetually searching for a magic elixir to planning. Be reassured that it is perfectly pragmatic to take some short cuts in your planning, and accept that you can and will make mistakes (which in themselves are important learning opportunities).

In the second camp, we have 'the minimalists' who tend to view planning as an onerous, long-winded and sometimes unnecessary activity. If this is you (which might be unlikely as 'minimalists' tend not to see the point of extensive planning, let alone researching for planning), then you need to really consider the fundamental purpose of planning, which is to help students learn. Hopefully, you can go beyond using the strategies below to superficially resolve your problems, and instead undertake some of the suggested *slow burners*, to really grapple with the complex pedagogy of planning. This should help you to see real value in the process of planning and evaluating lessons, in order to develop your own practice.

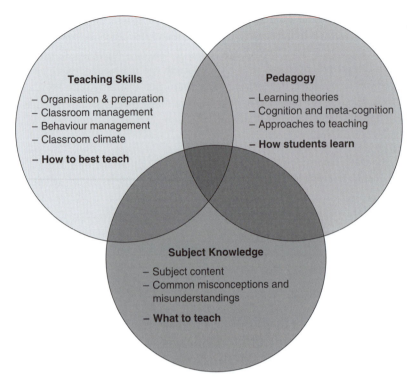

Figure 1.2 You should be clear that there is an obvious overlap between the three key aspects of planning teaching skills

Ultimately, you will find your own way of planning; some mentors might present it as a science, with a clear formula for success which trainees need to learn quickly. Others might present it as a more esoteric art form, which is not easily taught, based on trainees developing their creative skills over time. Hopefully, you can see the problem to both these views about teaching, in that the former oversimplifies the process of planning for learning, which sees it as a mere technical and procedural exercise. Indeed, I am sure your own experiences of spending hours of time procrastinating over your first lesson plans are evidence enough that it is not a straightforward process. However, the idea that it is only an art form is equally misguided, and in fact gives little hope to the average trainee, especially if they feel they lack the creative skills to plan effectively. Effective planning is certainly a mixture of both these approaches, and it could be seen as a *practical art* with a *scientific base* (Gage, 1978). Although a challenge, you will see in this chapter that there are a range of tried and tested strategies that will help you to find recipes for success and also support you in developing the less tangible skills of planning for learning.

In conclusion, no matter whether you are a 'perfectionist', a 'minimalist', or somewhere in between, you will all have encountered problems with your planning, or will at some stage be given a target relevant to your lesson planning. Ultimately it is a fundamental part of teaching and to coin (or in this case adapt) an often used phrase 'Proper planning prevents poor performance'. So use the strategies below to develop both the practical and pedagogical aspects of your own planning.

Targets

Plan lessons with a clear learning aim

Quick wins

- **Always have the end in mind**. Start your planning by establishing where you want all your students to get to by the end of the lesson.
- **Explain the purpose of all activities on your lesson plan**. For all tasks and activities ask yourself: 'Why am I doing this?' and 'How will it help students to achieve the learning objective?' By writing aims on to your lesson plan, it will ensure you are clear about why students are doing a task, which is likely to lead to your students experiencing your tasks as purposeful.
- **Plan to give students a concrete take-away** so they are able to walk out of your lesson knowing or being able to do something new. For example, at the end of the lesson you could ask students to name and demonstrate a cricket shot to a partner. Alternatively, you could ask them to share one new piece of knowledge they have gained from the lesson about Hindu wedding rituals.
- **Talk to learners**. Ask students if they know what they are learning, or if they can articulate the purpose of a particular activity in relation to the objective. You can do this informally, as they leave the lesson or when they are undertaking an activity, or more formally by interviewing students or asking them to complete an 'exit card' (see below).
- **Justify your choice of activities to your observer**. Even when you are not being observed, imagine an observer who will require you to answer the question: 'What was the learning point of that activity?'

Slow burners

- **Focus on pedagogy and always start with the learning objective** before considering which activities to use in a lesson. First, this makes pedagogical sense, by giving you a very clear focus to your planning, around which the lesson should be built. Second, it makes practical sense, as you will soon come to realise that for each developmental stage of the lesson, there are a range of activities you could undertake to achieve that objective. Over time, it will help you to begin to see patterns in your planning, and help you identify what works for similar developmental objectives with different classes or across different topics. It will also allow you to experiment with different tasks or activities, with different classes or lessons, when you are trying to achieve a similar developmental objective.

I often get trainees to try to match a series of short learning objectives to potential tasks and activities. They often come up with wholly different results, and the purpose is to help them see that there are often any number of activities you could plan to meet different objectives. For example, one of the objectives is for students to 'Know and apply each of the Spanish terms for household pets' and there is always a productive discussion about whether this would be achieved through a labelling activity, card-matching task, short video, or using textbooks to produce a table. In the subsequent discussion, it becomes clear that they are all potential activities. Many trainees thus leave the session having had that light bulb moment of realisation, that when the 'learning objective dog' wags the 'tail of tasks and activities', rather than vice versa, planning becomes much easier to negotiate.

One particular strategy you should trial to help you develop your focus on planning with the learning objective in mind, is to reverse engineer lessons. Look to observe a lesson yourself and try to deconstruct the learning which you see taking place. After the lesson try to design your own lesson plan, based on your observations, and share this with the class teacher. Consider how far your thoughts on the learning objectives and the purpose of each activity matched their own design. Discuss the teacher's rationale for the choices they made in the lesson, and which other activities might have served the same purpose. This will help you to deepen your own understanding about the nature of learning and pedagogy.

- **Be clear on the difference between lesson objectives and success criteria/lesson outcomes** so you can plan both what students will learn and how they will demonstrate their learning. The learning objective is the overall pedagogical learning aim of the lesson, whereas the success criteria, or outcomes, are what students will achieve in your lesson. Whereas a learning objective might be 'Know at least three advantages and three disadvantages of the UK First Past the Post electoral system', the lesson outcome might be 'Produce a speech supporting or opposing the current system for electing MPs to Parliament'.

When planning, you should always start with the general learning objectives before considering outcomes and success criteria (i.e. how you will get evidence that students have achieved the learning aim). Start by getting to the nub of what students are learning. Use this to set appropriate objectives which are based on the knowledge, understanding, skills or concepts that you want students to learn. As can be seen in the scenario below, it is helpful if you drill down into what you want students to learn in a particular lesson, rather than planning lessons around an aim which is too broad, such as 'Islam' or 'Electronics'.

Real life scenario

A trainee is discussing their learning aim for a lesson on Macbeth.

Mentor: What are they going to learn about?

Trainee: Macbeth.

Mentor: What do you want them to learn about Macbeth?

Trainee: About his character.

Mentor: What about his character?

Trainee: About how his character changes in the scene.

Mentor: So is that what you want them to learn?

Trainee: Yes.

Mentor: So how are you going to plan to meet that aim?

By setting a clear, overarching learning objective you can begin to consider, in very general terms, how you will differentiate the lesson to meet the needs of at least three groups of learners in your classroom: the least able, those who are of middle ability and the more able. A lesson focused on exploring the different interpretations of Oliver Cromwell might thereby be aimed at ensuring that the least able will be able to identify at least two contrasting interpretations; the middle ability will be able to explain a range of interpretations; while the more able should be able to evaluate how these interpretations have developed over time.

It is only once you have established these objectives that you will be able to plan the outcomes, which should allow students an opportunity to demonstrate their learning – perhaps by completing a table, drafting a newspaper article or delivering a speech. This is clarified in the table below.

Broad learning aim	Explore different interpretations of Oliver Cromwell		
Learning objective	The least able will be able to identify at least two contrasting interpretations.	The middle ability will be able to explain a range of interpretations.	The more able will be able to evaluate how these interpretations have developed over time.
Learning outcome	Create a table with two contrasting interpretations.	Create a mind-map that explains a range of interpretations.	Write an essay which includes an evaluation of changing interpretations over time.

Order and structure your planned learning activities more effectively to ensure that there is a clear sequence and flow to the lesson

Quick wins

- **Use a 'Think Aloud Protocol'** to see the process involved in planning. Ask an experienced teacher to think aloud and explain their thought processes as they undertake each stage of planning, while you observe.

- **Simplify your plan to see it as a three-course menu.** Whet students' appetites by planning an engaging starter, which introduces the learning objectives. Move into a more substantial main course, which develops their learning, and finish with a dessert that allows them to review and reinforce their learning.

- **Use the wheel, don't reinvent it,** by taking advantage of departmental resources, or asking other members of the department how they taught a particular topic.

- **Do discriminate,** and be very discerning in deciding the value of other people's resources.

- **Adapt the plans of others, and beware attempts to just replicate.** These will rarely work in practice, so ensure you review the plan, and the resources, to account for your own 'surface' and contextual knowledge of the class.

- **Personalise and modify** the plans and resources you pick up from others, or online, to suit your own teaching preferences. If you are less confident about getting students out of their seats – for example, when undertaking a whole-class debate, you can always ask them to draw a continuum in their books and justify where they would place themselves. It would have the same outcome but be less risky.

- **Ensure you clarify the purpose of all tasks** and articulate these to students. Make sure students can see the link between the planned activities they are due to undertake and the overall learning objective. For example, you might ask them to 'Explain the purpose of this card sort' or consider 'Why did we do that starter activity?' This will ensure that both you and the students are clear on what they are doing and why they are doing it.

- **Undertake student surveys** by giving students a structured questionnaire, which they complete during the lesson. The results should then help you understand the impact of your lesson plan, and improve your planning for the future. However, choosing the right students is important, to ensure that you get both honest and trustworthy feedback (choosing the best students in the class might seem like a good idea, but they might not be a true reflection of the class as a whole).

 Slow burners

- **Increase the cognitive demand across the lesson** by using Bloom's taxonomy (Bloom *et al.*, 1956). In essence, you should start with the less cognitively challenging activities, such as those ascribed to knowledge and comprehension tasks. You should then look to create opportunities for the application of that knowledge and understanding, before finally allowing chances for students to analyse, synthesise and evaluate what they have learnt.

This approach can help you to break up the lesson plan into separate and discrete sections, each of which is designed to build upon the previous section. Rather like building a house, it will help you lay the foundations of knowledge and comprehension before trying to get students to apply this and construct more complex analytical or evaluative thought processes. In a way, this approach is not dissimilar to the notion of the three-part lesson (starter, main and plenary), which was popularised during the educational initiatives of the Blair years, but is a more sophisticated way to break up the lesson plan into manageable sections. A starter can have a number of functions, such as settling students, recapping prior learning or engaging students (see below for more detail). The main section is where you will teach the main content of the lesson (see Chapter 4). The plenary is an opportunity to reflect on, review or apply learning which can occur in any part of the lesson, but is commonly seen at the end of a three-part lesson.

Take, for example, an English lesson which is based on a book review. The lesson could begin with students trying to identify the key characters in the text and recalling what they know about them and the story so far. Students could then be asked to predict what they think might happen in the next chapter, based on their own inferences. Having read the chapter, they could construct a brief precis or role play of the story. A final task might be to undertake a more complex evaluation of the motives of the different characters, or to compare and contrast two characters from the chapter. To really challenge the most able, they could be asked to create a completely new character and explain how they would fit into the story.

Quick click

In addition to a range of other useful lesson planning resources, the Canterbury College website (**http://bit.ly/2dalbKH**) includes a 'Bloom's Taxonomy Teacher Planning Kit'. This offers a really useful planning model, including keywords, actions, outcomes and key questions, which you can use to support your lesson planning. Use this model to move students from undertaking low-level to using high-level thinking skills across a lesson.

Slow burners

- **Use mini-plenaries** to support transitions between activities. A mini-plenary is an opportunity to undertake a brief learning review during the lesson. This can act as both an opportunity for pupils to revisit knowledge, and for you to judge which students might need further support in the next stage of the lesson. In some cases, it might help you to identify that fundamentally: 'They haven't got it'. This will prevent you from moving on to another activity when some students have fallen off the learning bus.

One very effective tool, which I have seen being used particularly well in lessons, is the mini-whiteboard. Use these boards to review and briefly check knowledge or understanding. In one notable maths lesson I observed, the trainee asked students to work through an answer on their boards. Not only did this allow the trainee to get a quick idea of who understood what they were doing, but it also opened up a ripe discussion about the different methods used to arrive at the answer. In this way the lesson was really lifted, and the students were engaged and challenged to discuss the different mathematical processes which would help provide an answer.

However, you do need to be careful not to overuse mini-plenaries, which can have the opposite effect of interrupting the flow of the lesson or mean that students don't have enough time to actually do the learning. Similarly, I often see mini-plenaries undertaken as artificial activities, which are designed to merely showcase to an observer that 'progress' is being made every 10 minutes. Indeed, I remember one particular lesson, which was so broken up with mini-plenaries that students didn't have enough time to process the knowledge or develop their understanding before being asked to review it.

Despite this, well-planned mini-plenaries can assist the transitions in your lesson from one activity to another, by acting as a bridge, in which students can see how the previous activity links to the next one. They can also introduce opportunities for genuine reflection, allowing students to consolidate learning before they are asked to extend or deepen that learning.

Key learning point

Remember that reflections are a key part of the learning process, and mini-plenaries should be viewed as an opportunity to build these into your lesson, rather than just another hoop to jump through to try to impress an observer.

Widen the range of teaching strategies and resources you use to support learners

Quick wins

- **Chunk** lessons into small manageable episodes of 10-15 minutes.
- **Break down extended activities** so that students can be given time to review progress or to refocus on the task.
- **Use thinking time** so that students can process information and questions. For example, introduce the 'Think-pair-share' model as a prelude to whole-class discussion. This will give students time to think for themselves and discuss their ideas with a partner first.
- **Remember 'variety is the spice of life' when it comes to planning activities**, so keep track of the types of activities you have used with a class over a series of lessons, and vary the length of time you spend on any one activity.
- Look to develop a rhythm to the lesson plan by achieving **a balance between pupil-centred activities**, such as paired discussion, group work or note taking, **and teacher-centred activities**, such as explanations, modelling or 'chalk and talk'. Remember the old maxim that 'pupils should always be working harder than the teacher in a lesson'.
- **Use technology** to support you in planning for engagement, progress or differentiation. With some schools now allowing teachers to book out banks of iPads, you could allow students to scan differentiated QR codes, which will take them to targeted articles, demonstrations or websites to suit their ability.
- **Pair off students so they** can support each other in their learning. Create different 'learning partners', where students might be matched to a different partner depending on the activity you are setting them. In this way, you can direct them to move into 'thinking pairs', 'writing pairs' or 'reading pairs'.
- **Prepare groups in advance** to ensure that time is not wasted on setting up groups, and to avoid the pitfalls of asking students to arrange themselves into groups, which is almost inevitably a disaster.
- **Plan for pupil movement,** rather than table rearrangement, when grouping students, so they become familiar with their 'working groups'. In addition to this, give clear direction to groups by assigning roles to individuals (such as chairperson, timekeeper or scribe). However, make sure you explain that any of them can be chosen as the summariser, who will report back for the group. This will ensure they are all individually accountable for the group task, as they could be the person called upon to feedback to the class.
- **Plan your questioning** by noting down the types of questions you might look to ask students when undertaking a Q&A session (see section on questioning). Consider the purpose of questions, the types of questions you are looking to ask, the order in which you might ask these questions, and which students the questions might be best targeted at.
- **Use explicit modelling** so pupils know what you want them to do. You can either model an example yourself, such as demonstrating a cricket shot, or complete this as a whole-class activity where you work through an example together.
- **Use exemplars** to help explain a task by giving students a completed example, so they can see what they need to do. For example, you might show them a completed section on a table, present them with a completed sculpture, or give students an example response to a question. A well-drafted exemplar, which is in need of improvement, can have the added benefit of encouraging students to spot, and thereby avoid, the obvious pitfalls in a response.

- **Make use of peers and colleagues,** who will undoubtedly be one of the richest sources of resources and ideas during your training year. I was often struck by moments of 'planner's block' during my training year, when I was unable to identify an appropriate task or activity to support a particular learning outcome. In these moments it was the discussions I had with peers or colleagues that provided me with a rich source of ideas and inspiration.

  In particular, look to organise 'planning parties' with fellow trainees. This can work particularly well when you are teaching a lesson with a similar focus or learning objective. The process of discussing a range of possible activities, possible misconceptions, the ways in which progress could be assessed, or the range of ways the lesson might be differentiated will really support your own development.

  Alternatively, compare lessons that have already been planned and taught, to consider the different approaches and strategies that you each adopted. These conversations will also force you to justify the pedagogical choices you made in designing the lesson, as well as providing you with alternative suggestions or ideas.

  One concrete method to develop your planning, using colleagues as a resource, is to undertake joint planning with an experienced teacher. My trainees always valued the time taken to go through all the stages of the planning process together. This allowed us to consider and discuss both the context of the lesson, and any 'surface' knowledge that might help planning, as well as the 'deeper' knowledge of progress, subject pedagogy, differentiation, assessment, and behaviour which informed the planning choices.

- **Make use of lessons which double up on your timetable,** so if you have at least two classes in the same year group, this will allow you to think deeply about the impact of duplicating, adapting or completely rewriting lesson plans. Initially look to repeat lesson plans and evaluate how far it led to similar outcomes for both classes. You should then look to introduce alternative approaches to adapt the lesson plan for each group, based on your evaluations of what seemed to work with each class. The final stage is to try planning completely different lessons for both classes with the same lesson objective, to evaluate which appeared to work better and why. As time goes by, you will start to recognise simple ways to adapt the same lesson plan to suit the learning needs of both groups.

Expand the range of approaches you use for starters and plenaries, to ensure lessons begin and end effectively

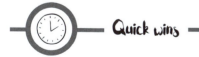

- **Make sure students 'get in and get on' with an extended starter**. Look to get students straight into the lesson by having a thought-provoking 'thunk question' (Gilbert, 2007) on the board, or asking them to complete a task which is on the board. This will give momentum and a positive start to the lesson, especially if you use it to reward those who are quickly on task. It has the added benefit of giving you time to integrate late arrivals, without disrupting the flow of the lesson.
- **Establish clear routines** for the start and end to lessons by reinforcing expectations, through your behaviour management strategies, so these become second nature for students.

- **Replicate and adapt starters,** to account for the different topics or age groups of the classes you teach. This will save lesson planning time, but will also help you consider what works with different groups, and allow you to reflect on why this might be the case. It should also start to give you an idea of what might be expected from different age and ability groups. For example, a quick starter might be to ask students to recap three things they learnt in the previous lesson.
- **Look to introduce learning objectives in a range of different ways**, without just reading them out, or getting students to copy them down (see the assessment section).
- **Be prepared,** especially when you are not able to set the classroom up before the lesson starts, by producing an activity sheet or a quick task which can be passed to students as they enter the room.
- **Use exit cards to give students a concrete 'take-away'**. Although progression is about long-term learning, it is important to get students to think about the short-term learning that has taken place. To help students set out the tangible learning they are taking away from a lesson, get them to complete 'exit cards' in which you ask them to state three things they have learnt, two things they are a little unsure about and one question they would still like the answer to. These are really useful guides for your future planning and will help you to discuss class progress with your mentor.

 Slow burners

- **Explore starters which have different purposes** and experiment by beginning lessons with starters which have a range of aims and purposes, such as the following.
  - **Settlers,** to encourage pupils to enter the lesson orderly and promptly, or overcome the problem of students arriving in a trickle from different lessons around the school. These create a calm environment with an individual activity such as reading, sequencing, or developing a list of factors relevant to the lesson.
  - **Recappers,** to review and consolidate prior learning. This could simply involve asking students to recall prior knowledge or summarise their learning from the previous lesson. However, you could make this more challenging by asking them to spot the 'odd one out' from a series of statements or images linked to the previous lesson, or undertake a 'heads and tails' activity, in which pupils need to draw links between one set of topic-related key terms, those labelled 'heads' and another set of topic-related key terms labelled 'tails'. A range of quizzes and bingo games are also useful ways to review key knowledge from the last lesson.
  - **Introducers,** to present the learning objectives, in a clear and engaging fashion. Instead of asking students to copy the objectives from the board, ask them to try to work out the objectives from a series of images, or following a brief demonstration.
  - **Engagers,** to 'hook' students into a lesson, and secure the interest and curiosity of students. Present them with a thought-provoking image, which will generate interest, or with different arguments about the lesson question, so they are drawn into the debate that surrounds the lesson. Similarly, come up with a well-posed question, which gets them thinking about the lesson. I would sometimes introduce the story of Thomas Becket by showing a picture of Henry II's penance at Canterbury. This always generated interesting questions about why a king would let monks whip him, or why he would not be wearing any shoes. This acted as a great way into the conflict between the Church and the Crown in this period.

– **Enquirers,** to get pupils to see the lesson as an exploration and a voyage of discovery. Try to phrase the lesson title as an intriguing question, or ask students to hypothesise about a question at the start of the lesson. This will focus students on trying to discover the answer to the lesson question and test or amend their own hypotheses as the lesson develops. In this way, a science lesson might be titled 'Why doesn't electricity spill out of sockets?' or a geography lesson on adaptation might be based on the question 'Why wouldn't polar bears survive in the Sahara?'

Quick click

There is a plethora of ideas and resource for starters and plenaries on the Internet, which can be easily adapted to suit your lesson aims. Try looking at **www.tes.com/teaching-resources** which is a useful starting point for shared resources.

Slow burners

• **Experiment with different plenaries, with distinctive aims.** Remember, a plenary is an opportunity for you to assess students' knowledge and understanding in order to adapt a lesson or guide your future planning and teaching.

– **Reviewing,** whereby pupils revise the knowledge, skills or understanding that has been the focus of the lesson. In its most basic form you can review substantive knowledge through a quiz or by asking students to play 'true or false', when given a series of statements. Alternatively, give students the opportunity to formulate a judgement on the lesson question, or to prioritise and rank factors from the lesson. Effectively, you are aiming to give students time to revisit and consolidate their learning.

– **Reflecting,** allowing students to formatively review their progress and explicitly reflect on their own learning. This should make clear what they have taken from the lesson, and what they are still struggling with. For example, get them to identify their concrete learning from the lesson using a different coloured 'progress pen'. This has the added advantage of making it easy for you to identify and respond to their reflections when you review their books.

– **Signposting,** to help students see how the current lesson links to their prior or future learning. Ask them to draw together links from previous lessons, or consider what questions remain unanswered around a topic. Where you have planned a series of lessons around a specific topic or enquiry, you should question how this might allow you to provide a stimulus, in order to prompt students to consider how they will be extending their learning in the next lesson.

– **Applying learning,** with structured opportunities for students to put their learning into practice and employ it for a specific purpose. An obvious way is to undertake an exam-style question, giving students in Key Stage 3 an insight into the format of exam questions, while allowing older pupils valuable exam practice, under timed conditions.

Ensure you appropriately plan the timing of activities to maximise learning (see Chapter 3)

 Quick wins

- **Keep an eye on the clock.**
- **Set a plenary alarm** at the start of the lesson, and tell students that when the alarm signals, it will be time to 'review learning'.
- **Record specific timings on your lesson plan**, so you are clear when an activity should be completed. Putting a specific time to undertake each episode of the lesson will allow you to keep on track, and is a better method than just noting down how long students are given for each lesson episode – for example, '10.38: Introduce card sorting activity'.
- For each activity you ask a class to undertake, **display a timer** which is visible to all students. Judicially guide them with how long is remaining at appropriate intervals and praise those who are on track to complete the work set.
- **Keep a copy of the plan** to hand, so you can review it at key moments in the lesson, such as when students are undertaking pupil-centred activities.
- **Use a student stop-watch** by asking a reliable student to keep a track of the time and remind you when there are 10 minutes left of the lesson, so you have time to wrap up the final activity and move on to a purposeful plenary.
- **Undertake a mental 'walk through'** of your lesson plan by going through each stage in your mind, mentally reviewing what you will be doing and what students will be doing across the lesson.
- **Develop a quick reference plan for the lesson** by condensing the main lesson plan on to one side of an A4 sheet so you can quickly reference the plan or check on timings throughout the lesson. Although a full and detailed plan will help with preparation, it might be hard to use and refer to in the heat of a lesson.
- **Add post-it notes** to your lesson plan summarising each point. Take these off the lesson plan in the correct order as a quick reference for what you are doing.
- **Rehearse the lesson** and time yourself delivering instructions or teacher exposition before the lesson, so you can realistically predict how long transitions between activities or different parts of the lesson plan are likely to take. Add about 2-3 minutes to each section to account for interruptions and distractions.

 Slow burners

- **Plan variable endings, so there are two or three different end points to the lesson**. This is a really useful tool in the early stages of your planning, especially while you are becoming familiar with the timings of activities. It allows you to plan for adaptions and will help you build flexibility into the end of your lessons. This means you can finish early, in a purposeful way, if time is running short, or extend the lesson if you have more time on your hands, without it seeming like unnecessary padding.

In my lessons, especially when I was being observed, I would often plan for at least two different plenaries, which would allow flexibility in my timings if things overran. One would be a simple review activity, such as asking students to consider one thing they could remember, one thing they had learnt, and one question they still had. The other plenary was usually a more challenging application activity, in which I might ask them to undertake a short exam question, or compile a brief radio report or tweet in which they would summarise their learning in the lesson.

Similarly, you might consider how you undertake feedback to minimise the number of responses you take, or by planning questioning to pick out only the key points you want to reinforce from an activity. Overall, being flexible and adaptable in your teaching is not an easy skill to master and, although time and experience will help you to think on your feet and 'reflect in action' (Schön, 1983), you should look to build this flexibility into your planning from an early stage.

- **Work on clarifying expectations** and establishing clear boundaries when you set up a task. Ensure you articulate timings and the minimum expectations for all students, when undertaking an activity. For example, you might state: 'In the next 15 minutes I would expect you all to . . . ' or briefly clarify that: 'You have 10 minutes to . . . '. Often it is worthwhile to ask a student to clarify these expectations before you let them begin, so that you can be confident that they are clear on what they have to do, and how long they have to do it.

Of course, you do need to ensure you monitor this as the lesson progresses, by rewarding those who are on task and on track to meet your expectations. You should look to praise those students who are working well, or those who have managed to move on to an enrichment activity. This will help you keep the whole class focused. Indeed, some students have an elastic view of lesson time and will look to stretch out any activity they are given for as long as possible. If you set clear and reasonable boundaries from the start and organise 'catch-up club', perhaps at break or lunchtime, for those students who are not meeting expectations, you will find that in the long run students are far more focused on using the allocated time effectively. A word of warning, however: be careful to ensure you are not unnecessarily penalising SEND students, who might need longer to process or act on what they are being asked to do.

Plan appropriate homework activities which are designed to sustain learners' progress and consolidate their learning

Quick wins

- Give students a **choice of homework**, which can be targeted at different levels.
- Encourage students to **further enrich their homework** and do more than the bare minimum. Set up a 'Must, Might, Could' homework, giving them a choice to do enrichment or more challenging work.
- Get students **to redraft a previous piece of work**, which they have had feedback on (see Chapter 7). Many schools now ask students to improve their work using a green pen, so it is obvious to see how the student has improved their work as a result of the feedback. This will also serve to reduce your marking load as you are not creating a whole new set of work to mark, but are merely checking that they have acted on the advice and feedback given.
- **Use peer teaching,** by giving students a topic or a subject to prepare to teach to their peers in the subsequent lesson. Pupils can be asked to become experts in their area in order to teach a peer or group of peers in the next lesson. You might also ask them to produce a handout to

support their teaching, which can be shared with the class. However, it is always a good idea to limit the word count on the handout or specify its format, to prevent them merely copying and pasting work from the Internet.

Slow burners

- **Plan for a flipped classroom,** where students undertake homework which is designed to allow them to develop their key knowledge and understanding of a subject. This might be through research tasks, guided reading, or reviewing specific online podcasts and videos. This will allow you to plan lessons which apply, evaluate, synthesise or analyse their home learning. Such a structure can encourage students to see the value of homework as a preparation for school learning, which looks to consolidate, build on and apply this learning. This flips the traditional view of homework as a follow-up activity after the lesson. It is certainly a useful tool for older students, who might need to take extensive notes in preparation for revision and exams. It thus reduces the necessity for this to take up valuable lesson time, which can be better spent allowing students to deepen and apply their learning.

- My A2 lessons often started with students using a whiteboard to write down anything they were unclear on from their preparatory reading. This would allow me to walk around the room and gain an idea of any particular points we would need to cover during the initial feedback activity. In minimising the use of lesson time to make copious amounts of notes, it meant there was much more time for students to apply that knowledge and understanding or to develop their own arguments and judgements. Alternatively, I got students to produce podcasts, which explained key concepts. These therefore became a valuable revision resource, and I sometimes set homework for subsequent classes to review them prior to the lesson.

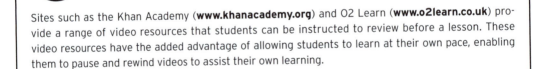

Quick Click

Sites such as the Khan Academy (**www.khanacademy.org**) and O2 Learn (**www.o2learn.co.uk**) provide a range of video resources that students can be instructed to review before a lesson. These video resources have the added advantage of allowing students to learn at their own pace, enabling them to pause and rewind videos to assist their own learning.

Develop your longer-term planning to ensure progress and learning over time

Quick wins

- **Bullet point the learning aims for future lessons** so you are thinking ahead with your planning, This will help you break out of seeing lessons in isolation, so you can clarify how the learning from one lesson will inform the next.

- **Undertake block planning** of lessons, in groups of three. This will help you consider progression over a series of lessons, but still enables you to make adaptions, based on your evaluations of how pupils are progressing.

- **Fully evaluate your lessons,** to reflect on the learning that took place, and set out how you might adapt future lessons to ensure pupils make progress over time. For example, you might identify some misunderstanding or a fundamental learning gap, which you should look to fill in subsequent lessons.

- **Move beyond simple lesson evaluations of What Went Well (WWW) and Even Better If (EBI).** Focus on how you will adapt your own practice, or future lessons, as a result of your EBI reflections.

- **Use Schemes of Work (SoW),** which most departments have in place, to plot out a sequence of lessons for a particular topic. Review these at the start of teaching a new topic in order to have a clear idea of progression over the topic.

- **Undertake simultaneous evaluations when you are being observed,** before hearing the lesson observation feedback. Ask the observer to also complete a detailed evaluation of the lesson, as if they had taught that lesson. Consider and discuss any similarities or differences in how you evaluated the lesson, and especially what you both felt were appropriate changes to practice or adaptions to future lesson plans that arose from these evaluations.

Slow burners

- **Use 'backward planning'** (Wiggins and McTighe, 2005) when you plan a series of lessons, by starting with the end point in mind. Establish the wider objectives and a focus across a unit of work. You should then use this to clarify what students should be able to do at the end of the unit that they were unable to do at the start. This enables you to break down the overall aim into smaller learning objectives, which can be covered in each lesson.

I have seen this work particularly well for practical subjects, such as music and PE, although the principles are the same for planning in all subjects. For example, a series of art lessons might be designed so that students can create an original piece of artwork to express ideas or arouse emotion. Once these desired results are established, the teacher can move on to consider any appropriate assessment evidence, which will allow them to know that students have achieved this desired result. This might take the form of a performance task, whereby students apply their learning from working with charcoal to the production of a self-portrait, or other evidence, such as observations and work samples so that the teacher can be clear on what students know and can do. The final stage is then for the teacher to plan lessons which will allow them to achieve the desired results. This should help clarify what activities, sequence, and resources are best suited to create their work.

- **Keep assessments in mind,** and try to think first like an assessor when planning units of work. Although there is a definite danger of producing both stale and repetitive lesson designs which 'teach to the test', it is still useful to have in mind how students will be assessed at the end of a unit of work, or in public exams. This can help guide your planning to ensure you have covered the relevant content, but also prepares students to face exams, whether in the form of written questions or practicals. It will ensure you are preparing them for the knowledge, understanding and skills that they will need to pass their tests. You need a detailed understanding of the programme of study or assessment criteria, so you have an awareness of what students should be able to do by the end of the unit of work. This will act as a rudder to steer the learning and ensure blocks of lessons are covering the content and preparing students for the final assessment they will undoubtedly face.

In summary

Planning is an aspect of your teaching which you will always be working on. Although the early days of your teaching will see your time dominated by hours spent planning and resourcing lessons, in the long run this will become easier. Time invested in planning will undoubtedly allow you to reap the rewards later on, as planning becomes an increasingly natural and intuitive process.

Before the lesson

- **Get to know your students** special educational needs profiles, strengths, weaknesses, likes, dislikes, attainment, progress, context, behaviours, etc.

- **Speak to other members of staff** about resources or activities for certain topics and what works with the particular classes you teach; bear this in mind when you are planning.

- **Be clear on the lesson objectives** and what you want students to learn.

- **Be organised**, have all materials ready to go.

- **Make a copy of the lesson plan** to refer to during the lesson.

During the lesson

- **Make an orderly start to the lesson** by ensuring students are able to come straight in and begin learning.

- **Have the title and objectives displayed (if appropriate) and work ready for students to begin as they enter**.

- **Provide clear explanations and instructions** so students are clear on what they are doing next.

- **Work on transitions between planned tasks** so students are clear on why they are doing a planned activity.

- **Don't be afraid to change the plan** or change direction. If it isn't working, you will need to develop the confidence to alter the plan during the lesson.

After the lesson

- **Evaluate lessons and reflect on your plan.** How far did students meet the learning objectives? Which activities supported them in their learning? Which activities failed to help them learn and why? What will you change in your plan to improve it for the next time?

- **Plan forward.** Where will the learning go in the next lesson? What gaps in knowledge and understanding will need to be covered next lesson?

Further reading

A range of books are available which give practical guidance in the form of short tips and ideas for enhancing your lesson plans. Perhaps the most useful and the easiest to negotiate is *Lesson planning tweaks for teachers: Small changes that make a big difference* (Abersonn and Light, 2015). Similarly, you might pick up some useful ideas from *100 Ideas for Lesson Planning* (Haynes, 2007).

If you want to find a little more about the practical processes and the key procedures in undertaking effective planning, it is worthwhile looking at either *Lesson Planning* (Butt, 2008) or *The Complete Guide to lesson planning and preparation* (Haynes, 2010). These both deal with the practicalities of planning and cover them in greater depth.

Last, if you are looking for a deeper understanding of the pedagogy of planning and research surrounding the different models of planning, then you should certainly look at Shulman's (1986) notion of pedagogical content knowledge and Peter John's (2006) rethinking of the dominant planning model.

References

Abersonn, M and **Light, D** (2015) *Lesson Planning Tweaks for Teachers: Small Changes that Make a Big Difference*, 1st edn. London: Bloomsbury Education.

Berry, A, Loughran, J and Driel, JH v (2008) Revisiting the roots of pedagogical content knowledge. *International Journal of Science Education*, 30(10): 1271–9.

Bloom, BS, Engelhart, MD, Furst, FJ and Hill, WH (1956) *Taxonomy of Educational Objectives: Cognitive Domain*. New York: David MacKay.

Butt, G (2008) *Lesson Planning*, 3rd edn. London: Continuum.

Gage, NL (1978) *The Scientific Basis of the Art of Teaching*. New York: Teachers College Press.

Gilbert, I (2007) *The Little Book of Thunks: 260 Questions to Make Your Brain Go Ouch!*, 1st edn. Carmarthen: Crown House Publishing.

Haynes, A (2007) *100 Ideas for Lesson Planning*, 1st edn. York: Continuum.

Haynes, A (2010) *The Complete Guide to Lesson Planning and Preparation*, 1st edn. London: Continuum.

John, P (1995) *Lessson Planning for Teachers*, 1st edn. London: Cassell Education.

John, P (2006) Lesson planning and the student teacher: Re-thinking the dominant model. *Curriculum Studies*, 38(4): 483–98.

Rusznyak, L and Walton, E (2011) Lesson planning guidelines for student teachers: A scaffold for the development of pedagogical content knowledge. *Education as Change*, 15(2): 271–85.

Schön, DA (1983) *The Reflective Practitioner: How Professionals Think in Action.* New York: Basic Books.

Shulman, L (1986) Those who understand: Knowledge growth in teaching. *Educational Researcher,* 15(2): 4–14.

Tyler, R (1950) *Basic Principles of Curriculum Instruction.* Chicago: University of Chicago Press.

Wiggins, G and McTighe, J (2005) *Understanding by Design,* 2nd edn. Alexandria: ASCD.

Wright, T (2010) *How to be a Brilliant Mentor: Developing Outstanding Teachers,* 1st edn. Oxford: Routledge.

2

Behaviour Management

Teachers' Standard 7 – Manage behaviour effectively to ensure a good and safe learning environment

This section is focused on supporting you in preventing, tackling and managing challenging behaviour to ensure a positive classroom environment. As with everything in effective teaching, this is underpinned by effective lesson planning.

- Establish a safe and stimulating environment for pupils, rooted in mutual respect (TS1).
- Demonstrate consistently the positive attitudes, values and behaviour which are expected of pupils (TS1).
- Impart knowledge and develop understanding through effective use of lesson time (TS4).
- Have a secure understanding of how a range of factors can inhibit pupils' ability to learn, and how best to overcome these (TS5).

Introduction

When I ask trainees what they are most concerned about before they embark on their teaching career, almost all say pupils' behaviour. It is a rational and understandable worry: the very premise of controlling thirty students, ordering them to do something and expecting them to do it without confrontation is a terrifying one. What happens if they just flatly refuse to do what you want? What happens if they see your fear, laugh in your face before banging on the desks, repeatedly chanting: 'You can't teach, you can't teach, you can't teach?'

This worry may have emanated from watching *Grange Hill*, *Waterloo Road* or countless representations of school in film or TV. It may be because you've seen groups of teenagers outside chicken-based establishments, earphones in and hollering with language that has more resonance with League Two footballers on a night out than children. Your fear might have manifested itself because you remember what you and your friends were like at school.

It might be hard to believe, but tackling behaviour is not as insurmountable as you think it is going to be. Learners – I use this word deliberately – are not necessarily what you witness in the playground, corridors, outside chicken-based establishments or at the bus stop after school; this is, after all, their natural habitat where their language and behaviours are matched to their audience and context. This is when they are just kids and not learners. Do you remember what that was like? Experimenting with words; with status; with each other; with technology; with who they are. It does not necessarily paint the most accurate picture of learners in a classroom when we judge them on how they are when they are just *being*. If we were judged on when we relax, perhaps in the sanctuary of our home or in the pub with friends, what would students think of us as human beings, let alone learners?

Managing behaviour in your training year – and beyond, for that matter – is challenging and at some point you will definitely have to deal with a challenging student, a challenging class or maybe a challenging school. But remember the words of Dr Pepper (not a real doctor of medicinal tasting drinks, or education, for that matter): 'What's the worst that can happen?' Prepare yourself for a challenge but don't assume it as an impossible, nightmarish task that will defeat you. Be positive, resilient and open-minded. You will succeed. That's not to say you won't face challenging behaviour and difficult students. You will. It just won't be as devastating as you think it will be.

There is a mantra to drum into your consciousness. You might not like it, some might disagree, but it does help when you come to terms with it.

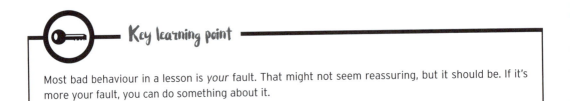

Key learning point

Most bad behaviour in a lesson is *your* fault. That might not seem reassuring, but it should be. If it's more your fault, you can do something about it.

There are many reasons why students misbehave, but the vast majority are within your control. For example, students may disengage if work is not pitched at the right level; boundaries for good behaviour are unclear or they don't feel valued by the teacher. This chapter will introduce you to a range of strategies you can adopt to achieve a calm, learning environment.

What targets does this chapter cover?

- Develop your classroom presence to establish a positive learning climate.
- Maintain a consistent and persistent approach; adopting clear rules and routines for behaviour.
- Develop effective relationships with students to create a good and safe learning environment.
- Minimise low-level behaviour to promote learning.
- Ensure students are responding appropriately to prevent calling out.
- Promote positive behaviour through effective use of praise.
- Ensure students are on task and engaged with learning.
- Challenge students who continually disrupt learning.

Proactive behaviour management

Taylor Swift might not be hailed as a leading educationalist but she, unwittingly, is an ambassador of sound behaviour management with such insightful observations as: 'Band aids don't fix bullet holes' (Taylor Swift, 'Bad Blood', 2015). I have observed many mentors giving trainees feedback on their lesson, advising them how to stem the 'bullets' of bad behaviour with a 'band aid' which is, of course, useful. But to effectively deal with behaviour, it is best done in a proactive way, not just reactively. Putting band aids over bullet holes is not going to completely fix the bad behaviour in a classroom. It might stem the bleeding in the short term, but what about later in the lesson? Or the following lesson? Or for the rest of the term? You will need a bountiful supply of band aids, but the more you plan for good behaviour, the fewer you will need over time. What Swift singularly fails to mention is that it is far better not to get shot at in the first place than it is to rely on band aids. When you observe experienced teachers, it might seem that they are bullet-proof (not using explicit behaviour management strategies) and behaviour in their lessons is exceptional. However, this is because they may have had years to establish expectations and develop a working rapport with students. Although it may be frustrating to you as a trainee teacher, behaviour management is something that develops over time, but there are certain things you can do to establish effective routines from the beginning.

Planning for good behaviour

There is an age-old debate in education about what comes first: effective lesson planning or behaviour management. One train of thought is that if the lesson plan is effective, differentiated and personalised, framed in an engaging and pupil-centred way, then behaviour will be better. Conversely, if you explicitly focus on the behaviour first, then the learning can flourish with clear and obvious boundaries already cemented. What is the correct answer? Well, as when one football team comprehensively beats another team and they ask pundits the question whether it was good attacking or poor defending, more often than not the inevitable response is 'a bit of both'. And it is.

A well-planned lesson can stop potential issues arising if the students are engaged so they are less likely to misbehave. Consider a time when you've been bored, perhaps during a lecture or a film. On these occasions, you were probably more likely to look at your phone, chat to a friend or simply give up listening. However, those who hooked you, whether through the delivery or the content, gave you less cause to be distracted. It's the same in teaching: a well-planned, engaging lesson is as much a behaviour tool as rewards and sanctions.

There are times, however, where high expectations and behaviour need to be the central theme before learning can flourish effectively. It might be redundant to do an innovative and daring starter if the class will not stop talking in the first place. It is important to integrate routines into a workable system and then teach that system through encouragement, discussion and modelling (Rogers, 2011).

Chapter 1 explains how to plan for pupil engagement and will prevent a whole host of behavioural issues if the strategies and suggestions are used judiciously and effectively so as to 'disarm' the students in the first place.

Key learning point

Behaviour management has a cyclical relationship with planning. A well-planned lesson can go a long way to minimise behaviour issues. However, if behaviour is not dealt with, even the best planned lessons can go awry.

Super Nanny, and other such parenting gurus, are seen as effective behaviour managers. You know the typical set-up for these sorts of shows: a bedraggled couple – let's call them Alim and Amandip. They are exhausted and frazzled as their daughter Niki is running amok, screaming, crying and generally being a destructive force of nature. They are at their wits' end. Super Nanny observes a typical exchange between parent and child.

Niki: I want a biscuit.

Alim: You know the rules. You've had a biscuit already.

Niki: But I want a biscuit. I'm starving! (begins to cry)

Alim: No, those are the rules. (Niki is now stamping her feet. She is making a horrendous noise that is getting louder and louder.)

Niki: Biscuit!

Alim: No Niki, love. You've already had one – no more today.

Niki: I hate you! You're not my best friend! I'm starving! (Niki begins to cry uncontrollably, wailing. Alim watches her and sees how sad she looks.)

Alim: Okay, but only one more. (Niki stops crying, takes the biscuit and smiles. Alim smiles back.)

Cue the hilarious voice over: 'Niki really is taking the biscuit.'

As Super Nanny will point out to Alim, he started well, reiterated the rules and stuck to them. When Niki's tears came, Alim immediately buckled, unnerved by his daughter's apparent distress. Super Nanny, in that slightly pompous way that self-professed gurus do, probes further: why did Alim give in so readily? Was Niki going to wither right in front of his eyes if she didn't get the biscuit? Is Niki's love of her father solely based around flour-based food products or might she get over the disappointment of not acquiring an additional custard cream? Super Nanny continues: so, giving in and giving her the biscuit, she stops crying. What about next time? What has this exchange told Niki about rules? What happens when Amandip maintains the line that she can't have another biscuit?

Let's consider the link to classroom practice. In unashamed shorthand: *the teacher teaches; the learner learns*. When there is negative behaviour that challenges the teacher – you – invariably, it isn't really about you. They are affecting 'the lesson', which is all about learning. Niki, the learner, needed to learn that rules are there for a reason and will be enforced. Alim and Amandip, the teachers, had set the rules for one biscuit in a day, a fair expectation. As soon as Alim allowed emotion into the situation, and perhaps sensing a quick fix, he bowed down to Niki's hysterics. It just showed Niki that she will, ultimately, get what she wants if she cries and stamps her feet. Alim is now creating an environment where rules are blurred and boundaries are inconsistent.

Key learning point

Respect and relationships are forged through a consistent and persistent approach. Learners need and want boundaries. Be strong, firm and fair, even when it's tough - and it will be tough sometimes.

It is sometimes hard not to see students' negative behaviour as a personal slight, but the best behaviour managers are the ones who can depersonalise. If you see the lesson as learning, is their behaviour affecting the lesson? Then they are affecting the learning. Of themselves. Of others. Therefore that can't carry on. It needs to be addressed. This is where staying cool and calm in situations like this can prevent further escalation and knowing that it is not affecting you is a liberating one. No one, even adults, like to be told what to do, or to be sanctioned in front of their peers. It is easier to challenge negative behaviour if you are calm, even if you are raging inside. It does not mean you are a robot. It just means that if you maintain a stance, it makes it clear to everyone what is expected.

Key learning point

Learning is paramount. Challenging behaviour is not affecting you, but it is affecting the lesson and impacting the students' learning.

Finally, returning to the proactive and not reactive ideal, being positive is crucial for an effective practitioner. You are not on the scout to find students doing the wrong thing; you're not going to relish when students have a detention; you're not there to enjoy defeating the gobby student who has had the audacity to question your authority in front of the rest of the class. You are there to promote learning; to promote doing the right thing and this is how you can do it.

Targets

Develop your classroom presence to establish a positive learning climate

Quick wins

- **Know your lesson inside out** so your attention can be focused on the students and learning rather than on the mechanics of where the books are or what the next activity is during the lesson.
- **Have all work and resources prepared before the lesson.**
- **Rehearse the lesson beforehand** with your friend, partner or dog.
- **Talk less, get students to do more.** If you are developing your confidence, plan so that the students are working harder than you. This means that you can focus on the delivery of what you are going to say and make the transitions clear and smooth.
- **Talk a little louder than you would do normally**, which might even out some of the cracks of your wobbly voice. This does not mean that you should shout, rather that you should be clearer in your projection.

- **Avoid the erring and fillers to give your voice control.** You need to know what you are saying and this comes with being prepared.

- **Use resources to support you to reduce your cognitive load.** You have a lot to think about during a lesson, so anything that can help you focus on learning, so much the better. For example, have instructions on the board to assist you; summarise your lesson plan and stick it to the table; have helpful reminders on PowerPoint slides, etc.

- **Eye contact** is important. It does not mean 'eyeballing' students, but it shows you are not scared even if you are petrified.

- **Be self-deprecating if things go awry.** Use gestures, facial expressions and words that show you are a human being rather than overreacting if things don't go to plan.

- **Give yourself time before sanctioning a student.** You need time to make decisions in the same way that students do. To do this, reflect on what the student has actually done and pause before issuing your sanction.

- **Stay calm even when you are angered, frustrated or annoyed.** Be physically prepared: have enough sleep, eat well and exercise where possible. If you feel lousy, you are going to communicate this to the class.

- **Be positive!**

Slow burners

- **Develop 'visible' confidence.** Imagine you've been seeing your doctor for a long time. You've probably built up a relationship with him or her. When they tell you not to worry, you trust them. When they say you need to pull yourself together, you know you are worrying about nothing. When they tell you what's going to happen next, you listen. Now, imagine you turn up and see a new doctor, fresh faced, eager and, a little nervous, how do you feel? Do you feel like being honest as you have done in the past? When the doctor tells you not to worry, is there doubt in your mind that they don't know what they are actually doing? When they tell you what to do, do you want to interrupt and say, 'Well, Dr X would know and I don't agree with you?'

This is how learners see new teachers. They are a break from what they have become accustomed to. Your face is new, so the process of recognition and trust has to begin again. You - as the patient - do not care that the junior doctor excelled in medical school; that they topped their class; that they know the medical code backwards. You see a nervous face and insecurity sets in - it's perfectly normal. If the doctor looked confident, spoke confidently and had an aura that they knew what they were doing, that would assuage some doubts and uncertainty.

Develop your 'visible' confidence even if you don't feel it. Don't hide by your desk, by the board or behind your lesson plan even if you feel safe there - it is counterproductive. Circulate the classroom and make the space your own; it's not their space - explore it. Have everything in hand. Know where the A4 lined paper is kept. Know where the spare pens are. If you are fortunate enough to observe the class you are going to take over before you start, circulate, talk to students, get to know names, get a feel for what it's going to be like when you start for real. Lessen the shock for the students when you do take over. If you go in cold, which might be the case, be positive; remember the doctor analogy. Appreciate it's going to take some time for them to warm to you. Empathy is a teacher's worthy steed.

When wanting the whole class to focus on you, implement a 'whole-class standing point' point which is a place in the classroom where you feel you have the attention of every student. A good place to stand is in the middle of the front of the class; if you could imagine putting your hands out as though you were weighing two melons, imagine the class in the palm of your hands. This reminds you that you have them in your hands even if you don't feel that they are. You could make this explicit to the class and tell them that when you stand there, they should be facing you and listening. Or, as the psychology of body language dictates, students will begin to subconsciously realise that you mean business when you take up that stance.

Ronnie O' Sullivan is described as one of the most charismatic and confident snooker players the game has ever seen, but even he had to portray confidence to win the 2016 Masters Snooker semi-final. *I don't feel great but I'm trying to kid myself that I'm confident* (*The Guardian*, 2016). Similarly, you'll see senior managers doing assemblies to the whole school and you might think that they are supremely confident. Ask them. I bet most will say their heart was knocking against their ribs. They were probably nervous but exhibited 'visible' confidence even if they didn't 'feel great'.

Key learning point

Teaching is sometimes a performance. Sometimes you need to 'act' confident to be confident.

- **Consider how you use your voice.** As a teacher, your voice is the conduit through which you communicate. It can also betray nerves, so it needs to be treated carefully. It is imperative that you pause and take time in your speech; sometimes the speed of your speech can show students a lack of dominance in the classroom (White and Gardner, 2012). You need to show control in your speech as well as your body language, so take your time. This is also to separate your emotion from your delivery as sometimes a lack of confidence can lead to overreaction and stress. Your voice and language might be affected by other external stresses. Don't let your emotion cloud your language. This does not suggest being robotic but being aware and in control of your emotions. While you will encounter many raw emotions from students and things that occur in the classroom will prompt strong feelings, remember you are the adult, the professional and the voice of reason.

Quick click

Read the following article by James Eison for some advice on building your confidence in the classroom.

http://bit.ly/2cKFYpR

Maintain a consistent and persistent approach, adopting clear rules and routines for behaviour

Quick wins

- **Be by the door as students enter.** This allows you to start the lesson in a positive way, pre-empting any behavioural issues as students enter the class.
- **Make protocols for behaviour in the classroom explicit to the students and feature prominently in the classroom.** It is also important for students to know the purpose of these rules and why they have been adopted.
- **Teach rules and consequences separate to curriculum matter if appropriate.** If lessons are constantly being disrupted to the point where learning cannot take place, then it might be beneficial to devote some lesson time on reiterating rules and expectations.
- **Be organised.** Have a protocol for following up on managing your classroom. For example, if a student came in late, and there is a clear rule for lateness, ensure you enforce it and don't forget. This could mean writing names on the board or on paper as a reminder to come back to these students.
- **If you propose a sanction, you have to go through with it.** Students are tuned into whether you mean what you say. Don't give hollow threats to students such as 'If you carry on with this, you'll have to come back on Sunday.'
- **Ensure you stay calm so you don't overreact to situations.** If you overreact and give out a sanction which isn't fair, you still have to go through with it. Therefore, give yourself time before issuing the sanction to ensure the sanction is well considered and fair.
- **Create a formal start and a formal end to every lesson** (see Chapters 1 and 3).

Slow burners

- **Create rules and apply them effectively.** A vital aspect of effective behaviour management is to ensure that students know that there are clear boundaries. This, coupled with a consistent and persistent application of the clear boundaries, can alleviate potential issues in the class. Don't be tricked by watching experienced teachers who appear to have a *laissez-faire* approach to rules; there are implicit techniques and strategies they implement to instil clear boundaries. Great artists and writers often break the rules, but they do so because they know the rules in the first place.

Classroom rules are an excellent tool to ensure that students know exactly what is expected of them. There is some disagreement among teachers about whether these rules need to be negotiated with the students, but again this is what works for you. Sharing rights and responsibilities is important, but does blur the line between who is in charge. It is essential that the teacher has control. You're in charge of establishing the boundaries within which learning takes place. It is within these boundaries that students can be allowed a degree of freedom and autonomy. It is your responsibility to control the climate of the classroom to ensure learning. You may decide on a large majority of the rules with one rule left for the students to come up with. This gives them a sense of ownership, but they do know that ultimately you are in charge.

- **Ensure that the rules are:**

  - simple and clearly communicated;
  - in line with the school's behaviour policy - consistency is massively important across the school;
  - used consistently and persistently to ensure fairness;
  - enforced positively with positive language such as 'do' rather than 'don't';
  - not overly draconian so they stifle students' creativity;
  - referred to when appropriate not to the point where learning is affected;
  - modelled by you.

If students know the rules explicitly, their application is made easier as it lends itself to the depersonalised approach. For example, Elle contravenes a rule that has a consequence. Let's say she swears in the class at another student which is a shared rule. She knows the consequence is a one-hour detention. When issuing her with the sanction, there is no need to be angry or upset as the only person who should be upset is Elle who has the detention or the victim of her language. The application of the rules ensures that it becomes the pupil's decision. It is out of your hands: depersonalisation. 'I'm sorry Elle, but you know the rules.'

- **Avoid the grey area.** Ask any student, regardless of ability, age or behavioural persuasion, what they want from a teacher in terms of behaviour management. They will invariably respond: someone who is firm but fair. It is as simple and complex as that. Whether your approach is more disciplinarian or relaxed than other teachers, as long as you are fair, students will come to respect your decisions. Students know exactly what justice is and they are finely tuned to it (Capel *et al.* 2001). Of course, consistency doesn't vanquish all behaviour issues; it just makes the application of such rules less confrontational and ambivalent. From a student's point of view, it is hard to argue if the teacher has been fair, consistent and clear about the behaviour. They might still argue, but logic is a powerful tool.

 **Real life scenario**

Matty is talking for the third time while the teacher is talking.

Teacher: Right, the next time you talk over me, Matty, you will receive a detention. You know the rules on talking through others in the class. Thank you.

[Matty nods. Thirty seconds later, Matty talks again.]

Teacher: Right, Matty, I can't believe you're talking. Right. This is absolutely the last time. No more. I've warned you. This is your last warning. The next time you do that, you will get a detention.

At the start of this exchange, the teacher has been clear, linked to the agreed rights and responsibilities of the classroom and has been positive with the 'thank you' at the end of the statement, showing there is an expectancy that Matty's behaviour is going to change. Firm but fair. A correct approach. Then, the teacher reneges on their comment. This communicates to Matty that the teacher does not follow through with their sanctions. The teacher is making it even harder to deal with behaviour as they are adding doubt and uncertainty. The teacher has issued a very clear instruction with a very clear consequence. Matty knows exactly what is going to happen if he repeats the behaviour. By then retracting this, he will not believe the teacher has the strength of his convictions. Perhaps the bigger consequence of this is where the grey area can be exploited by students if he does follow it up with another student doing the same thing in the lesson: 'Well, you let Matty off. This isn't fair. I'm not doing anything now.'

Read *Developing Behaviour Management Content for Initial Teacher Training (ITT)* by Tom Bennett, chair of the ITT Behaviour Working Group. This has a clear overview and rationale for behaviour management.

http://bit.ly/2cMUKur

Develop effective relationships with students to create a good and safe learning environment

- **Get to know students' names quickly and use them.** Makes sure you find out how to pronounce them and what their preferred name is: *Build personalised and meaningful relationships with pupils, including crucially, using each pupil's name* (Bennett, 2016, p10).

- **Smile genuinely at students.** Forget the myth of 'Don't smile before Christmas'. It does not mean you are not strict if you smile.

- **Do what you say you will.** If you say you will mark their work by Thursday, mark it by Thursday. Don't forget to follow through on what you say.

- **Actually listen to students when they answer a question.** So often, we are considering what the next task is and may reply to students with little or no enthusiasm, or not at all.

- **Use story-telling in lessons**. Use stories, personal or otherwise, to elucidate learning. If you don't feel confident about talking about yourself, that's fine, but I have always felt that students see you as a learner and a human being when you introduce appropriate stories.

- **Don't let any student become 'invisible' in your classroom.** Get to know their hobbies, likes and dislikes. It's not about becoming their friend; it's about showing an interest in their lives to build a positive working relationship.

- **Be patient and don't think you have to have an instant rapport.** Consider any relationship you have ever had. You may have disliked your partner or a close friend in the early stages but as you got to know them, things changed and vice versa.
- **Call home for positive reasons,** not just for the negative.
- **Avoid whole-class detentions.** This creates divisions in the class. It is simply not fair to keep everyone in for a detention if there are innocent students. They might side with the perpetrators if they feel an injustice.
- **Utilise Think-Pair-Share** or other ways to ensure all students contribute. This also builds confidence in the class and thus many more students will be likely to answer.
- **Treat students with respect.** Don't embarrass students in the classroom. How would you feel to be embarrassed or mocked in front of your peers?
- **Listen to students' feedback about the lessons.** Do allow students to offer feedback on what they enjoyed and what you could do to improve. There is a health warning attached to this: sometimes students don't know what's good for them. They might say they want more computer work, but this might be that they know this means less hard work.
- **Get to know students outside your lesson** – for example, on break duty, school trips, sport events, through form time, lunch-time clubs, etc.

 **Slow burners**

- **Use humour.** Students often say that they like a teacher to be funny and to make learning fun. I worked alongside a teacher who was exactly that: funny and liked by students. She regularly won teacher of the year awards and students clamoured to be in her lessons. But, in terms of pupil progress and attainment, she would be deemed ineffective. She would argue that she got difficult students engaged. True. But they did not engage in the learning. They engaged in *her* and *she* was not on the curriculum.

  I have observed teachers with limited humour but who are extremely effective practitioners where the students enjoy the lessons and have made excellent progress. I have seen genuinely laugh out loud funny teachers who are effective practitioners and everything in between. Humour has its place but it depends on when you use it, how you use it and to which groups. It can be an extremely powerful way to soften planning for behaviour (Canter and Canter, 1992 in Porter, 1996).

Key learning point

Humour does not mean cracking jokes to get students 'onside' but can be used to develop an effective student-teacher relationship. It could be a gesture, a smile and the ability to laugh at something funny.

The beauty of humour is that it can soften harsh situations or spikey issues. Humour can reduce boredom, which has a direct link to low-level disruption. It could be the simple case that if we are asked to do something in a light-hearted, warm manner, we are probably more likely to do it, if we respect the person saying it.

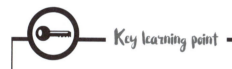

Quick click

Read how humour can bring cohesion to a class in this article.

http://bit.ly/2cK7Tal

- **Avoid overfamiliarity** *I see too many schools where head teachers are blurring the lines between friendliness and familiarity* (Sir Michael Wilshaw, *The Telegraph*, 2014). A possible danger of humour is that it can lead to overfamiliarity with students. The classroom is a place for learning and not for making friends with students. Overfamiliarity breeds the blurring of boundaries and this is unacceptable. Humour and a positive relationship is one thing but being overfriendly with students does not improve classroom management. Swearing and inappropriateness with the students does not make you one of them.

  Students don't see teachers positively if they consistently blur the lines between teacher and student. They might see the person positively, but when it comes to respect for their role as a teacher, this might be tarnished.

Key learning point

Effective relationships are built on trust. You are a teacher. They are the learner. If they don't like you but they respect you as a teacher, then so be it.

Minimise low-level behaviour to promote learning

Low-level behaviour is the most irritating of behaviours to confront as it is often subtle and difficult to put your finger on. Ofsted highlighted the negative impact that low-level behaviour has on learning. The statement that *pupils are potentially losing up to an hour of learning each day in English schools because of this kind of disruption in classrooms* (Ofsted, 2014, p4) is a shocking but a very believable statistic. In conjunction with this target, read Chapter 3, specifically on how to start a lesson effectively as this will prevent a host of behaviour issues from the outset.

Quick click

Read the Ofsted Report on low-level disruption: 'Below the radar – low-level disruptions in the country's classrooms' and the impact it has on progress.

http://bit.ly/1xW5E3m

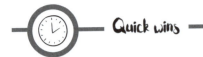

- **Establish clear boundaries and classroom rules and be consistent in the application of them (see above).**
- **Be prepared.** Have all materials and resources ready as dead time leads to low-level behaviour issues.
- **Speak lower *not* louder so students have to listen.** Sometimes speaking louder increases the noise in the class so students talk louder to be heard. Experiment with a range of volumes and tone.
- **Acknowledge the perpetrator in the middle of the sentence but do not lose flow** so attention is not drawn to the negative behaviour and learning can continue. Conversely, if this is continual, stop the class and direct the attention to the student, briefly describe their behaviour and insist on what they should be doing.
- **Minimise low-level noise with props.** If a student is prone to tapping, drumming, clicking their pen lid, etc., give them blu tack so they have something to fiddle with which doesn't make a noise. Also consider when to hand out materials so that they're not tempted to tap or play around with equipment.
- **Consider where you stand at different points in the lesson.** Position yourself where there are disruptions and move where you see the need. Vary where you stand during the lesson. Standing behind the students as they look at the board also draws the focus to the learning.
- **Use gestures or eye contact** to communicate with a student rather than **repeating a student's name.** If a particular student wants attention, you are giving it to them by saying their name repeatedly.
- **Tactical ignoring.** This is a dangerous strategy, which means you let some little things go. This is not advised for a student who you know will carry it on continuously. Tactical ignoring is best when you ignore secondary behaviours – the reaction to the sanction or punishment: *Choosing when to respond to pupil behaviours at a time suitable to the teacher; tactically ignoring secondary behaviours (less intrusive misbehaviour, such as whispering) to focus on primary ones (for example, getting the whole class on task) until such a point that the secondary behaviour can be responded to* (Bennett, 2016, p11).
- **Vary the pace of the lesson** so students don't get comfortable or bored in the lesson. Be aware of the class's focus. At times, you might want to encourage a faster pace when you sense lethargy; conversely, you might need to slow the pace down when students are struggling to keep up (see Chapter 3).
- **Use positive language when you talk to students.** Rather than saying 'please', say 'thank you' so students know there is an expectancy that they are going to complete the instruction. 'Please' has a tinge of desperation, especially if the tone that emanates from your voice is strained with stress.
- **Reframe students' behaviour.** For example, ask 'What should you be doing?' rather than, 'What are you doing?', which draws to the negative behaviour not what they should be doing. Consider how, in scenario B below, the teacher's prompt is about focusing on learning rather than honing in on the negative behaviour.

Real life scenario

Scenario A

Teacher: Why are you singing? (What answer does she expect?)

Student: I don't know. (He's responding to the inane question.)

Teacher: Don't answer back! (She asked the question – what did she expect?)

Scenario B

Teacher: What should you be doing?

Student: The work on the board.

Teacher: Anything stopping you from doing that?

Student: Er, no.

Teacher: Great, away you go, then.

- **Don't assume it is all the class talking** when sometimes it feels as if it is. Track the class very carefully to identify the students.

- **If you don't know who it is, issue a general comment to re-establish the rules of the classroom.**

Slow burners

- **Use seating plans.** There is not much dispute in the educational sphere that seating plans are a good idea, although there is some disagreement about whose space the classroom is. My firm belief is that it is not the students' space or an extension of the playground (Rogers, 2011); however, it is also not totally the teachers' space either. It is the teaching and learning space that the teacher cares for – if that doesn't sound too saccharine. If we link it back to the triangle of depersonalisation, it is the space of learning that is shared. The only caveat to this is that the teacher is the one responsible for ensuring that teaching and learning can occur, so let's say it's your space in which to ensure that learning takes place.

  There are many ways of structuring your seating plan; it is personal preference and you can experiment with a range of approaches (see below). At the start of your training, you might not know what works, so talk to experienced teachers about how they've set up their classrooms and their rationale. Again, some experienced teachers might not need or utilise a seating plan; it does not mean that you can replicate years of expertise and experience. The seating plan might need adaptation and frequent change. For some groups, it might work beautifully; for others, it might be an unmitigated disaster. But again, if you know this is the case, don't be despondent; you can do something about it and learn from the mistake. After all, you're going to make loads. It is always a good idea to change a seating plan regularly. Varying seating plans also avoids the 'this is my seat'. Why are you sitting in my seat? I've always sat in this seat.' Just be careful not to change it so much where it becomes counterproductive to learning and students don't know whether they are coming or going.

Before organising a seating plan, you need to consider the layout of the classroom that will best support learning. Sitting in rows is seemingly making a bit of a resurgence as some schools are keen for students to be pen in hand, ready to learn with no time taken up with off-task discussion if set up in groups. This could stifle creativity and discussions but is good when there is an emphasis on independence. Phil Beadle is unequivocal that learning should definitely take place in groups as this is the best way that students learn (Beadle, 2010). Yes, this might be effective in some scenarios but not for all work. Sometimes there needs to be a didactic approach with tables in rows as this tells the students that this is a different form of work. Exams are not sat in groups. Students need to be prepared for all different elements of work. It could be argued that in later life, we very rarely work individually in such a sterile setting, but we do have to be realistic: there are times in life where it is you, and you alone, answering a question. Outcome: vary where appropriate. If you are in your training year, this might not be possible, so do liaise with your mentor or classroom teacher.

Make sure your room is set up with the following advantages.

- There are no students' backs to the board and they have a natural body position.
- You can adapt and change where necessary depending on topic or task. There will be times when groups are ideal and other times when rows might be better. You need to liaise with your colleagues or anyone who shares the class with you.
- You can get everywhere in the classroom easily to circulate (see below).

- **You could try different seating plans as follows:**

  - **In register order.** It might make the seating plan random and thus break up potential disruption. It is also helpful if you are learning names in the initial weeks of getting to know the students. I would do this for a short period if you want to use this.
  - **High-ability students sit next to lower-ability students.** I am not a fan of this system as it is inherently flawed. The assumption that the higher-ability student will cascade their knowledge to the lower ability, thus raising their attainment is something of a misnomer. It is true that students learn from explaining to others but in different subjects, students are not always highly able and vice versa. Use this judiciously.
  - **Behaviour dynamics.** You could, after getting to know the students, or speaking to a colleague with experience of teaching the same group, carefully choose where students sit based on how they work together and their personalities. This, I have found from experience, is an effective method but requires a comprehensive knowledge of students. Dynamics are so important for students to work well together and this might need tinkering with until you find the perfect outcome. For example, two challenging girls who would talk across the room and cause mischief as they were not sitting together caused a problem for a textiles colleague of mine. It was clear that they were going to talk, no matter what. The textiles teacher sat them together after a lesson and made it clear that they would have two chances to prove

that it was best for their learning and the classes if they sat together. The two behaved well; they felt that they had been given a chance and their teacher was fair. Another teacher in the school tried the same with the same two girls. The result? Unmitigated disaster. The two ran amok, creating more disruptions than when they were split up. Their behaviour was even worse than before. What was the difference? Of course, there would be other contextual factors but, after further discussions, there was something different in how the teachers managed this. After talking to both, it seemed the textiles teacher made it crystal clear in their language that it was the teacher's choice to do this and not the students'. The other teacher had asked the girls what would make them work. Their assumption was that the teacher had succumbed to their behaviour and the negative behaviour had got them moved - thus, they felt in power. Remember, everything is your decision.

- **Negotiated seating.** Students are allowed to choose one person that they would like to sit next to and then the teacher places the pairs in the classroom. This is good as it gives students a sense that they are listened to but you have ultimate say where they go.

- **Students choose.** Allowing students to sit where they want is often shown as giving the power to the students and this assumption is correct. However, for some tasks, for some lessons, students might need to feel support from peers they get on with to fully engage with the learning. With everything to do with teaching, it is about purpose. If you think learning can be improved by allowing student choice, be bold - do it. It is whatever works. Remember the importance of language and control, though. Explain to students why you are doing this. It is their choice where they sit, but it's your choice to do this - not theirs. It is strongly advised that this approach is not used in the initial creation of the classroom environment. It is extremely difficult to re-establish control if this is utilised too early.

Ensure students are responding appropriately to prevent calling out

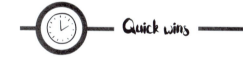

Quick wins

- **Praise responses which follow the protocol.** Praise those students who follow the rules, not only admonishing those who are not (Capel *et al.*, 2001).

- **Reiterate to the student the rule about answering in the class before they answer - this time with their hand up.** This is good as it trains them to follow rules and still enables the student to answer.

- **If a student shouts out, ignore their answer and ask another student instead.** Even if the student who is someone who does not normally answer, you can't change your rules. The more you accept this, the more students will see it as an appropriate form of behaviour.

- **Appeal to logic.** 'Please don't shout at me: I can't hear!' or 'I can't listen to everyone else if you shout.'

- **Don't ask open-ended questions.** If you ask the class 'What do you think about?' to no one in particular, or without the protocol for response, what do you expect to happen?

- **You could acknowledge the response with a hand gesture** before asking another student. Remember, you dictate what happens in your classroom.

- **Ask a question to which all students have time to prepare an individual response.** After some wait time, you can then select students to respond.
- Remember to be **consistent and persistent** in dealing with all calling out. If you have a rule of no calling out but you take an answer from them, it is going to be counterproductive.

Slow burners

- **Consider a balance between hands up/no hands.** Calling out might not be as negative as you first assume; it might come from a student being excited or engaged in the lesson and is desperate to show the teacher that they know the answer. It is always a balancing act to encourage participation without stifling a natural enthusiasm for the subject. However, protocols for how a student responds in class needs to be clear in your initial rules and expectations. Though it is important to punish shouting out, which has the intention to merely disrupt, enthusiasm and the desire to express learning should be channelled into an appropriate form.

  Make it clear to the students the protocols for answering questions. I would suggest a balance of responses. We have to empathise with the student who wants to respond all the time, but we do need to be mindful of the students drowned out by their responses.

  First, try to be explicit when you want hands up or no hands. You could have an image on the board which specifies whether you will accept hands up or not.

Real life scenario

The teacher is about to ask a challenging question. It will stretch many of the students in a Year 9 citizenship class.

Teacher: Okay, this next question is challenging and will need some thought, so no calling out, thanks.

[Here the teacher is giving kudos to the question and making it clear that thought and reflection are required. The 'thanks' at the end highlights that it's an expectation.]

Teacher: I am going to accept hands up first and then I am going to choose other people to answer as well.

[Here, the teacher is giving the confident student who likes to answer a chance to answer first before others contribute; there is an expectation of how they will answer. This could, of course, be reversed and the teacher could select students before opening up to others with hands up.]

It might seem mechanical, but in those formative times with the class, these expectations need to become embedded before students know the routine. I am not advocating robotic teaching, but I am wholeheartedly advocating structure of response until it becomes subconscious and students know that calling out is not a feature of your classroom. In this context, the teacher asks for hands up first as it is a challenging question and also to give those enthusiastic students a chance to respond.

There are two main ways of taking student oral feedback: taking hands up and no hands. If it is a 'how do you feel question' then all students will be able to answer it as it is their opinion so no hands could be used. However, if you asked a particularly challenging question, you might expect only a few members of the class to respond so a hands-up approach would be appropriate. Both approaches have their advantages but consistency is paramount: if you say no hands and then accept hands up, then you are creating that grey area to be exploited.

Promote positive behaviour through effective use of praise

 Quick wins

- **Try to praise more than you criticise.** Look to make three positive comments for every negative one.
- **Try to catch students being good to reward them.** Some students don't like public acknowledgements that they are doing the right thing, so a personal reward to a student when they weren't trying for a reward might be productive.
- **Arrange a meeting with the head of year, head of department or even the headteacher to praise the student.**
- **Make positive phone calls home.** These are often seen as a very positive reward and also bring parents into pupil progress. This might lead to a reward at home but shows that when the student acts positively, good things happen.
- **Send cards home for good effort, behaviour, progress and community spirit.**
- **Display students' good work**. For example, spotlight specific students, use the visualiser or display work on classroom walls. The work you display should vary and be taken from a range of students.
- **For smaller groups, have a large chart on the wall with students' names on them which tracks their efforts and successes.** This becomes a visual representation of behaviour and highlights the positive rather than the negative.
- **Stickers on good pieces of work.** Contrary to belief, most ages like this and students in Year 11 still like a sticker, especially the boys.
- **Develop rewards that add to the school experience and develops cultural capital**, such as theatre trips, experiences, visits, speakers coming into the school, etc.
- **Rewards need to be used in a consistent and persistent manner so it is fair for all students.**

 Slow burners

- **Make use of genuine and judicious praise.** When it is justified and apt, praise is an excellent way of providing pupils with motivation. However, injudicious praise when giving feedback on learning can be damaging (see Chapter 7). I have observed lessons where almost any student action is greeted with a string of superlatives. This does not help learning and progress. Students need to be resilient for the world: that means honest, fair and positive criticism as they are going to get all their lives. It is how you couch this that makes the difference.

Also, consider what you are actually praising. Praise does not mean just praising the successes; it's praising the effort to achieve the success. They might not achieve their goal, but you need to give the students the encouragement that they can so they can do it again with the next task. Praise acts as a way of building resilience if done correctly. Look at the difference between the two scenarios.

Real life scenario

Scenario A

Teacher walks over to a student who is working. The student doesn't normally write much but has written a short paragraph discussing gender bias in sport.

Teacher: Alex, that's brilliant! Well done! That's a reward. Keep it up.

What is the teacher praising here? The teacher is praising the fact that Alex has written something, anything. Did the teacher actually read the work? When the teacher takes Alex's book in, it lacks deeper understanding. The student may now be under the impression that any work is 'brilliant' work.

Scenario B

Teacher: Alex, I'm really pleased that you have made the effort to start [specific about the praise of effort]. It's good that you have understood what gender bias is [praise specific success]. Now can you give me an example of where this might be shown in sport?

Alex: In tennis? Men get paid more than women, don't they?

Teacher: They do, you're right [encouraging through conversation but not labouring praise]. What else do you know about it?

Alex: Some people think that men get more people to watch them and less people watch women so they should get paid more.

Teacher: Yes, that's what some people think. Good stuff.

This is where the targeted and specific nature of the praise given in scenario B will enable the student to replicate the behaviour in future lessons. We need to ensure that effort is rewarded as this is the pathway to learning and progress. It can't just be, however, to make students accept a lack of progress even to the point where they feel good about it (Dweck, 2016).

Key learning point

In short, if students are consistently praised, they might lose sight of what they are actually being praised for.

Another issue with praise is making sure it is not just for the children who don't follow expectations the first time around. It could be the case that a difficult child is praised for picking up a pen, or not rocking on their chair, or simply doing what is expected. Although you may praise the more challenging student for perhaps doing something that they should be doing in the first place, it is important to make sure you are praising the students who quietly and consistently conform to the rules and expectations every lesson.

When and where praise is administered also needs to be considered. Some students abhor being publically praised as it tells their peers that they have tried, or that they have worked. Some students don't want this and it could be counterproductive. One challenging student I taught preferred a quiet, private word of praise. She still found it hard to hear because hearing praise is difficult, especially face-to-face. I once publically praised a Year 7 student, Ajay, for an outstanding speaking and listening exercise where he recounted a tale from his primary school when he was hit in the face with a football. I praised him extensively saying that it wouldn't be amiss for a GCSE presentation. He loved it. The other students loved it. The problem? When it came to reading and writing, he did not have the same ability and found it hard to feel as if he wasn't as good as that moment. 'You said I could do my GCSEs,' he said. I didn't, but I could see why he thought this. Using praise is important in creating a positive classroom climate, but we don't want to enforce a fixed mindset that could be counterproductive in the longer term (Boyd et al., 2015).

- **Motivate learners.** Students should, in a perfect world, be working for themselves, not for a merit, or for a Gummy Bear, or for a voucher for a local shopping centre. If that is what they deem a reward and what success looks like, we are setting ourselves up for a fall as the novelty soon wears off. Of course, students might put the extra effort in if a chocolate snack is made available, but what about the next time they have to answer a question when there isn't a chocolate snack on offer? Will this affect their motivation? *Incentives rarely produced long-term results because it reduced the perception that pupils were doing that task of their own free will* (Paton, 2009).

Of course, it is naive to think that all students can be intrinsically motivated at any stage of their development. Self-discipline takes time to develop. Many students struggle to delay gratification. Such students may need help to see the long-term benefits of behaving in a lesson. While rewards aren't wrong per se, they do little to foster intrinsic motivation in your students (see Chapter 4).

In my NQT year, I had a challenging Year 9 group (all boys plus one girl called Lyndsay who was delighted to be in the same room as the tricky duo of Chris and David last period on a Friday). I used a reward system: if they could work perfectly for 40 minutes, in the last 20 minutes they could play games while eating donuts. My rationale was that it was better to have 40 minutes of learning rather than an hour's battle with no tangible work done and detentions a plenty. Their behaviour was impeccable. So rewards work. No discussion. Period. Or so I thought.

I also had them on the following Monday. No rewards for effort or behaviour were on offer. It was Monday, so back to normal. No donuts, just work on *Much Ado about Nothing* and the playful linguistic conflict between Benedick and Beatrice in preparation for SATS. Their behaviour was considerably worse than the week before. I spent a large portion of the lesson explaining the absence of donuts, flustered that they were not behaving as they had done on the Friday. 'It's not Friday,' I responded, stress etched on my face. Monday, for them, was a million miles away from the Friday before and the Friday to come.

Ultimately, no motivation had been built up and their desire for engagement in the lesson was not about the subject, it was about what they were going to gain. What they were going to get. It was a short-term fix. I was inexperienced and I made other mistakes (read back over the last paragraph – what other mistakes did I make?) but I used rewards as the only way of engaging in learning. The five detentions I gave out that lesson were entirely my fault.

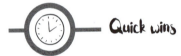

Key learning point

Rewards are a short-term measure and the real target should be getting students to be intrinsically motivated to succeed.

Ensure students are on task and engaged with learning

Quick wins

- **Create activities which are purposeful and engaging.** Ensure that you plan lessons that are going to engage students (see Chapter 1). If, for whatever reason they are not engaged, make them realise the purpose and importance of the task.

- **Ensure lessons have a degree of choice.** Consider giving students options to reach the learning outcomes. This is not pandering to the students. You are getting the desired learning but giving the students choice is a liberating thing (see Chapter 4).

- **Differentiate activities:** You need to make sure the work is differentiated so there is challenge and support for all students in the class (see Chapter 8).

- **Praise the students who are on task and engaged in learning.**

- **Develop take-up time to put the onus on the students.** If students say they know what to do but are slow to settle, write the time in the margins of their work. Set a realistic amount of time in which you will return to check. If they haven't done sufficient work, sanction in line with the school's behaviour policy.

- **Circulate.** If you make sure your presence is felt tangibly around the room, honing in on specific areas of the classroom, this can have a positive impact on behaviour. When circulating, question the level of work and ask students to justify any absence of work.

- **Make sure transitions are swift, as dead time leads to disengagement** (see Chapter 3).

- **Regularly check students' books at the end of the lesson.** Those students who seem to have been on task might not have produced either the quality or quantity of work expected. This is always a good barometer of how on-task students have been in the lesson and creates a motivating expectation that their work is important.

Slow burners

- **Explain tasks clearly and make expectations explicit.** First, students need to know exactly what they are going to do in tasks so your instructions need to be clear, explicit and time specific. You might try breaking down the instructions or slowing down the delivery so that students are not overwhelmed. Some teachers use the technique of asking a student to repeat back the instruction to ensure that they are listening and to ensure the rest of the class understand. Use this judiciously. Overuse of this can slow down the pace and lead to off-task behaviour. These instructions could also be on the board as well as on a handout so there is no confusion on what students should be doing.

- **Establish the level of noise you want in your classroom.** If you continually shut down all noise in the classroom, you are going to make a rod for your own back. The classroom does not need to be silent all the time, which can be counterproductive; a little noise can actually be a sign of a positive learning environment. It is important for you to know the difference between 'work' noise and 'off-task' noise. This is difficult at the start of your practice as it is hard to differentiate. Home in on conversations and listen to individual voices. If someone from the back row asks a question and you can't hear them, this could be a barometer that the classroom is too loud. You could also have a line on the board and mark it to indicate where the noise levels are; this is a good non-verbal way of making students aware that the noise is too loud.

A moment for caution about the gimmick in teaching. A colleague of mine identified that the noise in his lessons was getting too much so he invested heavily in bulky traffic lights that monitored decibel levels. The traffic light would take pride and place at the front of the class and when the noise level was acceptable it was green; amber was borderline and red was dangerously high. It sounded like a great idea when he had mentioned it in Monday briefing. When I spoke to him at the end of the day, he looked a broken man. 'You feeling okay Tim? How did the traffic lights go?' I said. 'Not great,' he replied rubbing his temples, his eyes half open, 'the devils have spent all day trying to make it go red.' He never used them again.

Challenge students that continually disrupt learning

Quick wins

- **Pre-empt disruptive behaviour.** Keep your eyes and ears open for early signs of disruption.
- **Use a distraction technique.** With students who seem to be going off-task, rather than sanction them, try to set them a task with some responsibility like handing out equipment or asking them a question.
- **Effectively use the seating plan** to ensure that specific students are separated or away from potential disruptions (see above). Move the student if the seating plan is not working for them.
- **Adopt and perfect 'the look'.** Develop a way to look at a student who is not following an instruction, which screams silently 'stop'.

- **Criticise the behaviour and not the student so as not to exacerbate the situation.** For example, rather than saying, 'Charlotte, you are rude and are not listening,' say, 'Charlotte, the behaviour you are showing now is stopping others learning.'
- **Use calm, assertive energy.** Change your voice when behaviour escalates. If you raise your voice for minor misdemeanours, your impact will be diminished if a more serious incident occurs.
- **Don't slow the pace of the lesson to admonish a student.** If students see that you stop the lesson every time they interrupt or disrupt, this might make them do it even more as they become the focal point of the lesson.
- **Allocate students a role or responsibility** to show they have a part to play in the class.

- **Get to know different students.** The start of this section stated that most behaviour problems emanate from the teacher. There are, however, times when it is simply out of your control. Remember, you are in the business of working with young minds, bumbling their way through adolescence.

If you have an idea about possible reasons for pupils' bad behaviour, you are in a better position to be able to deal with it (Leaman, 2007). Before you react to behaviour, you need to consider where this behaviour comes from. Before taking any lesson, it is good practice to get an indication of the students you are going to teach: background, contextual factors, behaviour, family life, etc. Liaise with the appropriate people in the school so you can pre-empt any issues which might occur in the first place. It does not mean you stigmatise or make a judgement on them – it simply means you are aware. To understand is not to excuse and sanctions need to be applied fairly but knowing that student's circumstances will help you exercise professional judgement. Should you sanction a girl for being late to registration, when you know that she is a young carer who has to support her two brothers as well as taking three buses to get to school? What about the normally well-behaved boy, struggling with his parents' acrimonious divorce, who argued back at you? It is important not to lose focus of what it was like to be a teenager. It isn't easy.

Key learning point

A key aspect of behaviour management is knowing your students well enough to understand the roots of their behaviours.

Every student is different, but there are common behaviours that teachers contend with in the classroom. For each of these types of students, and the ones who don't fit tidily in a label, you need to get to know the student and understand where these behaviours have come from.

The attention seeker

- **Ensure that they do have a chance to have a voice.** If you are always shutting them down, this might lead to resentment. For example, let them lead a group, present their work or give them responsibilities.

- **When giving praise, use the student's name. Avoid overuse of their name for negativity** as this becomes a way of being noticed; utilise non-verbal approaches where possible.

- **Don't let them derail the lesson.** Try not to keep stopping the lesson to have a one- to-one discussion with the student, which says that their attention seeking works.

The negative student

- **Be enthusiastic as much as possible to model positivity.** If you're disinterested or downplay the importance of the work, students will mirror this.

- **Use humour to diffuse the situation**. Employ mirroring. If they say, 'I hate you and I hate this lesson', try something like: 'I'm not crazy about me right now but I have to go home with me. You're the lucky one.' It's hard to be angry with someone who doesn't rise to the bait.

- **Depersonalise comments**. 'This lesson is boring.' This might be covering a student's own back if they are finding the work difficult. Try something like: 'Well, we can have a chat after the lesson about it and how it can be improved.'

- **Be patient and adopt a long-term approach**. 'You might not like it now, but I guarantee that by the end of the year, you will love it.' It's amazing what students might think at the start of the year compared to the end of it

- **Listen to students' concerns. Remember, they might be right.** A Year 8 girl once told me that my lessons were boring. I, of course, shrugged this off as it was just a student trying to get a rise out of me. That was until one of my quieter students came to me at the end of the lesson, cocked their head slightly embarrassed and said, 'It has been pretty dull, sir. We've done the same activities for the last two weeks.' And we had.

The argumentative student

- **Do not rise to the argument.** Remember depersonalisation. If a student wants to argue with you, don't rise to the bait: adopt a calm and authoritative tone of voice.

- **When issuing a sanction, use a clear, non-accusatory voice making sure you are explicit** about what the problem is.

- **Do not issue sanctions in front of another student or a group,** which will exacerbate the situation. Do this quietly and privately, making sure the student has time to reflect on their behaviour. There is an episode of *The Simpsons* which is excellent at showing this. Bart is punished for breaking Grandpa's false teeth. He is sent to his room as a punishment and as he starts to realise he won't get dinner, he considers that actually his behaviour needs to change. Homer, thinking he is doing the right thing, slips him some pizza. Bart laughs and says, 'sucker!'

- **Give options** to the student so there is no sense of injustice: 'Do you want me to take the ball off you now or do you want to put it in your bag?' This gives them two choices and both outcomes are what you desire. Saying 'Give me the ball' is only going to lead to a confrontation.

- **Ignore the secondary behaviour** (see tactical ignoring above).

The aggressive student

- This is where **knowing the school's behaviour policy is imperative before you teach any lesson.** You need to know where students go if their behaviour is compromising others, including your own.

- **Carefully look for signs of aggression from the student**. There might need to be a pre-emptive conversation. This might be due to the previous lesson or their own personal situation. You might want to offer them a 'breather' or some time out to calm down.

- **Talk to the student quietly and privately before anything happens.**

- **Always look to de-escalate the situation.** Fighting fire with fire doesn't work. You're the adult. It's hard to remain angry with someone who is calm, controlled and reasonable.

- If something physically aggressive happens, this might result in the student being **removed from the classroom**. The aggression should not be tolerated and will be sanctioned, but if another student has caused this response, they also need to be dealt with.

- It could be that you **move the student to another designated classroom** or to the Head of Department. Again, these protocols need to be agreed beforehand.

- **Aggressive behaviour could lead to call patrol, on call** or whatever system the school has in place to remove the student for this lesson.

The swearing student

- **Model appropriate language at all times.** You set the tone.

- **Ensure the school policy on swearing is adhered to.** If the swearing is directed at a student or yourself, it needs to be dealt with because it has been used aggressively.

- **Don't make a student's swearing personal.** Consider where the student has come from and their background. Some families use swearing as punctuation and thus it becomes the norm for them to replicate. This is not to condone the swearing and the sanction should be applied, but they might not understand the significance or seriousness of their language.

- **Do not get overly offended or shocked by swearing**. This might have been the intention in the first place, so stay calm.

In summary

Every teacher – every single one – has suffered from a difficult class in their career. Effective behaviour management takes time. It takes learning from mistakes and it takes patience. If you take these steps, it will go a long way to prevent, tackle and manage challenging behaviour.

Before the lesson

- **Get to know your class**: strengths, weaknesses, likes, dislikes, attainment, progress, context, behaviours, etc. Create a profile of them as much as you can.

- **Be clear where you are going in the lesson** and in future lessons.

- **Be prepared and organised,** have all materials ready to go.

- **Understand the school's behaviour policy.**

- Make sure you are **confident with the lesson's content.**

- **Plan engaging lessons that are differentiated, pupil-centred and challenging.**

During the lesson

- **Have clear rules and routines from the very beginning**: be by the door, dealing with behaviour, being positive and smiling to greet them.

- **Stay calm** and make sure you depersonalise any negative behaviour.

- **Ensure your pace is varied** and there is no dead time that breeds negative behaviour.

- **Pre-empt behaviour** issues by being vigilant.

- **Give clear and explicit instructions** both orally and in writing.

- **Praise positively and judiciously.**

- **Circulate the classroom.**

- **Value students' responses and ideas.**

After the lesson

- **Evaluate lessons and reflect on both what went well and areas to improve.** Where you have experienced negative behaviour, what are you going to do next?

- **Make sure you follow through on rewards and sanctions administered in the lesson.** For example, if students were asked to stay behind but didn't, make sure you follow this up through the necessary channels. If you said you would call home for Ed's excellent effort, or poor behaviour, make sure you do it. If you promised house credits to the winning group for their dramatic reworking of photosynthesis, make sure these are accredited to the students.

- **If it is the best lesson ever, it does not make you an amazing teacher. If it is the worst lesson ever, you are not a terrible teacher.** Learn from what you did well and what you need to improve. Every footballer has a terrible game. Every actor has a terrible performance. Every teacher has a terrible lesson.

Further reading

Rogers, B (2011) *Classroom Behaviour: A Practical Guide to Effective Teaching, Behaviour Management and Colleague Support*, 4th edn. London: SAGE.

A comprehensive and extremely readable guide to behaviour management approaches is *Classroom Behaviour* by Bill Rogers. The timeless nature of the strategies will help you in your training year and beyond. There are also some interesting insights into developing teachers' emotional literacy.

McPhillimy, B (1996) *Controlling Your Class: A Teacher's Guide to Managing Classroom Behaviour.* Chichester: John Wiley & Sons.

Despite *Controlling Your Class*'s relative 'old age', this book gets to the heart of controlling a classroom environment and demonstrates how effective behaviour management techniques should not be fads, gimmicks or knee-jerk reactions to the latest interpretation of the Ofsted framework.

Tauber, RT (2007) *Classroom Management*, 4th revd edn. Westport, CT: Praeger.

A text that balances the theory and the practice is *Classroom Management: Sound Theory and Effective Practice*. It offers discipline suggestions that can be seen as quick wins as well as more difficult to implement discipline models.

References

Beadle, P (2010) *How to Teach*. Bancyfelin: Crown House Publishing.

Bennett, T (2016) *Developing Behaviour Management Content for Initial Teacher Training*. London: Department for Education.

Boyd, P, Hymer, B and Lockney, K (2015) *Learning Teaching: Becoming an Inspirational Leader.* St Albans: Critical Publishing.

Capel, S, Leask, M and Turner, T (2001) *Learning to Teach in the Secondary School*, 3rd edn. Abingdon: Routledge.

Department for Education and Skills (2005) *Key Stage 3 National Strategy Behaviour and Attendance Strand Toolkit Unit 2. Everyday Policies: Rewards, Sanctions and Promotion of Positive Behaviour*. London: DfES. Available at: **http://dera.ioe.ac.uk/6293/1/84ea41b4e7e54c59c558a35bbe234925.pdf** (accessed 19 September 2016).

Dweck, C (2016) 'Praise the effort not the outcome? Think again'. *The Guardian*, 29 January. Available at: **www.tes.com/news/school-news/breaking-views/praise-effort-not-outcome-think-again** (accessed 19 September 2016).

Eison, J (1990) Confidence in the classroom: ten maxims for new teachers. *College Teaching*, 38(1): 21–5. Available at: **www.uwo.ca/tsc/resources/pdf/Confidence%20in%20the%20Classroom%20 College%20Teaching%20Article.pdf** (accessed 19 September 2016).

The Guardian (2016) 'Ronnie O'Sullivan reaches Masters semi-final with Mark Selby win'. *The Guardian*, 14 January. Available at: **www.theguardian.com/sport/2016/jan/14/ronnie-o-sullivan-masters-semi-final-mark-selby** (accessed 19 September 2016).

Leaman, L (2007) *Dictionary of Disruption*. London: Continuum.

Paton, G (2009) 'Classroom rewards do not work'. *The Telegraph*, 13 November. Available at: **www.telegraph.co.uk/education/6563040/Classroom-rewards-do-not-work-work.html** (accessed 19 September 2016).

Porter, L (1996) *Student Behaviour History and Practice for Teachers*. St Leonards, NSW: Allen & Unwin.

Rogers, B (1997) *You Know the Fair Rule*, 2nd edn. London: Financial Times/Prentice Hall.

Rogers, B (2011) *Classroom Behaviour*, 3rd edn. London: SAGE.

White, J and Gardner, J (2012) *The Classroom X Factor: The Power of Body Language and Nonverbal Communication in Teaching*. Abingdon: Routledge.

3

Pace

Teachers' Standard 4 - Plan well-structured lessons: impart knowledge and develop understanding through effective use of lesson time

This section is most relevant to Teachers' Standard 4, and aims to support you in establishing strategies to ensure that you make the best use of time in a lesson. Pace is one of the most common targets a trainee is given in the formative stages of training to teach. There are many links between Teachers' Standard 7 and Chapter 2 on behaviour management, especially when setting the right tone at the start of the lesson.

- Demonstrate knowledge and understanding of how pupils learn and how this impacts on teaching (TS2).
- Set high expectations which inspire, motivate and challenge pupils (TS1).
- Manage behaviour effectively to ensure a good and safe learning environment (TS7).

Introduction

Without doubt, at some point in your training year, and beyond for that matter, using pace effectively in a lesson will be a target. Let's be fair: you've only just started your journey as a teacher, so how are you expected to know how long activities should last for? How to move seamlessly between transitions when you're desperately just trying to remember what's on the next PowerPoint slide? How to use your voice authoritatively to improve the lesson's momentum when Neil's own version of momentum is to repeatedly pound a basketball on to an innocent girl's face?

In a past role as an English subject mentor, I once set a target that the trainee needed to improve the pace in her lesson. The trainee asked me how they could improve. I replied: 'Don't worry, improved pace in a lesson really comes with experience.' It was meant to reassure but it did the exact opposite: the trainee felt a sense of frustration that getting the pace right was something you would only get to grips with in the distant future. On reflection, it was not useful advice and arrogant to boot. What I said to the trainee wasn't totally wrong, of course – there is no getting away from it: experience does help you with pace, but there are easy to use strategies to exorcise this ghost.

Experience does give you a strong indication of how long a chosen activity *might* take. In those early days, when you're planning a lesson, you might set the task: 'Write a paragraph responding to the question: "Was Macbeth a butcher?"' At first, you allocate five minutes in your lesson for this activity; however, you need to consider the following.

- What sort of responses would you expect in such a short space of time?

- What deep thinking can a student realistically do in five minutes? What parts of Macbeth's character are butcher-like? What parts of his character contradict this?

- Could you, a subject specialist with a degree and an unquenchable passion for the Bard, complete this task effectively in five minutes?

- Therefore, is five minutes enough time for this activity to address the learning aim?

The answer is of course no, so how can you expect the students to? This activity clearly requires more time to allow students to access deeper learning. Conversely, you could set the following task: 'You have ten minutes to underline four words linked with photosynthesis.' What deep thinking needs to be done for this to require such a lengthy time? The students may finish in a minute and then what? Dead time. Off-task behaviour. Disengagement.

Targets

What targets does this chapter cover?

- Improve pace at the start of lessons.
- Ensure there is no 'dead time' in a lesson; make sure students are working productively.
- Improve timings to maintain an appropriate pace.

So how do we define the term pace?

Maintaining a good pace is about making sure the speed at which students are enabled to learn is appropriate. There is no 'dead' learning time and there is a seamless link between activities; all students have time to think and they do not have to rush through learning.

The pace will vary according to different stages of the lesson and for the purpose of the activities. It could also depend on the learners in front of you. Higher pace could be more appropriate for lower level basic skills and younger students, whereas more demanding content for older students might be better suited to a slower pace to allow pupils to develop understanding (Muijs and Reynolds, 2011). However, an overly slow exposition might demonstrate a lack of passion, even though you are brimful of ideas and verve which might lead to student disengagement. It is important that you are aware of how variations in pace can affect your learners' motivation and also how they view your dynamism and passion for what you are teaching them.

Key learning point

Effective pace in a lesson is not necessarily about doing things quickly.

You do need to embrace real, spontaneous moments of learning and truncate tasks when you see it is falling flat or it is not fulfilling its purpose. Just because it's in the lesson plan, does not mean it is sacred. A plan is a plan. The lesson is a different beast entirely. A lesson breathes, a lesson plan does not. Teachers should relish – where appropriate, of course – pupils' input as you might miss out on something truly special. You need to think on your feet and sometimes react to pupils' responses for real impact (Glazzard, 2014). Consider the following scenario.

Real life scenario

Scenario A: Slave to the lesson plan with students studying the language of Shakespeare:

Pupil: Miss, I think a hugger-mugger is someone who is adulterous.

Teacher: Sorry, we don't have time for that; we need to move on.

Scenario B: Using the question as a learning point

Pupil: Miss, I think a hugger-mugger is someone who is adulterous.

Teacher: Interesting, how so?

Pupil: Well, a hug is something you do to someone you love. A mugger is someone who steals, so it would make sense that this person is stealing a heart as it doesn't belong to them.

Teacher: So what does that show about that word's meaning?

I think it is worth embracing the saying a 'lot about a little' principle rather than superficially touching on ideas and paying lip service to learning. Rattling through content actually devalues the content you are endeavouring to impart at such speed. The lesson becomes about 'getting through it' rather than the enjoyment of 'deeper learning' and electing to use tasks to move learning forward. It pains me as a university tutor to see trainee teachers speed through content 'to get to the end' where they have lost sight of what the end actually is.

In conclusion, pace makes a real difference. Get it right early and other things will fall into place. Effective use of pace in lessons helps improve student engagement; behaviour management; pupil progress; student reflection and, significantly, it helps us as we should not be working as hard as the students in our classrooms.

Targets

Improve pace at the start of lessons

 **Quick wins**

- Where possible, **be in the room five minutes before the lesson begins.** If the room is not free, ask the classroom teacher if you can set up while they finish their lesson. Most teachers are accommodating and will allow this.
- If you are in another room the lesson before and have to move, **make sure you pack up in good time** so you are not late to set up for the next lesson.
- **Have all materials (equipment/exercise books/resources/worksheets, etc.)** ready prepared either on the tables or ready for you to hand out when needed. Load up a box with the resources needed for each of your lessons that day.
- **Check the technology in the room beforehand.** Have the PowerPoint/IWB up on the screen before students enter. Make sure everything works (not just the day before - things can happen unexpectedly).
- If you want the students to sit in a **seating plan, have the classroom diagram displayed prominently on the screen and direct students verbally as well.** Avoid clutching a flimsy piece of paper as they come in individually, talking to one student at a time while the other students lose focus.
- **Have the date and title on the board** to prevent the question: 'What's the title?' which Year 7s, in particular, seem to be obsessed with.
- **Give timed reminders** about when the lesson is formally going to start in an authoritative and confident manner, reminding the students of the expectations. Use non-verbal gestures such as raising a hand or moving position in the classroom.
- **Use positive language** when talking to the students. Say 'thank you' rather than 'please' when you want them to complete a task, indicating that your expectations should be met. The question 'What are you doing?' draws attention to negative behaviour, but 'What should you be doing?' draws students' attention to the task at hand.
- **Praise those students who are following your instructions** rather than demonising the ones who are not. You could write the names of those behaving positively on the board; avoid writing the names of those not doing the work as this is counterproductive.

- **Leave non-essential administration** until a more suitable part of the lesson.
- If there are latecomers, acknowledge their lateness but deal with this at the end or at a more suitable part of the lesson. Do make a note so you don't forget to deal with it later.

Slow burners

- **Ensure a formal start.** This might seem a contradictory strategy, but it is for the long-term benefit of improved pace in a lesson, especially for the more challenging groups. You need to establish clear routines at the start of every lesson. Insist that students know what is expected of them and what will happen if they are not met. Do they line up outside? Do they know they need to complete the task on the board? Is there a school or departmental policy for this? It will inevitably take time to get the expectations clear and take more time to implement but, in the long run, will improve pace at the start of a lesson and have a knock-on effect to the main body of the lesson as well.

Students need to be in no doubt about the expectations and boundaries in the classroom and this could take time but the long-term effects will be hugely rewarding. You could go as far as to send them out again and rehearse entry into your classroom, or ask them to stand behind their desks and not start the lesson until it's the way *you* want it. You might say 'What about when I want to do an unusual starter to engage? I don't want to keep on doing the same thing.' This is a fair point, but the expectations you establish are an essential platform for more creative starters and future learning (see Chapter 2).

Make it your policy not to deal with individual queries until the class is settled and on task. If students know that they just need to ask you a question, and you lose track of what you need to be doing, they will persist on doing it. It is not rude to say, 'Thanks, John Paul, but I'll come to you when we're settled'. As long as John Paul knows that you will go to him at some point and not forget about him, then he will be appeased. If he isn't, remember: *you* control everything that happens in a classroom. You are not 'shutting them down'; you are saying, it is not convenient at that precise moment. The lesson is paramount. If students know that you don't entertain trivial questions or things that *you* deem irrelevant, the questions will diminish and, after a while, cease entirely. If it is a real issue with particular students or a class, you might allow them a set number of post-it notes per lesson to pose a question or to make a comment and then you can deal with this if you deem fit. More often than not the question will not be worthy of a complete interruption of learning. I had a student called Charlie and, as was always his opening gambit, he would state with his churlish smile: 'I have two questions; well, actually three . . .' . After realising that this student's questions were, more often than not, frivolous, and normally variations on a theme, I issued him with 'Charlie blocks' (three pieces of Lego) and he had to give me a piece every time he wanted to ask a question. He soon started to evaluate the validity of his questions and only used a 'Charlie block' when he definitely needed to know the answer. However, if the Lego became a distraction to learning, I would not have used it (beware of using a gimmick).

Key learning point

Be consistent and persistent in the way you manage the start of lessons.

- **Position yourself strategically to establish an orderly start to the lesson.** At the start of the lesson, as students enter the classroom, position yourself by the door, body half in and half out. Engage in dialogue with the students to ensure that they know what to do and direct them towards the task as well as greeting them into the learning environment. While you are doing this, you can tackle any uniform, equipment or behavioural issues as well as creating a positive, classroom environment. If these minor issues are ironed out at this point, *potential* disruption can be avoided in the main part of the lesson. This should be carried out in a positive but pleasant manner. Always consider how you, as a human being, like to be spoken to. 'Morning, Sam, good to see you. Tuck your shirt in, thanks. Your task is on the board.' This is better than 'Tuck your shirt in now. You look a mess.' Or, 'Why are you dressed this way? You know the school rules.'

Think of a boss you have worked with. Imagine them getting you to do something. How would you want to be treated? With respect? Certainly. With humour? Possibly. But you want to feel as if you are trusted. Therefore, ask yourself, 'What do I want? I want Sam to tuck her shirt in and do the work.' Then ask yourself, 'How can I get her to do that without creating unnecessary confrontation?'

Avoid the patronising comment. Be positive. Be pleasant. Be firm. You want Sam to do the work and you want her to be smartly dressed in line with the school's policy. You can do that pleasantly and politely, avoiding a potential confrontation and disagreement, and not affect the pace of the lesson. If she becomes defiant, you can escalate your approach.

 — **Key learning point**

Do as you would be done by. How would you want to be treated by someone in authority?

When the class starts to swell, and students in the classroom become the majority, this is when you might gravitate more inside the classroom, leaving the position by the door. This is where you might move to the back of the room, so you can deal with students coming into the room, but then the focus is on the board and the work you want them to do (see immediate engagement, below). Students are then not looking at you, and the focus is on the board rather than on you.

- **Ensure there is immediate engagement.** Have a task on the board for students to do as they come in. You need to grab them; hook them; hold them and, let's be honest, calm them down sometimes, but it does not mean necessarily that they just come in and write the learning objectives. It might settle, but does it engage? (See Chapter 1 - lesson planning-starters and plenaries'.) For some classes, this will be fine. Therefore, develop bell/through the door/do now/entry tasks as soon as they walk into the classroom. These are activities that the students do as soon as they enter the room. This will give the students focus as they enter the classroom and immediately get them engaged in learning. Here are some examples you could use.
  - **Thunking questions** (Gilbert, 2007) are open questions that promote thinking skills. 'Is a paper bag art? Would you rather sit or stand forever? Is it ever right to bully a bully?'

The three thunking questions promote the following thought processes:

1. Not necessarily a right/wrong answer.
2. Use of prior knowledge.
3. Develop higher-order thinking.

Quick click

Explore the world of Ian Gilbert's thunks and experiment with bell tasks and starters.

http://bit.ly/2cMUWd4

— **Shock tactics or challenging statements** to encourage debate and discussion: 'Should we feel sympathy for the parents of a killer?' 'Men should earn more money than women.' 'Mobile phones should be banned in schools.'

— **Music can prime the mind** for learning (Jones, 2014). For example, in history, you could play *La Marseillaise* as they enter and students consider what the lyrics and the music tells them about the aims of the French Revolution. In English, you might play *F.E.A.R.* by Ian Brown as they enter and ask them to speculate what is interesting about the lyrics (all the verses use the acronym of F.E.A.R. and could potentially lead to a lesson on structure, poetry or as a listening exercise).

— **Problem-solving activities** – for example, using a cryptogram, or puzzles, or what's the missing number/word?

— **Word webs** where students start with a word and link using the prefix and suffix to generate other words. For example, starting with the word 'transfer', students might generate other words like 'transport', 'transmit', 'transgender' and then they could consider what the prefix 'trans' means.

— **Recap quiz/questions** from the previous lessons.

It is not just about keeping students occupied while you do something at the front of the class. Make it purposeful. Link it to the lesson. Shock the socks off them.

Real life scenario

In a citizenship lesson, the teacher had this on the board: 'Make notes on the following question: What would you find in a cigarette? For example, nicotine.'

This was a simple enough bell task to get them to consider the topic of the lesson. The students completed this as the teacher did the register and spoke to a child who did not have the correct equipment, which she accomplished quietly and privately. When she took some of the responses using no hands, which consisted of nicotine, paper, tar, etc., she then revealed:

Rat poison.

Cue a tirade of 'Err!' and 'That's disgusting!' Register done. Student spoken to. Learning set up. Students engaged.

Two minutes elapsed.

Ensure there is no 'dead time' in a lesson; make sure students are productively engaged

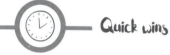 Quick wins

- **Consider the nature of tasks** you ask your students to do: cutting out a sheet then sticking it in might take longer than just giving them out the sheet already prepared. Yes, it takes you more time but pointless admin tasks leads to 'dead time'.
- **Clarity of instructions.** You don't need to explain everything you are doing in the class. Limit your own talking time so that your commands are clear and punchy to avoid over-dwelling where you repeat the same instruction (Muijs and Reynolds, 2011).
- **Use positive, imperative language** ('now', 'move', 'next', 'go', etc.).
- **Ask yourself whether students really need to do 20 examples or whether after five, you can move on,** making sure that consolidation is built in later (if required). In maths, for example, making students complete 20 similar questions could lead to disengagement whereas less, more steadily challenging questions could increase productivity and engagement (see Chapter 8).
- **Avoid asking the students to repeat the task.** Consider why you are doing this. It slows things down. You might ask a student who you think is not listening to get their attention, but if you ask four or five students what the task is, this will slow down the flow of the lesson (see circulation, below).
- **Have timings on your PowerPoint/IWB slides** to denote how long the task should take so you don't forget.
- **Use gestures** as well as verbal communication: stopping the class to admonish a child for chewing gum is counterproductive to learning. Miming removing the chewing gum could be more effective and can be done quickly with no loss of learning time.
- **Use a time keeper in group work** so students become more invested in their own time management. Hand the responsibility to them.
- **Always be two steps ahead.** While pupils are working, prepare for the next activity (by writing on the board, distributing the next resources, setting up the room, etc.).

Slow burners

- **Circulate to ensure that students are on task at all times.** A lot of time is taken by trainee teachers tearing around the classroom in search of a student to ask endless questions for no discernible reason. Develop how to read the room before circulating. Wait for around a minute at the front of the classroom so you are a clear presence, and scan for issues or 'pockets of need' before circulating. Consider the clothes shop analogy: there is nothing worse than going into a clothes shop to have a shop assistant ask you if you need help in fourteen seconds of setting foot in their establishment. I've only been in your shop a matter of seconds – how can I possibly know what I want, how I'm doing or if I have any questions? It's the same for students working on a task: let them settle and, if you're sensing they are not on task, then you can use gestures or move to their group to put 'pleasant pressure' on them. This should come with clear expectations prior to the task, so don't just expect students to be able to do what you're thinking. This will help improve pace as by going around injudiciously to each group you could actually slow down their learning rather than aiding their development; your involvement with one group might trigger another to go off task. This is not to say that you shouldn't circulate, but consider the purpose. Why am I going to certain groups? Why am I talking to a group who know exactly what they are doing and doing it effectively?

- **Develop transitions to maximise productive engagement.** Transitions are the bridge or the movement between different parts of a lesson and they can make or break the flow of learning. You need to consider how you use transitions in lessons effectively. Transitions are vital and are often the time when 'dead time' occurs and learning is lost, sometimes irreparably.

  There is no harm in having bullet points or a PowerPoint print-out on your desk to refer to if needed. It is not ideal, but it can remind you where you are going and what is coming next. If you work better with technology, you could have a sentence on the bottom of the PowerPoint/IWB about what is about to come.

  Also, consider if you are planning for too many activities which will require more transitions. This 'fragmentation' (Muijs and Reynolds, 2011) can cause the lesson's flow to diminish with a seemingly never-ending paper chase or succession of a thousand chunked activities that don't allow for deeper learning (see Chapter 1).

  Your voice is also important in transitions to signal a change. Consider the language you use when you want to approach a transition. Be clear about what you require students to do when you issue an instruction such as 'Everybody listening'. Does this command mean students can continue on the task as long as they are listening or does this mean you require their total attention?

- **Maximise learning time during whole-class feedback.** It is important to get feedback from students in your class, which can be achieved in many ways. If you have circulated effectively, you should have an idea about what they have learnt, therefore negating the need for lengthy whole-class feedback. Don't spend too long asking questions they know the answers to, which is pointless. Move to the more challenging questions or to the next activity. Remember purpose: What is the point of questions? To move the learning on. If they have got it, don't labour it.

  One of the most common errors made by trainee teachers in terms of whole-class feedback is that every group/individual presents back to the class, one by one. I have seen a thousand lessons where the student/group presents to the class as the rest of the class sit passively, disengaged by their peers chuntering on about something or other, nervously pointing to an overpopulated PowerPoint screen or a terribly drawn poster curling at the edges as some youngster desperately tries to keep it up. This is then repeated, so everyone presents. Why? Why is there a need for every group to present in this way?

- **There are other ways to share learning and still maximise learning time.**

  - **Speed dating.** This can be done in many ways. For example, students are each given a question on a chosen topic to do with their subject. They have to sit with someone else who has the same question. They then work together on creating the best possible answer using their ideas, notes and any other resources at their disposal, becoming experts on that question. They then split up and 'speed date' with the other groups (maybe five or six), sharing their best answer and hearing the other students' responses, which makes learning active and engenders effective working relationships (Zepke and Leach, 2010). It's pupil-centred and there is no wasted time. Of course, it needs to be set up with clear expectations and instructions about what is required.

  - **Carousels.** This is an interactive way for students to move from one group to the next. At the stops on the carousel, students discuss, reflect, share, etc. (anything you want them to do). For example, business studies students, in groups of four, are given a new approach to motivation in the workplace. In their groups, they investigate a particular approach. When this is done, two of the students go around to all the other groups to discuss, reflect and share findings. The other two students stay and they explain their approach. Of course, the two students who stay won't hear the other carousels, so when the other two students return, they need to teach them everything they have learnt about different approaches to motivation in the workplace.

    If you wanted to still have whole-class involvement, what are the other students going to do while they watch the presentations or performances? They could have questions to answer from the presentation. They might need to ask three questions at the end. They might need to make bullet points on the main ideas. You might randomly select a student to summarise the key points of the presentation.

- **Involve students in their own learning.** It is important to make goals clear for students and to outline the learning journey. Whether you believe in the validity of learning objectives, no one can argue that the teacher needs to know where the learning is going and what knowledge or skills they want from the students at the end of the lesson or schemes of learning. It is easier said than done, however, and it could be argued whether students really understand their own learning journey. Whether they can chart their progress against the exam specifications is debatable, but students do benefit from knowing what's coming up in the lesson and beyond. It does not mean that at every turn, in every transition, in every mini-plenary, they need to be referred back to the learning objective to 'see' how well they have done as this can become counterproductive. While signposting is important, it should never take priority over learning itself. A simple strategy is to use a task checklist to help students know what steps to take to achieve their learning outcomes and prevent the endless questions about 'What do we do next?'

- **Deal with disruptions that lead to dead time.** Cowley (2003) says that teachers in their first year should wait for students to be quiet before proceeding. I have always disagreed with this. I absolutely stand by the idea that you do not talk over any students but there are more effective, time-conscious ways to deal with the chatty student. Why should *you* wait for them? Why should *you* have to fold your arms? Feign that *you* are gazing out of a window? Feign knitting? Remember: *you* are in control of the classroom. Why should students, who are ready to learn, have to wait for the other students to decide when they want to be quiet? This leads to dead time and can create a ripple effect to the other students as they have nothing discernible to do. Students get very frustrated at the perceived lack of control demonstrated by a teacher. I appreciate that there are times when you need to pause and this can be effective. It just can't be all the time. Pausing for a few seconds before formally starting the lesson is useful because it allows the class to settle, know that the lesson has begun and could save time in the long run.

As for the whole-class detention, where you put a minute on the board regardless of the innocent, this is a reprehensible idea, likely to encourage more students to feel you haven't got the wherewithal to deal with behaviour authoritatively and students might side with the troublemakers. I have seen trainees, and experienced teachers for that matter, use whole-class punishments and when I make this point, they say, 'Yes, but it worked.' I will always agree and ask them to consider the longer-term effects of such a punishment. When I was a teacher, our whole staff were reprimanded by the Senior Leadership Team for not marking our books. The Senior Leadership Team knew exactly who this applied to, so why were they punishing those teachers who were doing the right thing? That meeting lasted for over an hour and applied only to a few teachers, so it wasted a lot of time. You can imagine how the majority of the staff felt who had done everything expected, and more, of them.

If there are low-level disruptions, identify the student(s) and deal with them rather than affecting the whole-class progress. Expectations should be set up from the very beginning to pre-empt some of these issues (see Chapter 2).

Improve timings to maintain an appropriate pace

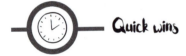 Quick wins

- **Wear a watch and use it.**
- **Plan your lesson thinking about what pupils will be asked to do, not what you will be doing.**
- **Plan for 5 minutes less than your lesson time** to give you some extra leeway.
- **Vary tasks** so there are not just static activities; break them up with some more active ones – where appropriate and purposeful.
- In your lesson plan, **indicate the activities you could take out without an impact on the 'learning journey'.** This means you can skip these if other parts of the lesson overrun.
- **Ensure that you factor in modelling to your lesson plan** so that students know what is expected of them, what the challenge looks like and how they can independently achieve the learning outcomes (see Chapter 4). This may take longer, but students will know what to do and will perform better.
- **Do the task yourself** and then consider the thought behind the task. Do they need thinking time for this? Is it straightforward? Consider every pupil doing this task.
- **Observe the processes of learning** and how they engage with the task. Mentally take note of how well they complete tasks.

○—🕐—**Slow burners** ————————————————————

- **Plan effective activities.** The 'effective use of lesson time' (Teachers' Standard 4) starts with lesson planning - most things normally do. Lesson planning, if you stripped it down to its core, is all about purpose. Every activity you employ needs to serve a purpose in the 'learning journey' of the student. Shaping these activities and planning the time they should take is a daunting prospect but there is a way into this. Consider: What thinking time needs to go into the activity? How complex is the task that you are asking the students to do? Where in Bloom's taxonomy (Bloom *et al.*, 1956) does it fall? Is it a recall exercise where the information should be easily locatable? Does it require the more complex approach of evaluation, which means they have to look at more than one idea or issue to draw together conclusions?

○—🔑—**Key learning point** ————————————————————

Maintaining pace is very important as a common problem is often that teachers allow the activity to drift; it then dominates the lesson time and, consequently, the planned learning opportunities don't actually take place or are rushed or lose their value (Bartlett, 2015, p35).

There is often a real desire as a trainee to shove everything that you have learnt into a lesson when you are being observed. Effective teaching is not about gimmicks. It is not about ticking boxes. It is about the most appropriate activities for students to achieve the learning outcomes. Consider a well-known cookery show. The contestant who does the overly complicated thirty-four element dish of grilled orange with tartan, mustard marshmallows might be exciting, but most people would take the good, old steak and chips cooked perfectly every day of the week (apart from vegetarians, that is). A very well-cooked lesson, with perfect seasoning delivered every time is favourable to the unpredictable orange disaster that tastes decidedly of sawdust. This does not mean you shouldn't take risks; it means that you need to perfect the basics first before you try to subvert or be radical in your planning.

Lewis Hamilton learnt to drive in a go-kart after being obsessed with radio-controlled cars. He did not learn to drive in a Formula One car.

The danger of packing lots of things into a lesson is where the focus wrongly shifts to the teacher rather than the learner. You don't need to show *everything*; it is more impressive when you select the most appropriate and judicious activity, which might not necessarily be the all singing and dancing one - which enables the students to make progress. Observation or not, this should be the rule for planning.

In the initial months of planning, start with the 'less is more' approach. The strict three-part lesson (see Chapter 1), even though it has its limitations, is a good starting point. Focus on planning for key activities, especially if your transitions are an issue as this is when the noise begins to escalate (Rogers, 2011).

- **Control the time of the activities.** Don't be afraid to truncate or extend activities, but remember you are in charge of the pace. You could extend the time because you feel that the students would benefit from more time not because they have failed to use the time wisely. You are the barometer of time. You shorten time when you realise they don't need the time. Remember: you are in control of the time of an activity. If they need longer because they genuinely need longer, give them it but be clear to them why you are extending the time. It is not just that they haven't worked hard enough. Your lesson plan is simply that. Don't be afraid to adapt where necessary.

In summary

You will invariably be set a target based on pace, especially at the very start of your training. After every lesson, every week, every term, as long as you critically reflect on your use of timings, the pace of your lessons will improve. Remember, pace is not just about doing things quickly, it's about giving the appropriate amount of time to what you want to achieve.

Before the lesson

- **Know your lesson plan inside and out.**

- **Try out the activities yourself to gauge how long they might take for different abilities.**

- **Pre-empt issues that might slow the lesson down (technology, understanding of tasks, admin, etc.).**

During the lesson

- **Be prepared and organised,** have all materials ready to go.

- **Leave unnecessary admin until an appropriate time in the lesson. Give time reminders.**

- **Give clear and explicit instructions** both orally and in writing.

- **Have timings on your PowerPoint/IWB slides.**

- **Ensure your pace is varied so there is no dead time.**

- **Circulate the class effectively to ensure on task behaviour.**

After the lesson

- **Reflect on the lesson** and how the length of activities may have affected progress, engagement and behaviour.

—— Further reading

There are no definitive texts on pace as it is different from other weightier topics such as behaviour, lesson planning or assessment, for example. These topics – and you will understand this when you see the myriad of literature available – can fill countless bookcases. Pace, on the other hand, does have a ceiling point. A book that has pace referred to throughout is the comprehensive and readable *Learning to Teach* by J Glazzard.

Glazzard, J (2014) *Learning to Teach*. Maidenhead: Open University Press.

—— References

Arends, R (1994) *Learning to Teach*, 3rd edn. New York: McGraw Hill.

Bartlett, J (2015) *Outstanding Assessment for Learning in the Classroom*. Abingdon: Routledge.

Bloom, B *et al.* (1956) *Taxonomy of Educational Objectives: Cognitive Domain*. New York: David MacKay.

Cowley, S (2003) *How to Survive your First Year in Teaching*. Chelmsford: Ruskin Press.

Gilbert, I (2007) *The Little Book of Thunks*. Bancyfelin: Crown House Publishing.

Glazzard, J (2014) *Learning to Teach*. Maidenhead: Open University Press.

Jones, R (2014) *Don't Change the Lightbulbs*. Bancyfelin: Crown House.

Muijs, D and Reynolds, D (2011) *Effective Teaching Evidence and Practice*, 3rd edn. London: SAGE.

Rogers, B (2011) *Classroom Behaviour*, 3rd edn. London: SAGE.

Zepke, N and Leach, L (2010) Improving student engagement: Ten proposals for action. *Active Learning in Higher Education*, 11(3): 167–77.

4
Teaching and Modelling

Teachers' Standards 2 and 4

This chapter discusses different approaches to teaching and modelling concepts in the classroom and aims to provide you with a range of different strategies to present different ideas to students. The chapter will cover the following Teachers' Standards.

- Be aware of pupils' capabilities and their prior knowledge, and plan teaching to build on these (TS2).
- Demonstrate knowledge and understanding of how pupils learn and how this impacts on teaching (TS2).
- Reflect systematically on the effectiveness of lessons and approaches to teaching (TS4).

Introduction

Over the years I have spent in the company of teachers, I have heard teaching compared to many different things, such as the following.

Teaching is like lighting a flame.

Teaching is like training an animal.

Teaching is like riding a bike.

Teaching is like herding cats.

Teaching is like weaving.

Teaching is like sowing seeds.

These might sound like poetic and impractical ways to describe teaching, but how do any of these descriptions help you to go and teach that difficult group on Friday afternoon? While these descriptions of teaching might not help you to plan your next class (and for some more specific suggestions, see the quick wins section below), it is worth reflecting on what kind of activity you think you are doing when you teach. This chapter will introduce you to a number of different models of learning and also to practical strategies that arise from those models.

─────── Targets ───────

What targets does this chapter cover?

- Widen the range of teaching strategies used in your lessons.
- Encourage student-led learning to increase independence.
- Support the development of students' metacognitive skills.

Different models of teaching

Different understandings of teaching lead to different approaches in the classroom. For example, in the early part of the last century, teachers borrowed ideas from a group of psychologists known as the behaviourists. You may have heard of Pavlov's experiments: when he fed the dogs in his laboratory, he rang a bell and he noticed that when he rang the bell without offering the dogs their food, they would drool at the mouth. Pavlov argued that the dogs associated a stimulus (the bell ringing) with a response (drooling). Teachers apply Pavlov's ideas to the classroom even in the present day. If you want Jemima to continue to work hard, you can associate the behaviour with praise or a reward: 'Well done, Jemima, great effort!' and you can link behaviours you want to suppress with punishments: 'Put it away, or you will lose your break time.' The behaviourists applied the same principles to learning as well as to behaviour. Learning was seen as the transfer of facts from the teacher to the student, and learning could be stimulated by associating it with rewards. For example, students might be tested and punished or rewarded to encourage correct answers and to suppress incorrect ones.

You may feel that teaching knowledge in your subject is more complex than associating a stimulus with a response. Later thinkers, such as Jean Piaget and Lev Vygotsky, argued that students' learning was more complicated than had been suggested by experiments carried out on laboratory animals (for a brief introduction to the work of Piaget, Vygotsky and other thinkers discussed in this chapter, see Bates, 2016). They noted that learners arrived at lessons with their own ideas, which interacted with information from their teachers. Piaget, Vygotsky and other writers, labelled constructivists, argued that rather than thinking of teaching as transferring knowledge to students, a better model was to imagine that the learner constructed their own personal understandings of the world. A teacher then cannot directly transfer facts from their head to their students, but must engage with the models that students develop and encourage them to resemble those of experts in the subject. For example, after several lessons of teaching a group about the planets in the solar system, one student raised her hand and asked if Pluto was called a dwarf planet because dwarves lived there. This student had developed her own, not unreasonable inference, presumably from an early comment I had made about Pluto no longer being considered a planet. This led to an interesting discussion of what the word dwarf meant in the context of a planet and it turned out that a number of students had assumed that Pluto was the size of a football or a house. The constructivist model highlights that knowledge doesn't transfer directly and it is important to check the understandings your students are developing.

Quick click

For a brief introduction to Piaget and Vygotsky's ideas about learning, the clips below from the Khan academy, are a good place to start.

www.youtube.com/watch?v=xoAUMmZOpzc

www.youtube.com/watch?v=-p_-On2f35o

This discussion might seem a little removed from the demands of planning for the classroom but, by looking at the examples below, you will hopefully gain some insight into how different assumptions about what learning is like can guide your actions in the classroom.

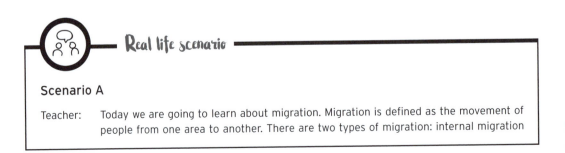

Real life scenario

Scenario A

Teacher: Today we are going to learn about migration. Migration is defined as the movement of people from one area to another. There are two types of migration: internal migration and external migration. There are many different reasons why people may leave an area, called push factors, such as the occurrence of natural disasters or high unemployment. In addition, there may be reasons that attract people to a new area, such as better climate or higher standards of living. These motivations are known as pull factors. Student A, what does migration mean?

Student A: When things move around.

Teacher: No, student B?

Student B: The movement of people from one area to another.

Teacher: Correct.

Scenario B

Teacher: Today we are going to learn about migration. Has anyone heard of the word migration before?

Student A: We learned about migration of animals in biology.

Teacher: Tell me what you know about it.

Student A: Well, it's when animals move from one place to the next.

Teacher: So why do animals migrate?

Student B: To look for food, or because it's cold.

Teacher: Interesting, is that the only meaning of the word?

Student C: In computer science, migration is about moving information.

Teacher: Are those ideas different?

Student A: Well, they're all about stuff moving.

Student D: Like immigrants are people moving into a country.

Teacher: Exactly. Migration is the movement of *people* from one place to another. Talk to your partner and come up with at least three reasons why people might migrate. For an extra challenge, explain the differences between immigration and emigration.

These examples are exaggerated, but the teacher's different assumptions about learning affected the manner in which they taught. In scenario A, the teacher adopted the role of the sole source of knowledge and judge of correctness. In scenario B the teacher acts as a facilitator encouraging students to develop their own ideas and understand their assumptions. Though the behaviourist model may be useful in some situations – for example, drilling factual knowledge or in behaviour management – constructivist teaching is widely accepted as a powerful approach for teaching complex ideas. However, you may not necessarily agree. Through your own experiences in the classroom, conversations with colleagues and reading research, you will develop opinions about the statements below that will affect the way you teach in the classroom.

- The teacher should be the source of knowledge in the classroom.

- Learning is a personal process and no two students learn in the same way.

- Learning some topics occurs best through social interaction.

- Knowing facts lies at the heart of good learning.

- All the students in your class are capable of reaching the learning goals set by the curriculum.

As you develop an awareness of your beliefs about learning, you may find it interesting to look through a range of different learning theories – Schunk (2014) is a good place to start. It is best not to think of these theories as either right or wrong, or to assume that there is always a best approach for all contexts. Though the constructivist model of teaching has, for good reasons, become dominant in many education systems, there are things to be learned from studying other models of learning.

Key learning point

There are many different ways to think of learning - your assumptions about what learning is will affect the way that you teach.

Using a variety of explanations

One assumption of the constructivist understanding of learning is that every learner develops a personal understanding of the world. You may feel, as an expert in your subject, that you know the single correct way in which to understand a concept or topic. However, try talking to other teachers in your subject and you will find they construct the same ideas in slightly different ways. This is not to say you will disagree about key facts, but they may emphasise different features or use different forms of explanations. It is tempting to become attached to the way of understanding the world that has worked for you, and be surprised and frustrated when others make sense of the world in a different way. An effective teacher is one who is able to present an idea in a variety of different forms to allow students to select elements that make sense to them and so develop a personally meaningful understanding. Consider the example below.

Real life scenario

Teacher: What do these representations have in common? Can you think of other representations that would fit?

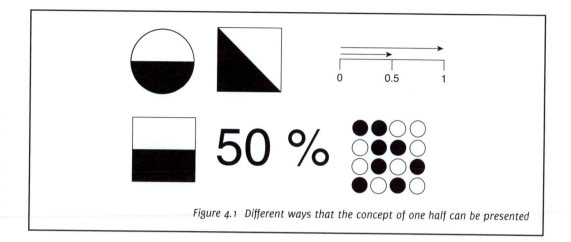

Figure 4.1 Different ways that the concept of one half can be presented

It may be that when you think of the concept of one half you visualise a particular type of representation. I tend to think of the pie-shaped image in the top left of the box above. However, other people may understand the concept through a different representation. In the example above, by presenting a range of ways to understand the concept of one half, the teacher is allowing students multiple routes to grasp the concept. In addition to finding a representation that is meaningful to them, presenting a range of different explanations enables students to understand that ideas can be represented in multiple forms and they may have to work through a number of different types of explanations before they reach one that works for them. It is important here to emphasise that I am not arguing for the notion that learners have fixed preferences for learning through certain kinds of representations. The notion of fixed learning styles – that is, some learners will prefer to learn through visual, auditory or kinesthetic approaches – has been largely discredited (Pashler *et al.*, 2009). Rather, I am arguing that all learners will be supported if new ideas are presented to them in a number of different ways.

When using visual representations, it is important to explain to students the assumptions that are used in the images. I was told a story by a colleague who had shown their class a diagram of the male reproductive system. A very worried-looking boy came to see my colleague after the class and said they were troubled as they had two testicles but the diagram showed it was normal to have only one. The teacher is now always careful to point out that the diagram of the male reproductive system is a cross-section and to show an additional representation drawn from a different angle. Do not assume that students will automatically understand the conventions of the representations you use in your lessons, and spend some time making the assumptions clear.

Key learning point

Bear in mind that there are multiple ways to come to understand a topic. Try to offer your students alternative routes to making sense of a concept.

Using metaphors and analogies

One of the ways we can learn is to link unfamiliar ideas with concepts we already understand well. Our language is saturated with these kinds of metaphorical links. For example, we say things are looking up or I was boiling with rage. When encountering a complex concept for the first time, linking it to a better understood situation can be a powerful tool for encouraging learning. However, there are challenges to using comparative situations – consider the example below.

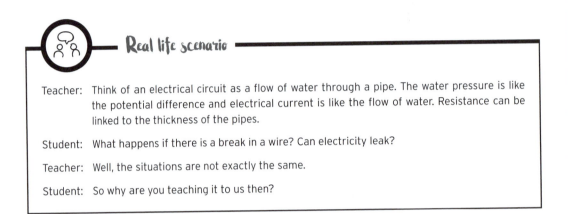

Real life scenario

Teacher: Think of an electrical circuit as a flow of water through a pipe. The water pressure is like the potential difference and electrical current is like the flow of water. Resistance can be linked to the thickness of the pipes.

Student: What happens if there is a break in a wire? Can electricity leak?

Teacher: Well, the situations are not exactly the same.

Student: So why are you teaching it to us then?

The insightful student in the example has grasped that analogies are not perfect matches for the situations they model. This may seem obvious, but you may be surprised at the connotations students will take from a metaphor. For example, if I proposed that the Cold War was like two arm-wrestlers locked in competition, what message might your students take from the image? Possibilities include: the sides in the war were of equal strength; the conflict involved two protagonists; the situation during the Cold War looked static from the outside. You may feel that all of these implications are part of the message you wanted to convey. However, it is worth taking a little time to introduce and make explicit the associations you wish to foster in the comparisons you use.

In general, it would be helpful to indicate to your students when you are using a comparison in a non-literal way. It may be a useful activity for students to describe where the comparison is apt and where it is not. For example, rather than just likening Hitler's rise to power to Vladimir Putin's path to leadership, you might provide scaffolding to allow students to consider different facets of the comparison. How was the leaders' use of media the same or different? How did they deal with dissenting voices? A stimulating approach could be to ask students to generate their own analogies and consider the strengths and weaknesses of their comparisons. This approach can be a useful technique as it encourages students to become critical of analogies they encounter. This can be considered a metacognitive technique (see section on metacognition below) – that is, it requires students to think about their own learning in addition to the concepts of the subject you are teaching. Encouraging students to reflect on their own thinking can be a powerful tool for learning in general and will be discussed in detail below.

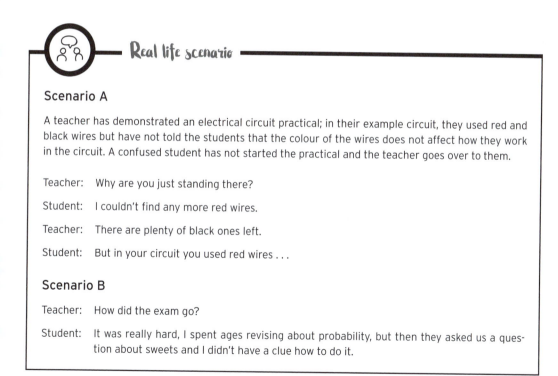

Key learning point

Analogies and metaphors can be useful tools for encouraging learning, but take care to discuss the rules and assumptions underlying the comparisons you use.

Showing and telling

Imagine trying to teach someone to dance over the phone. It is theoretically possible: you could transfer all the information related to the sequence of the positions of feet and hands to your student, but they will struggle with finding the right forms to take without seeing an example. The same thing occurs in the classroom. I have observed trainees who have stated all the information that students require to achieve a task, yet the students have struggled to begin the activity as they have not been shown what to do. Giving a suitable example can be a useful way to ease students into a new activity. However, there are some potential difficulties with presenting students with particular contexts. Consider the two scenarios below.

Real life scenario

Scenario A

A teacher has demonstrated an electrical circuit practical; in their example circuit, they used red and black wires but have not told the students that the colour of the wires does not affect how they work in the circuit. A confused student has not started the practical and the teacher goes over to them.

Teacher: Why are you just standing there?

Student: I couldn't find any more red wires.

Teacher: There are plenty of black ones left.

Student: But in your circuit you used red wires . . .

Scenario B

Teacher: How did the exam go?

Student: It was really hard, I spent ages revising about probability, but then they asked us a question about sweets and I didn't have a clue how to do it.

Researchers have pointed out that learning is often situated (Lave and Wenger, 1991) – that is, students link ideas to a particular context and have difficulty transferring the material to a novel situation. The student who wanted to precisely replicate the circuit the teacher had set up should be complemented on their observation. However, the teacher should try to pre-empt this kind of confusion by explicitly describing which features of practical equipment are significant for an experiment and which are not. Students who are unfamiliar with a context may struggle to understand which features are significant and which are not. The second scenario above suggests that you need to think carefully when choosing the kind of examples you present and also the questions you then set for your students. It can help students if they encounter a wide range of contexts in which they can practise applying their skills. You may wish to explicitly teach the metacognitive skill of stepping back from the surface detail of an exam question and reflecting on what knowledge or skill the problem might best be solved with.

In a similar way, you should give plenty of consideration to the examples you choose when explaining a new concept. Is it representative of all the situations a student will encounter? Are all the strategies a student will need represented in this example? You may want to give a number of examples to indicate different issues that may arise. When you are setting questions, also consider covering as wide a range of scenarios as you can, otherwise your students may struggle to apply their learning to new contexts.

Key learning point

Examples can help to show rather than tell students how to achieve a learning aim, but consider using a range of scenarios to avoid situated thinking.

Motivation

'What's the point?' may be the kind of existential question a teacher dreads hearing. One of the most important and challenging roles of your job is to find a genuine answer to the question in the context of every lesson you teach. If students are not motivated to learn, the most well-planned and tightly managed lessons will have little practical outcome. In every lesson you teach, imagine that very question and ensure you have considered this in your planning. Motivation is often divided into two types: intrinsic and extrinsic (Sansone and Harackiewicz, 2000). Intrinsic motivation is when behaviour is seen as end in itself, rather than extrinsic motivation where the behaviour is the means to a separate outcome. Consider the following list of reasons why a student may want to learn in your lesson.

- They want to become a doctor so need good grades.
- They enjoy getting praise and rewards.
- They want to compete with a sibling.
- They want to avoid conflict.
- They want to please you, their teacher.
- They find the activity interesting in itself.

Only the last of these might be considered an intrinsic motivation, although some people might argue that all motivation is ultimately intrinsic. There continues to be a heated debate in psychological literature about the effectiveness of extrinsic motivations such as rewards and sanctions (Eisenberger and Cameron, 1996). It is likely that you will not have complete control over the reward and sanctions structure in your school. However, as a classroom teacher, you can attempt to increase your students' motivation by considering the manner in which you present the purpose of learning in your lessons.

There is evidence that a number of different strategies may be used to increase the motivation of students (Cordova and Lepper, 1996). The role of the teacher is to convert the sometimes dry and abstract learning objectives into motivating learning opportunities. When I am planning and teaching, I have an internalised student voice asking me: 'Why do we have to learn this? What's the point? I don't need to know this. I am going to be a professional football player.' This is a challenging and provocative question, but your knowledge and enthusiasm for your subject will provide a valid answer to this question. For example, an abstract skill such as calculating percentages may seem useless in isolation, but placing it in a financial or sporting context may make the acquisition of the skill more motivating for the student. Look at the following ways to introduce Shakespeare's *Romeo and Juliet* to students.

- This important play has had a significant influence.

- This play that helps us understand the complex feeling of being in love,

The second statement contextualises the learning objective in a manner that is motivating to students, meaning there is a greater likelihood that students will want to engage with the material.

The second strategy that may motivate students is to give them an element of choice within a lesson. When people are given a choice over which tasks to work on and how much time to spend on them, they perform better than people who have those decisions imposed on them (Zuckerman *et al.*, 1978). Clearly, there are some areas that students cannot have control over, like exam syllabi and means of summative assessment. However, it is worth reflecting on what decisions you allow your students to make. Self-determination is seen as a human right, and, though it can seem frightening to hand some power over to your students, you may find motivation increases if students are given greater autonomy over their learning (see strategies, below for some ideas on this theme).

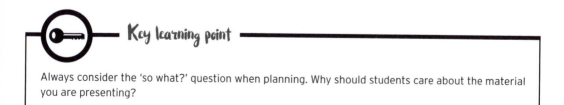

Key learning point

Always consider the 'so what?' question when planning. Why should students care about the material you are presenting?

Metacognitive teaching

Imagine these internal dialogues in the heads of two students looking at a problem in your subject.

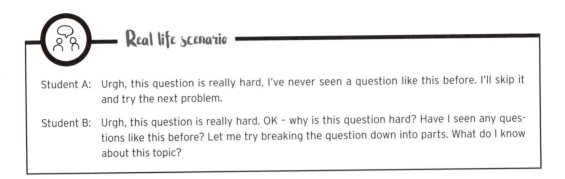

Real life scenario

Student A: Urgh, this question is really hard, I've never seen a question like this before. I'll skip it and try the next problem.

Student B: Urgh, this question is really hard. OK - why is this question hard? Have I seen any questions like this before? Let me try breaking the question down into parts. What do I know about this topic?

It may be that these students have the same knowledge available to them but they approach the difficult question in different ways. The first student lacks strategies to deal with the situation, the other has acquired strategies to try to control their own thinking to make progress. Your role as a teacher can be thought of as having two parts – teaching students factual knowledge about your subject, and teaching students to regulate their thinking to resemble the strategies used by experts in your subject. This kind of thinking about thinking or knowing about knowing has been labelled metacognition (Flavell, 1979). A part of metacognitive knowledge is the student's understanding of the strategies they can use in various learning situations. For example, a student might possess knowledge about a topic but be unable to write a well-structured essay on a theme, or have the knowledge to solve a problem but be unable to apply it to a particular question. It has therefore been argued that teaching students to be aware of their own thinking and to develop the skill of controlling their use of strategies may be a powerful way to raise achievement (Kolenick and Hillwig, 2011).

Quick click

For a good introduction to metacognitive teaching, watch the following video of Dylan Wiliam discussing the power of teaching metacognitive skills.

www.youtube.com/watch?v=bojaoVYrBmE

One way in which you can encourage students to think about their own thinking is to focus on the language you use. Costa (2008) suggests that teachers should use a form of language called 'cogitare', which emphasises the cognitive processes that are involved in learning. For example, consider the differences between the scenarios below.

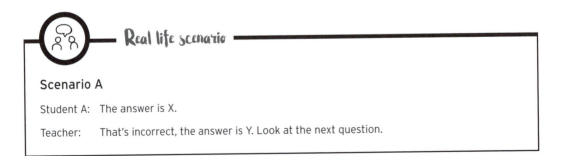

Real life scenario

Scenario A

Student A: The answer is X.

Teacher: That's incorrect, the answer is Y. Look at the next question.

Scenario B

Student B: The answer is X.

Teacher: That's incorrect but let's think about why you ended up with that answer.

In scenario B, rather than just giving the answer, the teacher is encouraging the student to develop the ability to think about their own learning. Whereas student A is likely to be less well equipped to attempt the next question, student B will have greater insight into the process of their learning as well as the answer itself. Therefore, when you are modelling a problem, it could be useful to highlight your own thinking. If possible, try to simulate the kind of difficulties students may encounter and strategies that may help to overcome them, as in the example below.

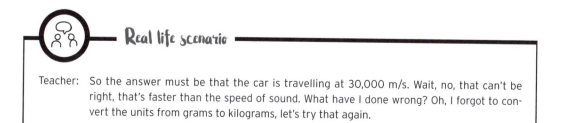

Real life scenario

Teacher: Okay, I have read the essay question through and the focus is on whether an actor used their skills effectively. First, I think it's important to examine what the words in the question mean, what might different facets of effectiveness be. Let me make a list: use of voice, their movement, facial expressions, etc. [Directed to the students] Can anyone help me out? What else might I look for?

Although it may seem at times that teaching is only about transferring factual knowledge to your students, a better representation might be that you are acting as a role model of expert thinking in your subject. Giving students an insight into your thinking processes by thinking aloud, can be a powerful tool for supporting learning. Some trainee teachers worry about making mistakes in front of their students. While it is important that you have a secure understanding of the content knowledge in your discipline, even the most experienced teachers will, occasionally, make mistakes in front of the class. Show that you monitor your own thinking and have strategies to check your answers. This will serve as a more useful model for students than a teacher who seems to pluck the answers out of the air, as shown in the example below.

Real life scenario

Teacher: So the answer must be that the car is travelling at 30,000 m/s. Wait, no, that can't be right, that's faster than the speed of sound. What have I done wrong? Oh, I forgot to convert the units from grams to kilograms, let's try that again.

Many teachers and researchers recommend teaching students metacognitive techniques. For an introduction to these ideas, McGuire's (2015) *Teaching Students How to Learn* is a good place to start.

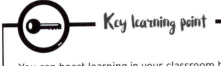

Key learning point

You can boost learning in your classroom by helping students become aware of the mental strategies they use to learn.

Quick click

A good place to compare the evidence for the effectiveness of different teaching and learning strategies is the Education Endowment Foundation website, below. The teaching and learning toolkit lists a range of different approaches such as mastery learning and metacognitive teaching, and compares the evidence to support claims and the time taken for the strategy to become effective.

https://educationendowmentfoundation.org.uk/evidence/teaching-learning-toolkit

Teaching for deeper understanding

Some educationalists make a distinction between rote learning factual information and more desirable types of learning such as understanding (Newton, 2012) or meaningful learning (Ausubel, 2000). It is worth reflecting on your own view of what the goal of successful teaching might mean. If there is more to learning than simply acquiring facts, what are those other factors and how might you teach them in your classroom? The next sections give you some ideas of the processes that various writers have linked to deeper forms of understanding.

Successful learning is interconnected – joining together ideas from different contexts and domains can lead to an increased sense of understanding (Newton, 2012). However, students often struggle to make the links themselves and end up with learning that consists of a set of isolated facts. When you are teaching a new idea, try to uncover what students already know that might be relevant and encourage them to develop links to pre-existing knowledge. This can not only make the learning more meaningful, but will help to motivate learning by highlighting the relevance of the new material.

Seeing the bigger picture – students can feel that school is a fragmented experience. They go from learning about ox-bow lakes to the enzymes in the digestive system to designing a new kind of trainer, in the space of a few hours. You can help your students to attain a deeper understanding by occasionally, metaphorically, stepping back and focusing on the bigger picture. Ox-bow lakes are one example of the same forces of erosion that have shaped many of the features in the world, the action of enzymes are evidence of evolutionary forces that have driven our bodies' adaption to a particular niche. Joining the dots to see the position of specific pieces of knowledge in a larger scheme can be powerful.

Successful learning is coherent – students often have both knowledge learned in school and ideas about the world they have developed themselves. Learners don't simply discard their old ideas when new material is taught in school. There will be a period when different ideas coexist and students struggle to form a coherent understanding. It can be useful, both for you as a teacher and the students themselves, to be made aware of the misconceptions they hold about the world and to come to understand how these ideas interact with what they are taught in school. For example, a common bias is for people to assume that violent events in the news, such as air crashes, are more common than they actually are (Kahneman, 2011). By making your students aware of their, sometimes non-conscious, assumptions about the world, you can help them develop a more coherent understanding of the world. If you are interested in teaching for understanding, Tina Blythe's and colleagues' *The Teaching for Understanding Guide* (1998), discussed at the end of this chapter, is a good place to start.

Key learning point

There is more to successful learning than simply knowing some facts. In your planning and teaching, consider how you might develop broad and flexible understandings in your students.

Social interactions and teaching and learning

Some models of education highlight the important role of interacting with other students for the learning processes of an individual (Vygotsky, 1978). Students may learn effectively, in certain contexts, by interacting with their peers. When I observe lessons in which a teacher has chosen to set a group activity a number of questions spring to mind: Is this an activity in which group work has an advantage over other approaches? Will all the students in the group benefit from this approach? Could more learning be achieved by another means? In some classrooms there appears to be an implicit assumption that group work is always superior to other approaches, regardless of the learning aim. Group work is a useful technique in a number of scenarios, such as when learning aims that do not have a clear right answer and the objective is to develop argumentation and critical thinking skills. For example, students may work in a group to discuss different possible energy generation strategies for the future. Allowing students to formulate their ideas, develop arguments, critique and be critiqued by others can be a powerful learning experience.

However, when students are developing their skills in a particular context, for example, learning how to do long division, practising the skill is an inherently personal task. There may be scope for students to work together to support each other, or to assess each other's work. However, students must have the opportunity to practise the skill by themselves. Similarly, I have seen teachers give the same worksheet they give to individuals to groups of students and ask them to complete it collectively. It is likely that a small number of dominant students will supply the answers, and the remainder of the group may contribute and learn little from the task. Group tasks should contain an authentic element of social interaction. Do think carefully about how the interpersonal relationships will contribute to the learning of all participants.

A second challenge with group work is in planning and structuring activities such that students can engage in productive social learning. Working in a group is a skill that takes time to develop. Some students may struggle to engage in discussion with their peers, groups may be dominated by a single student, or spend time discussing minor or irrelevant issues. Assigning roles to students and structuring discussions such that each member contributes in some way can, to some extent, avoid these difficulties. It may be useful to spend some time at the start of the activity talking to students about what effective group work looks like and suggesting strategies for cases such as one student not contributing or conversation drifting off topic. Students may find it difficult to challenge the ideas of their peers, it may be worth discussing the nature of academic debate and drawing clear boundaries between the personal and the academic.

Quick click

There is a useful checklist for areas to reflect on before setting group work in the following issue of the Stanford University teaching newsletter.

http://web.stanford.edu/dept/CTL/Newsletter/cooperative.pdf

Certain kinds of learning can be supported by students working with their peers, but do be careful to consider the purposes and manner in which you structure group work.

Targets

Widen the range of teaching strategies used in your lessons

Quick wins

- **Make sure tasks feel purposeful.** It is difficult to learn from a task when the purpose or desired outcome of the activity is unclear. This does not mean that every task must come with a set of learning objectives. However, it should be clear to the students that, at all points during the lesson, they appreciate the purpose of what they are doing and how it contributes to a larger goal.
- **Reiterate the main ideas.** Build opportunities into your lesson to reiterate the main ideas. It is easy for students to forget the main purpose of the lesson and several quick summaries during the lesson can be helpful.
- **Bridge the gap from other lessons.** Remember that your students may have come from a lesson where they have been engaged in a completely different type of learning, or may just have been exercising or socialising. In each lesson, you need to facilitate a smooth transition for your students into the world of your classroom. This may mean reiterating expectations, but it could also means priming knowledge from the previous lesson.

- **Link tasks to the students' experiences.** If you are teaching abstract knowledge, try to link it to contexts that are familiar to students. For example, calculating percentages could be related to a sport or hobby that is popular among the students. This will require sensitivity to the interests of your students and a light touch. I can imagine a lesson that teaches chemical reactions in the context of Harry Potter's potion classes as both a triumph and a disaster, depending on how it is handled. Make sure the context doesn't overwhelm the learning.

- **Break down your explanations.** Even if you understand a topic well, it can still be challenging to explain it to others. Before you teach, try to break down the material into a sequence of statements and ensure they flow logically. Try rearranging the order and reflect on what assumptions are required to understand each statement.

- **Try out your explanations**. Trial your explanations on people who aren't experts in your subject. Can they follow your argument? Ask if there were any steps in the reasoning that were difficult to follow.

- **Use mnemonics and songs for rote-learned knowledge.** There are areas of the curriculum in most subjects where students are required to rote learn some information. Don't just present the information, but make up a mnemonic or search for a song that will help with the rote learning. Do not assume that your students will be able to develop their own strategies to rote learn without support.

- **Include an element of competition.** Many students will find competition against others motivating. If you feel that some students may find competition threatening, you could set up a comparison against personal bests or past behaviour. You can decide whether individuals should compete as teams or as individuals, depending on the learning goals. Students may find it motivating if you structure the scoring and questioning to match a well-known television quiz.

- **Chunk complex information.** It is claimed that our working memory can hold between five and nine pieces of information (Miller, 1956), depending on the individual and type of information. Plan explanations and activities so they don't overload your students' working memory. Break explanations into short chunks, divide complex tasks into simpler stages and provide external aids such as instruction sheets to support students' ability to complete tasks.

- **Add an element of chance to rewards in some games.** Although this may seem counterintuitive, and is certainly not recommended as a formative assessment strategy, recent research (Howard-Jones et al., 2015) has suggested that adding an element of randomness to the scores students received in an informal quiz increased their learning. Researchers found that when the reward for answering a question successfully was uncertain, determined by spinning a 'wheel-of-fortune', engagement and learning from the quiz increased.

Quick click

To hear more details about the effect that uncertain rewards may have on motivation and learning, the link below will take you to a BBC Radio 4 documentary about Paul Howard-Jones's research. The programme also includes some more general discussion of how findings from neuroscience research can be applied in the classroom.

www.bbc.co.uk/programmes/b04g8qfg

Slow burners

- **Plan to use multiple forms of representation.** When you look at the learning objectives for a particular lesson, try to imagine different ways in which you could explain the idea. Keep in mind that an explanation or model that helped *you* understand might not work for all learners. If possible, prepare a number of different ways of explaining the same concept, as below.

Real life scenario

Teacher: In a displacement reaction, a more reactive element takes the place of a less reactive one in a compound.

Student: I don't get it.

Teacher: Imagine two students in a relationship, which are like the two elements in a compound. If a more attractive person, who is analogous to a more reactive element comes along, he or she can take the place of the less attractive person in the relationship.

Student: I still don't get it.

Teacher: Okay, imagine two magnets that are stuck together. If a stronger magnet is placed near the pair, it might be able to pull one of the magnets away to form a new pair that is harder to pull apart.

Student: That doesn't make any sense.

Teacher: Have a look at this animation . . .

Consider different ways of representing the knowledge. Is it possible to have a visual representation? Can you show a video clip? Is there a way in which students can physically engage with a model or materials while they learn about the idea? Such multimodal representations may not be available in all topics and you shouldn't feel forced into presenting every idea through different media, but do consider preparing as many different versions of a potential explanation as you can to allow students different insights into the idea. If you present multiple representations, do think about the difficulties that students may have in understanding how the representations can work together. For example, if you present an animation and a static diagram of plate tectonics, are the same features shown on each? It could be useful to highlight the assumptions that each representation makes and to discuss with your students its strengths and weaknesses in representing the phenomenon you are discussing.

- **Show as well as tell.** There is a crucial difference between simply stating a piece of knowledge and teaching it to your students. If teaching just involved telling, anybody could turn up in your classroom, read out the set of statements on the specification and be considered a teacher. When you plan, consider the following questions.

- What prior knowledge do students need to learn this concept?

- What is challenging about learning this concept? How might it be misunderstood?

- What are different ways of approaching the teaching of this concept? Which one would be most suitable given the class of students I teach?

- How can I use examples, models, simulations, practical equipment, videos, diagrams or other forms of representations to explain this notion?

- How will I know whether my students have understood?

Consider the two different routes to explaining some of the factors behind the rise of National Socialism in 1930s Germany, as described in the two scenarios below.

Real life scenario

Scenario A

Teacher: Political rallies made use of popular songs targeting scapegoats and the energy of large groups to promote a feeling of belonging to a larger group of people.

Scenario B

Teacher: Think about a sports match or music festival you have been to. What made you feel part of the crowd? How might the emotions you felt in these situations be similar to those of people who attended National Socialist rallies?

In the second scenario, rather than simply asserting that certain techniques induce feelings of group membership, the teacher draws on the students' personal experiences. The teacher hasn't just told the students an idea but has built on what the students already know, which may develop a more integrated understanding.

- **Gamify your classroom.** The idea of gamification, making the activities in your classroom like games, has been growing in popularity (Faber, 2015). The trend stems from the observation that certain features of both traditional and video games make them highly motivating and players are often driven to spend hours trying to solve complex puzzles. It is hoped that transferring some of the principles used by game designers to the classroom can make lessons more engaging. The following strategies may make help you to gamify your lessons.

  - Allow students multiple lives: when they complete a problem incorrectly, rather than just moving on, let them have multiple attempts at finding a solution.

- Provide feedback as quickly as you can; video games provide near-instantaneous feedback on actions, so students can change strategies rapidly. Use approaches such as online, self-marking tests or peer marking by another student to speed up the feedback process.

- Lessons can sometimes seem like a never-ending journey towards a far-off goal. Create a visual representation, perhaps a series of pictures representing the different sections of the course, so your students can get a sense of their progress towards a final goal.

- **Use spaced practice sessions.** Evidence suggests that spaced repetition of skills or activation learning is an effective way to boost retention. Rather than simply teaching an idea on one occasion and moving on to new material, it is more effective to revisit the idea on multiple occasions interspersed with breaks. Typically, the gaps between practice sessions should lengthen as the material is acquired. This technique is well suited to learning factual material such as lists of vocabulary or facts. For example, you may wish to use the starters to a series of lessons to repeatedly test a set of facts. Do not assume that simply because you have taught an idea once, your students will have committed the idea to long-term memory. Consider setting up a series of opportunities to practise the material in a series of spaced sessions at increasing intervals - for example, after one day, after three days, after a week, after a month.

- **Experiment with moving from the specific to the general and vice versa.** Sometimes it may be engaging to start a lesson with a specific example. For instance, in art, when introducing the topic of surrealism you could begin by discussing a particular example, such as Dali's *Metamorphosis of Narcissus*. Abstract concepts such as surrealism might be difficult for students to grasp and beginning with a specific example can provide a route into more abstract and deeper learning. Similarly, in psychology the complex debate around nature or nurture could be approached through a news story about identical twins who have taken different paths. In mathematics, a teacher may put their students in the scenario of painting their bedroom to introduce the concept of calculating areas. Be aware, in this approach, that students may assume the examples you have introduced are the only valid forms of the concept.

Alternatively, you may want to introduce a general idea before looking at specific cases. For example, you may want to introduce the concept of a financial depression; this might take the form of a word association activity around the term depression, before examining specific cases of financial depression. In biology, a teacher might wish to describe the criteria for classifying a living creature as a mammal before introducing examples. In Religious Studies, the notion of the afterlife could be defined before students explored the different religious interpretations of this idea. However, some students may find it challenging to apply a general concept to a range of cases.

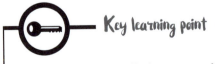

Key learning point

Both starting from particular cases or from a general idea are valid approaches. Experiment with different strategies for different topics.

Encourage student-led learning to increase independence

 Quick wins

- **Encourage students to self-explain.** Try asking your students to think aloud when they solve a problem or write an essay. Encourage them to reflect on the kind of strategies they are using and model successful approaches.
- **Teach students strategies to use when they are stuck.** Use the C3B4ME model – students are encouraged to seek support from three peers before asking the teacher for help. Alternatively, students could follow the five B model – that is, they should consult their own Brain, the Board, their Book, a Buddy, before asking the Boss (teacher).
- **Limit teacher talk.** Get an observer to time how long you spend talking compared to the time students spend on task.
- **Students answer their own questions.** If a student has a question, they write it on a post-it note and endeavour to answer their own question by the end of the lesson. If their question still remains, this question can either be answered by another student or set for homework.
- **Rather than telling students the answer, elicit the answer from the students.**
- **Don't spend too long on superfluous explanations.** Students can often carry out tasks with brief but clear instructions.

 Slow burners

- **Give your students an opportunity to make choices.** Though there are some aspects of teaching in the classroom that are not appropriate for your students to determine, it can be highly motivating for students to have some sense of control over lessons. Listed below are some strategies for achieving this aim.

  - Set some open-ended, investigative projects in which you provide some guidelines for assessment and the students are free to develop the work in their own style. For example, you may ask them to research a topic but allow them to present it in a style of their choosing (a blog, a film, an animation, etc.). Think carefully about how you set objectives that ensure students cover the information required from the curriculum but also have some freedom to choose other areas of interest. You could provide a checklist of what must be covered.
  - Allow for some teaching time in which the class can vote for a topic within your subject they would like to learn about. This need only be 10 minutes on a Friday afternoon in which you teach about ideas that are off the curriculum but the students find interesting. For example, demonstrating exciting experiments that are not on the curriculum, analysing their favourite song lyrics, or playing an unusual sport such as kabbadi.
  - You could offer your students a menu of possible approaches to teaching a topic and allow them to choose. For example, offer them teaching interspersed with a video, hands-on activities or group discussion and take a class vote. Where possible, it could be effective to let

different students take different approaches. However, all the options you offer must create valid and constructive learning opportunities. For example, a student choosing to use a poster or model to represent their ideas may show artistic talent, but display very limited evidence of learning about the topic.

- **Help students see the bigger picture.** If you were asked to memorise this set of numbers - 27456381 - you may find the task both challenging and somewhat meaningless. However, if you noticed that the sequence consists of increasing even integers (2 - 4 - 6 - 8) alternating with decreasing odd integers (7 - 5 - 3 - 1), the sequence may become easier to learn. In a similar way, understanding how a piece of knowledge fits into a larger pattern can help students to appreciate why it is meaningful and increase their motivation for learning. There are a number of ways to achieve this aim.

  - When introducing a new idea, show students a mind map of how the idea relates to other concepts they already know and those they will learn in the future.
  - Even though a particular activity may be specialised - for example, learning about a particular text or mathematical approach - place an emphasis on the generally applicable skills the students are acquiring: critical thinking, clear communication or argumentation.
  - The ability to make connections between ideas developed in different fields is an important intellectual ability. Encourage your students to develop this skill by asking questions such as: 'I wonder if this relates to any of your other subjects?' 'Does this remind you of something that was in the news recently?' Not only will this approach lead to an understanding of particular links that exist, it may model to students the cognitive process of seeking links between new ideas and knowledge they already possess - a process that may stimulate understanding.

- **Encourage students to teach each other.** There is an old piece of wisdom in teaching that argues you haven't really understood something until you have tried to teach it to someone else. Ideas that I thought I understood proved more challenging when I attempted to explain them to students. The process of developing a clear progression of ideas, with no gaps in reasoning, helped me come to a better understanding of the concept I was trying to explain. In a similar way, allowing your students the opportunity to teach each other can be a powerful learning experience for both the 'teacher' and the student. However, the activity needs careful structuring and planning and may only be appropriate with certain groups of students and in certain topics. I have seen the approach used successfully in a number of different formats.

  - Each student in a class is assigned a learning aim from the curriculum and is ask to develop a five minute introduction to the idea. This feature could become a routine starter for lessons and their presentation could be followed by questions from the class.
  - Students are divided into a number of groups and work together to become 'experts' on a particular topic, using resources provided by the teacher. The students then form mixed groups including one expert on each topic who explains their area of focus to the other members of the group (sometimes called a jigsaw task).
  - If a student finishes their work, while the rest of the class is still on task, they can be asked to adopt the role of a peer educator to assist others in the class.

- **Increase time on task.** You will doubtless have had the experience of someone explaining to you how to use a new piece of software or play a sport, and felt the urge for them to stop talking and let you get on and try the activity for yourself. Many educationalists have emphasised the importance of direct engagement with an activity or learning, often called experiential learning

(Dewey, 1938/1997). There is a balance to be struck between the amount of time you spend explaining how to do a task and the time the students spend engaged on the activity. In general, you should aim to give the shortest possible explanation that will allow students to successfully complete the task. I find I tend to over-complicate instructions in the classroom and have a natural tendency to want to keep talking, giving additional information and helpful hints – I am, after all, a teacher. However, I have found that students tend to cope with tasks just as well with shorter explanations provided you think through which pieces of information are key. Plan lessons to give your students as much time as possible to engage with the tasks themselves. It is possible that, for some students, some of the time, listening to a teacher talk can be an active learning experience. I am sure you can recall lectures that you found really stimulating and which engaged your ideas. However, it is also difficult to follow your train of thought and check your own developing understanding if you are listening to someone else talk.

When you are writing a lesson plan, reflect on how much of the lesson allows students to be actively engaged with learning about the concepts. There will necessarily be time taken up in administrative activities such as coming into the classroom, handing out books, or getting practical equipment, but try to develop techniques to maximise the time which students spend actively engaged on a task. Could you place their books on their desks before the lesson? How could you arrange practical equipment to reduce set up time? Reflect on the kind of activities that most actively promote learning in your students and consider which will be most effective to meet the aims of that lesson.

- **Try flipping your classroom**. In the traditional model of teaching, the teacher is seen as the main source of knowledge in the classroom. The teacher may spend a significant portion of the lesson talking about content knowledge and the remainder of the time is allocated to students carrying out tasks and receiving feedback. However, it has been argued that a teacher is most effective at stimulating learning when they interact with students who are engaged with tasks to give personalised feedback. The delivery of content knowledge could be achieved just as effectively by students watching a video or reading a text in their own time. This has the advantage that they are able to control the pace of their learning and seek additional support if required. More lesson time could therefore be made available for assessing students' understanding and developing their learning. Recently, an approach to learning which shifts the acquisition of content knowledge outside classroom time has been developed – for example, students could be asked to watch three interpretations of Hamlet's famous soliloquy in Act 3, Scene 1 at home, with guidance for areas of focus. This allows the teacher, in the subsequent lesson, to focus on examining students' personal and critical responses, rather than spending lesson time watching videos. This approach is known as the flipped classroom (for a clear introduction to flipping your classroom, see Bergmann and Sams, 2012).

Quick Click

One very well-known source of videos for use in the flipped learning is the Kahn Academy.

www.khanacademy.org

In a TED talk, the founder of the website, Salman Khan, discusses how flipped classrooms may be used to stimulate learning.

http://bit.ly/1loHtf7

To give another example, rather than have a teacher explain the topic, students might be asked to watch a video on Pythagoras' theorem, including a number of example problems, for their homework. The next lesson would begin with a set of problems for them to complete, with no direct teaching at the start of the lesson. There is evidence that, in some contexts, the greater emphasis on engaging with tasks in the lessons can boost achievement. However, there are a number of challenges with setting up a flipped classroom: a) difficulty in finding resources that match the level of your students and use terms that match the course you are teaching; b) students may not engage with the resources in depth or at all outside the classroom; c) some students may not have access to online resources. It is worth experimenting with the technique. It is unlikely to be appropriate for all your classes or for all topics, but it may be useful with particular groups of students in particular contexts.

Support the development of students' metacognitive skills

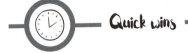
Quick wins

- **Teach the skills of interpreting analogies and metaphors.** Teachers often use analogies and metaphors to explain complicated ideas and they are a really good way to help students make sense of a novel concept in terms of knowledge they already have. However, it is easy to assume that students, even more advanced students, are clear about the assumptions that you are using in making a comparison.
- **Ask students how they arrived at a response.**
- **Praise approach to thinking as well as the outcome.** For example, 'Even though that's not the correct answer, I like that you broke down the key words in the question.'
- **Encourage students to develop multiple ways of approaching problems.** Discuss their advantages and disadvantages.
- **Think aloud when you are doing tasks** such as solving an example problem or planning how to write an essay. Model the process of thinking as well as the practical steps your students will need to take. Try to model some of the difficulties students will encounter and how you would like them to respond.
- **Encourage students to share their own cognitive strategies** with the class. For example, what do you think about when you first read an essay question on an exam? What do you do if you reach an exam question that you think you know nothing about?
- **Make students write a list of their strengths and areas of development in your subject.** Discuss what actions they should take to remedy the areas of development.

Slow burners

- **Question your assumptions about learning.** Learning is a complex process and you should reflect on what you are seeking to achieve in your classroom and how you will know if you have been successful. It might seem a straightforward assumption that ultimately you are paid to get your students the highest possible exam results. Few teachers would disagree that helping their students to get the best qualifications they are capable of is an important part of their career. However, how you achieve this goal is dependent on what you believe about the nature of learning. Thinking about learning might seem an abstract topic that is removed from the everyday realities of planning and marking, but every teacher, implicitly or explicitly, makes assumptions about what approaches will lead to the most effective learning in the classroom. You will be better placed to make key decisions about your teaching if you have thought and reflected on how students learn.

You may find it useful to join your subject association which may publish a magazine or journal outlining the latest research and present a discussion of ideas in your field. The *Times Educational Supplement* is also a useful place to find discussions of novel pedagogies and debates about different models of learning. Some teachers have found carrying out their own small-scale research projects has led to improvements in their practice. Some schools encourage networks of teacher-researchers to carry out investigations or share their ideas with each other. Studying for a Masters degree in education, which can be done while teaching full-time, is a route to finding out more about the nature of learning and carrying out research into your own areas of interest.

Quick click

If you are interested in finding out more about educational research, researchEd, an organisation that promotes evidence-based practice, is a good place to start. The website has links to research across a wide range of contexts and they hold regular conferences across subject areas with presentations from teachers, policy makers and researchers.

www.workingoutwhatworks.com

- **Develop critical thinking in students**. Focus on the idea that your job as a teacher is not only in helping students acquire knowledge of particular content areas, but that you are also nurturing a particular way of approaching thinking and learning. The most effective learners are capable of reflecting about their own thinking and regulating their learning. When you are writing a lesson plan, look for opportunities to make thinking skills explicit. Encourage students to internalise the processes of self-reflection and critical thinking. Model the skill of examining ideas as they occur. The first answer that occurs to you may not be the most appropriate and should be critiqued. When you are using questioning to probe a student's assumptions, encourage the class to adopt a similar approach with their own ideas. You might brainstorm a list of questions students could run through when proposing an idea. What evidence exists for this position? What counter-arguments could be proposed? In what circumstances does this idea work and where does it not apply? Are there multiple ways of understanding this concept?
- **Vary the contexts of the tasks you set**. Try to set as wide a range of tasks as you possibly can. When students first encounter a concept, they will find it easier to apply ideas to a narrow range of contexts. However, if they only encounter problems in a small range of contexts, students are

likely to develop situated or context-dependent knowledge. This may cause problems in formal assessments where they will be required to transfer ideas to novel situations. A student once complained that their end of topic test was unfair as they were asked to describe how a seal was adapted to its environment and they hadn't 'done' seals. It can be helpful to point out to your students that assessments tend to use new contexts and they need to be able to transfer ideas. Students who are not prepared for encountering novel contexts may simply assume that they don't have any appropriate knowledge to deal with the apparently new situation. For example, if students are learning to critique the validity of different sources of information, include the broadest range of contexts you can - for example, tweets or statements by teachers and other students. When learning to analyse poems, encourage students to apply the skills to songs, football chants and advertising jingles.

Another useful metacognitive skill for students to learn is to understand in which contexts an idea can be appropriately applied. The skill or knowledge you are teaching may work well in some situations but not others; it can be an effective teaching approach to introduce a range of contexts in which the technique works more or less successfully. This encourages students to be critical about learning rather than simply accepting new ideas as completely true across all situations. For example, in teaching that the angles in a triangle add up to 180°, the teacher might introduce a triangle drawn on a globe and encourage the students to discover that the internal angles will sum to more than 180°.

In summary

Your main role as a teacher is to support learning in your students. Your planning, assessment and management of behaviour should all be underpinned by a desire to maximise opportunities for learning in your students. Moreover, during your lessons you should develop a sensitivity to the amount and type of learning that is occurring and be able to alter your teaching in response.

Before the lesson

- **Reflect on your model of learning**. Think about what successful learning means to you and how you might know if it has occurred in your lesson.

- **Keep the learning objectives in mind**. For every activity you plan, reflect on what you want students to learn from the activity.

- **Plan for activities that offer different ways of explaining ideas.** Different students will make sense in different ways and need different kinds of support.

- **Plan for assessment.** Build in opportunities to check that the learning you planned for has occurred.

- **Use assessment information to guide planning.** Your teaching will be most effective if you build your lesson plans on your knowledge of students' misconception and their individual strengths and weaknesses.

During the lesson

- **Be sensitive to the level of learning that is occurring.** Develop a sense of whether students are 'getting it'. If learners are finding the lesson too easy or difficult, be prepared to deviate from your plan.

- **Be responsive to assessment.** Use the information gathered from mini-plenaries and other assessments during the lesson to vary your approach.

- **Ensure you clarify the aims of learning and provide a motivation for the importance of the content**. Ensure that all tasks feel purposeful and meaningful.

- **Reflect on the nature of learning that is occurring.** Are students just repeating what they have been told or is there evidence of deeper learning?

After the lesson

- **Reflect on the level of learning that has occurred.** Use any data from assessments to develop plans for future lessons.

- **Reflect on the kinds of approaches that were successful.** Think about the techniques that fostered successful learning in particular students and try to replicate those techniques in future lessons.

------ Further reading ----------

Hattie, J and Yates, G (2014) *Visible Learning and the Science of How We Learn.* Abingdon: Routledge.

John Hattie is well known in educational research for developing a large analysis of thousands of research studies to find out what works in the classroom. Written with Gregory Yates, the book introduces ideas from psychology to develop a range of recommendations for teachers in the classroom. The nine principles of good teaching they set out in the introduction are a really good summary of effective teaching. Though the book builds on theoretical ideas, it lists many practical ideas, grounded in research, to develop effective practice:

Bates, B (2016) *Learning Theories Simplified . . . And How to Apply Them to Teaching.* London, SAGE.

If you are interested in learning more about different learning theories, Bob Bates's book provides an introduction to many of the major thinkers in education but also includes practical ideas for the classroom. Bates summarises the ideas of important educationalists such as Piaget and Vygotsky in a few bullet points and then provides suggestions of how their ideas can be applied in the classroom.

McGuire, SY (2015) *Teaching Students How to Learn.* Sterling, VA: Stylus Publishing.

A recurring theme of the strategies discussed above is that encouraging students to be more aware of their own learning and to be able to regulate and direct their thinking, may have a powerful affect on achievement. A good introduction to applying these kinds of metacogntive skills in the classroom can be found in Stephanie McGuire's book.

Blyhe, T and Associates (1998) *The Teaching for Understanding Guide.* San Francisco, CA: Jossey-Bass Publishers.

This chapter has suggested that there is more to successful learning than simply memorising facts. Some teachers feel that the goal of education should be, alongside acquiring knowledge, to develop an understanding of a subject. Tina Blythe's book provides an accessible introduction to the teaching for understanding movement.

—— **References** ——————————————————————

Ausubel, D (2000) *The Acquisition and Retention of Knowledge*. Dordrecht: Kluwer Academic Publishers.

Bates, B (2016) *Learning Theories Simplified . . . And How to Apply Them to Teaching*. London: SAGE.

Bergman, J and Sams, A (2012) *Flip Your Classroom: Reach Every Student in Every Class Every Day*. Eugene, OR: International Society for Technology in Education.

Cordova, DI and Lepper, MR (1996) Intrinsic motivation and the process of learning: Beneficial effects of contextualization, personalization, and choice. *Journal of Educational Psychology*, 88(4): 715–730.

Costa, AL (2008) *The School as a Home for the Mind: Creating Mindful Curriculum, Instruction, and Dialogue*. Thousand Oaks, CA: Corwin Press.

Dewey, J (1938/1997) *Experience and Education*. New York: Touchstone.

Eisenberger, R and Cameron, J (1996) Detrimental effects of reward: Reality or myth? *American Psychologist*, 51(11): 1153–1166.

Faber, M (2015) *Gamify your Classroom*. New York: Peter Lang.

Flavell, JH (1979) Metacognition and cognitive monitoring. *American Psychologist*, 34(10): 906–911.

Howard-Jones, PA, Jay, T, Mason, A and Jones, H (2015) Gamification of learning deactivates the default mode network. *Frontiers in Psychology*, 6(1891): 1–16.

Kahneman, D (2011) *Thinking, Fast and Slow*. London: Penguin.

Kolenick, PL and Hillwig, SA (2011) *Encouraging Metacognition: Supporting Learners Through Metacognitive Teaching Strategies*. New York: Peter Lang.

Lave, J and Wenger, E (1991) *Situated Learning: Legitimate Peripheral Participation* (Vol. 95). Cambridge: Cambridge University Press.

McGuire, SY (2015) *Teaching Students How to Learn*. Sterling, VA: Stylus Publishing.

Miller, GA (1956) The magical number seven, plus or minus two: Some limits on our capacity for processing information. *Psychological Review*, 63(2): 81–97.

Newton, DP (2012) *Teaching for Understanding* (2nd edn). Abingdon: Routledge.

Pashler, H, McDaniel, M, Rohrer, D and Bjork, R (2009) Learning styles: Concepts and evidence. *Psychological Science in the Public Interest*, 9(3): 105–19.

Sansone, C and Harackiewicz, JM (eds) (2000) *Intrinsic and Extrinsic Motivation*. San Diego, CA: Academic Press.

Schunk, DH (2014) *Learning Theories: An Educational Perspective*. Harlow: Pearson Education.

Vygotsky, L (1978) *Mind in Society: The Development of Higher Mental Processes* (trans M Cole). Cambridge, MA: Harvard University Press.

Zuckerman, M, Porac, J, Lathin, D and Deci, EL (1978) On the importance of self-determination for intrinsically-motivated behavior. *Personality and Social Psychology Bulletin*, 4(3): 443–6.

5
Questioning

Teachers' Standards 2, 4, 5 and 6

This chapter will introduce ideas related to questioning and outline a number of strategies to support your use of questioning in the classroom. The chapter is most relevant to the following Teachers' Standards.

- Be aware of pupils' capabilities and their prior knowledge, and plan teaching to build on these (TS2).
- Make use of formative and summative assessment to secure pupils' progress (TS6).
- Give pupils regular feedback, both orally and through accurate marking, and encourage pupils to respond to the feedback (TS6).

Introduction

Consider the beginning of Lewis Carroll's *Jabberwocky* and the example questions posed by Thelen (1984, p2):

> Twas brillig and the slithy toves
> Did gyre and gimble in the wabe;
> All mimsy were the borogroves,
> And all the mame raths outgrabe
>
> What were the toves doing?
> Where were they doing it?

You might expect that most readers would supply the answers that the toves were gyring and gimbling and they were located in the wabe. This admittedly contrived example illustrates a kind of questioning that is all too common in classrooms – that is, questioning that requires students to repeat back factual information they have recently been told. Students can give the correct answers to such questions while lacking a deeper understanding of what they are being asked. The strategies introduced below will suggest some approaches to assessment that assess more than factual recall.

Questioning is one of the most important skills you will develop. Teachers are reported as asking on average 400 questions in a day, accounting for a third of all classroom time. A teacher may therefore pose two or three million questions over the course of their career (Hastings, 2006, p67). However, though questioning may seem at first like an easy skill to develop, we are all after all used to asking questions, developing the skill of pedagogic questioning requires some practice.

Questioning might seem to be largely about assessment, and you might assume that questions are only used to determine the extent of your students' learning. A more useful conceptualisation is to consider questioning and learning as inextricably linked (Elder and Paul, 1998). Rather than a process that occurs after learning has finished, you should see questioning as a device for moulding and shaping understanding. Students may come to internalise some of the behaviours of the classrooms they experience, and therefore learners who encounter well-crafted and challenging questions may develop the skills of critically assessing new information when they encounter it. When I started teaching, my mentor would ask me a series of questions when giving me feedback after a lesson. For example, did all the students learn? Why did Jo switch off in that activity? Why did Summer engage so much better this lesson? I still return to those kinds of questions and they have become part of my evaluation process.

Too often questioning becomes a ritual that is carried out without reference to learning. I have seen trainees ask questions without listening to the responses while organising equipment for the next activity; waste time on questions which do not provoke further thought; and respond overly positively to an answer which contained some misconceptions. The process of challenging and questioning knowledge you use in the classroom is critical as it has a strong influence on students' learning.

Key learning point

Questioning should be seen as a significant learning opportunity rather than as a purposeless activity done to fill lesson time.

This chapter considers some key research on questioning to address the following targets.

Targets

What targets does this chapter cover?

- Ensure all students are included in questioning.
- Ask a wider range of questions.
- Use questions to encourage higher-order thinking in students.

Types of questions

- What is the population of London?

- Why does the population of London change?

These questions clearly have very different educational aims. The first checks the presence or absence of a piece of factual knowledge. It is worth noting that even an apparently simple question might lead to a series of interesting follow-up questions: how do we define the boundaries of London? How long does someone have to stay in London to be included in the count? Does the population include temporary residents? The second question seems to require a more complex kind of answer. However, a student may answer with a rote-learned list of factors that do not evidence any deeper understanding than knowing the value of London's population.

Reflecting on the nature of the demands a question places on a student is an important aspect of planning questioning. You must make a decision as to the criteria you will accept as evidence that a student has fulfilled a learning aim. Supplying the answer to a closed question may fulfil a learning aim related to knowledge – for example, to know London's population. However, assessing the learning objective of understanding the factors that affect population change may require more extended questioning. Therefore, it is important you are aware of different categorisations of questions and how they may be used to assess different forms of knowledge. Perhaps the most common categorisation is based on Bloom's taxonomy, a hierarchy of learning skills (Bloom *et al.*, 1956). One way of expressing

Bloom's taxonomy is via a list of processes (Krathwohl, 2002) which can be linked to a type of question. See the history example in the table below.

Level in hierarchy	Example question
1.0 Remember	When did the Wall Street Crash happen?
2.0 Understand	What factors contributed to the economic depression?
3.0 Apply	What parallels can be drawn between the Wall Street Crash and the recent banking crisis?
4.0 Analyse	Look at the financial data from 1925. Are there any indications a crash was about to occur?
5.0 Evaluate	It has been argued that the Versailles Treaty led directly to the Wall Street Crash, to what extent do you believe this to be a valid argument?
6.0 Create	Investigate a number of historical financial crashes, formulate an understanding of their causes and explore how the Wall Street Crash could have been averted.

Although the use of this kind of hierarchy of cognitive processes is commonplace in teaching, it is worth remembering that several critics have raised objections to the classification (Pring, 1971) – for example, the ranking of understanding as a lower skill than evaluation seems difficult to justify. Despite the debatable ordering of the skills in the taxonomy, the categories can be a useful way to focus thinking about questioning. For example, Wragg and Brown (2001, p21) report that out of a thousand teachers' questions recorded in primary schools only eight per cent were higher-order – that is, they required the students to do more than remember facts. I have observed lessons in which the majority of the questions, both oral and written, were low level and closed (they had a limited number of correct responses). For example, in a history lesson exploring the causes of the English Civil War, the teacher did little more than assess students' ability to recall rote-learned knowledge without exploring more complex themes.

Although it may seem intuitively that students should be engaging with more higher-order questions, there is no correct distribution for the types of question expected in a lesson. Rather, the distribution of questioning should be appropriate for the learning aims of the lesson and the abilities and needs of the students. You might wish to probe the presence of prior factual knowledge, in a lesson that is setting the scene for future learning, and the question distribution may appropriately skew towards recall prompts. Once a teacher is assured that their students know the necessary information, a subsequent lesson may focus exclusively on higher-order questions.

Key learning point

There is a role for all types of questions in the classroom; often probes of knowledge are a route into more complex questions and deeper learning.

A different categorisation of questioning highlights the difference between convergent and divergent questions, based on the number of possible acceptable answers to a prompt. Convergent questions have a single expected correct answer, whereas divergent questions may have a number of different acceptable responses (Wittmer and Honig, 1991). Therefore, you might use convergent questions to assess if students possess certain pieces of knowledge, whereas divergent questions could be used to encourage students' thinking. For example, a convergent question might ask: 'Who does Hamlet stab through the arras?' The single expected answer is Polonius. A divergent question, on the other hand, does not have a single correct solution – for example, 'Is Hamlet's madness genuine or a performance?' Clearly, these questions are performing different functions and prompt different kinds of processing in students. When asking divergent questions, you should indicate to students that there is no single correct answer to the question. Divergent questions can be a difficult proposition for students who assume that school is about the acquisition of factual knowledge and that the teacher is the source of learning. Therefore, it can assist students if you highlight that divergent questions are an opportunity to focus on how they justify and argue their case, not just getting the right answer. The assertive questioning approach (Petty, 2009, pp281–7) described in the strategies below, suggests that for such divergent questions the role of the teacher is not in assessing if an answer is correct or incorrect, but in supporting students to understand the features of a good argument. As has been discussed with Bloom's taxonomy of questions, both kinds of questions can be useful to a teacher and the spread of convergent to divergent questions in a lesson should be determined by the aims and context of the class.

Wait time

Good questioning is about more than just the type of questions you ask. A particular problem among trainee teachers is firing out questions in rapid succession, like a machine gun, giving students little opportunity to compose their responses. This has been the case for many years. Researchers reported that teachers often waited only a single second between posing a question to a student and moving to a different question or selecting a different student (Rowe, 1986). The wait time, the period from a teacher asking a question to issuing another prompt or focusing their attention on another student, is a significant factor in the success of questioning.

Real life scenario

Scenario A

Teacher: Vijay, what are the features of a fugue?

Vijay: Er . . .

Teacher: No, Paris?

Paris: Um . . .

Teacher: Anyone? Come on, we learned this last lesson!

Scenario B

Teacher: Vijay, what are the features of a fugue?

Vijay: Er . . . [Teacher waits]

Teacher: Okay, give it some more thought. I'll come back to you. Give me a wave if you remember. Paris, any thoughts?

Paris: Um . . . [Teacher waits] . . . Isn't it like a round when people sing different parts?

Teacher: That's a good start. Vijay, you're waving.

Vijay: Like there are two tunes going on at the same time.

Think about what it feels like when someone pounces on you with a factual question. Can you always answer straight away? In scenario A, even though it's a recap from a previous lesson, the teacher gives no time for Vijay or Paris to recall learning that may have occurred several days before. The teacher in scenario B, by allowing the students time to recall the answers themselves, will have strengthened the accessibility of those memories for the students. An improvement on both these cases, which allows students even greater thinking time, is shown in scenario C.

Real life scenario

As students enter, the question 'What are the features of a fugue?' is displayed on the board.

Teacher: Have a look at the question. Twenty seconds. Think of as many features as you can. Remember, we did this last lesson. I'll be asking someone at random [Twenty seconds of silence pass.] Okay. Vijay?

Vijay: Two tunes going on at the same time?

Teacher: That's a good start. Paris, can you add anything?

Paris: It's when people sing different parts.

Short wait times may be appropriate in some circumstances – for example, for drill-like practice of memorised material. However, rapid questioning may induce anxiety in your students and cause you frustration, as depicted in scenario A. For questions that have a higher cognitive demand, research indicates that an extended wait time can enhance student achievement (Tobin, 1987). As well as allowing students more time to think, teachers also benefit from the additional time to rehearse their next probe and it is therefore unsurprising that longer wait times are linked with enriched classroom dialogue. Trainee teachers often find it difficult to increase the wait time after a question: they may feel the pause suggests to students they have not planned thoroughly or are not in control of the class. However, it is worth persisting until a longer wait time becomes an automatic part of your questioning.

Asking an observer to measure the average wait time you apply in a lesson can be an effective technique for focusing your attention on the issue.

Styles of questioning

Questioning does not necessarily end with a student's answer to a teacher's question: the answer may present opportunities for following up on ambiguities or clarifying meaning. A typical exchange in the classroom might follow the pattern shown in the scenario below.

Real life scenario

Teacher: Why do people migrate from less developed countries to more developed countries?

Student: To find jobs.

Teacher: Good.

This type of interaction, which involves a teacher initiating a question, a student's response and some kind of evaluation or feedback from the teacher is sometimes referred to as IRE, or initiation, response and evaluation questioning (Mehan, 1979). In the scenario above, the question is simply an assessment of a single element of knowledge. This kind of assessment may be appropriate in certain circumstances, but the student is not expected to justify or engage with the assumptions of their answer. Moving away from the IRE pattern can allow you to probe student thinking in more detail – for example, in the 'reflective toss' interaction, the onus for justification is returned to the student (van Zee and Minstrell, 1997).

Real life scenario

Teacher: Why do people migrate from less developed countries to more developed countries?

Student: To find jobs.

Teacher: Are there more jobs in more developed countries?

Student: Well, maybe to find jobs that pay more, or for a better quality of life.

The questioning can be opened up to other students to critique or evaluate the points made leading to an active engagement in the construction of knowledge that moves beyond the teacher acting as a simple checker of facts. This model of questioning is powerful as it encourages students to develop the skills of critical thinking. Students may internalise the teacher's prompts and rather than simply accepting the first answer they think of, may develop the skill of critiquing and questioning the assumptions of their own ideas. This idea underlies the Socratic questioning approach (see strategies below). Jane Jones and Dylan Wiliam (2008) suggest teachers move away from a model of questioning as 'serial table tennis' to a style that resembles basketball, with many students participating in different roles in the questioning (for a further discussion of this technique, see the strategies section below).

Effective questioning lies at the heart of good teaching. Certainly, at the start of your practice, you can't expect to come up with good questions while you are teaching: effective questioning requires careful planning. You should always consider the timing and purpose of questions. If you are asking questions in order to assess understanding, what will you do with the information? If your probes are to develop students' thinking, how might the questions be phrased to stimulate learning? What follow-up questions might be appropriate? The next section outline some strategies that you can use to improve the questioning in your classroom.

Targets

Ensure all students are included in questioning

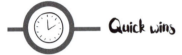 Quick wins

- **No hands up.** Train your students that when you ask a question, you will choose who answers it. This means you are in control of the direction of questions and all students must rehearse an answer.
- **Support students' ability to respond.** For certain kinds of questions, allow students to think individually before talking to a partner or drafting a written response before you choose a respondent.
- **Encourage multiple students to contribute to developing the best possible answer.** After one student has answered a question, ask another student to reflect on the answer and see if they can add any additional information.
- **Idea, develop, challenge.** Ask any student to share their idea on a particular question. Another student is then asked to either develop or challenge the first student's response. If a student cannot contribute, they may offer a new idea.
- **Allow students to ask for help from peers.** Directing questions at students may be anxiety inducing, so clarify that once a certain time has elapsed, or the chosen student has made some attempt to answer, they may ask a classmate for a hint.
- **No passing.** Develop an expectation that students are not allowed to respond with 'I don't know'. They are expected to volunteer some relevant information or make an attempt at a solution. This technique may not be appropriate for certain kinds of classroom or for certain kinds of questions. For example, when testing French vocabulary, though it might be argued that if a student doesn't know the word for giraffe, forcing the response of a long-necked horse develops the skill of attempting to communicate even when gaps in vocabulary exist.
- **Plan questions.** Questions asked at the right moment can stimulate learning. Carefully plan the wording of your questions, even write them out and add them to your lesson plans. Consider your follow-up questions for different responses and which students you might target.

Slow burners

- **Consider how you target questions**. You may wish to ask an observer to monitor how you target your questions. One way of achieving this aim is to ask the observer to mark a lesson plan with the locations of students you questioned as below.

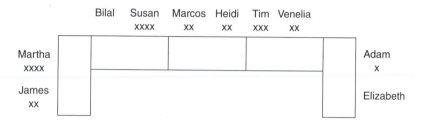

Figure 5.1 An example of the distribution of questions across a classroom. The crosses indicate students who have been asked a question.

You may discover you have some unconscious bias to areas in the classroom, genders or ability levels in the direction of your questions. You may wish to reflect on where you stand when you ask questions or to use a tool, such as those described in the next section, to ensure your selection of students is fair. A different line of analysis involves asking your observer to write down verbatim the questions you ask and the student to whom they were addressed. This will help you to reflect on the phrasing and distribution of types of questions and whether the level of the question was appropriately matched with the student. You may wish in your planning to write questions that are appropriate for specific individuals in your classroom.

A strategy to ensure that you fairly distribute your questions is to write the names of the students on to pieces of card. Draw the cards from the pack without replacing to select a student. You could write the target level of the student on the card to enable you to match the question to the student's ability. PowerPoint slides and websites that perform this function are also available.

Quick click

The website below allows you to copy and paste a class into the yellow box and then offers various random selection methods.

www.classtools.net/education-games-php/fruit_machine

This technique of randomisation, which is sometimes done with lollipop sticks, comes with a warning: questions should be appropriately targeted to students. This method is simply a tool to help you ensure that all students are engaged and involved in the lesson. As you gain more experience, you will be able to include all students without such props.

- **Use the 'assertive questioning' approach (Petty, 2009)**. Ask an open or divergent question (see section on types of questions above) to the whole class and then encourage students to talk in pairs or larger groups with the aim of reaching an agreed answer. During the time students are working on their answers, you should monitor their thinking and ask if they require any additional information but not judge their process or provide the answer. You may give hints to any students who are really stuck. After a set time has elapsed, choose one member of the group to feed back the answer that has been agreed upon by the members of the group, again without passing judgement on the answer. The answers may be written up on the board and the whole class is asked to comment on which answers they feel are stronger or weaker. It is only after these stages in the process have been completed that the teacher can either indicate stronger responses or comment on the quality of the arguments in the students' answers.

Real life scenario

Teacher: You've had a chance to think about the question on the board. So now talk in pairs and share thoughts on 'What is an appropriate training strategy for a marathon runner?' I'll give you five minutes and I will choose one of you to feed back.

[Teacher circulates, gives encouragement but does not judge emerging answers.]

Teacher: We'll start with this group. Fernando, what has your group come up with?

[The teacher writes Fernando's idea on to the board without judgement and continues to collect responses from all groups.]

Teacher: Now we've got these ideas, on your own decide which five are the most effective.

- **Use techniques to assess whole-class understanding**. Using techniques that give you an understanding of the overall position of a class can be a powerful diagnostic tool for a teacher. Consider giving students cards labelled A, B, C or D, mini-whiteboards, using movement to labelled corners in the room, holding up a number of fingers, and even smartphone apps to gain an understanding to the overall learning of a group. Plan for how you will respond to the distribution of answers. What will you do if a majority of the students display a particular misconception?

A key consideration with all questioning is what you do with the information you've gathered. One approach is the hinge point question – a question that determines the future direction of a lesson. This works particularly well when your assessment leads to information about the learning needs of the whole class, rather than an individual. For example, you might set the class a single multiple-choice question and direct students who choose different answers to carry out a different worksheet or activity (Brock, 2007). For example, you might ask students to choose between different models of the way current flows, including common misconceptions such as that current flows out of both ends of the battery; only one wire is required for current to flow from a battery; and current is used up around a circuit. Depending on their answers, students could be directed to different practical activities that are structured to encourage them to move away from their misconceptions. This kind of approach is effective as the activities are personalised to the students' current understanding (for further information, see Chapter 6).

Ask a wider range of questions

 Quick wins

- **Plan higher-order questions before the lesson**. It is easier to think of low-level questions while you are teaching, but a well-rounded higher-order question can take some planning. Consider the phrasing, timing and follow-up questions before you begin teaching. Higher-order questions are significant moments in a lesson. Ensure that students have the necessary factual knowledge and are given sufficient time to think about these questions. Plan how you will assess and provide feedback on their responses.

- **Reflect carefully on the processes students will use to respond to a question**. The question: 'What were the causes of the first world war?' may, for some students, prompt critical thinking, for others it may simply stimulate a rote learned list of responses. If your aim is to encourage critical engagement, consider follow up prompts that may encourage more than a memorised response. This might be to prioritise causes or to encourage them to think about counterfactual 'what if . . . ' questions.

- **Consider statements as prompts for discussion**. Rather than asking a direct question, ask students to discuss the validity of a statement which can be a powerful approach to stimulate thought. For example: 'Talk to your partner about this claim: Higher taxes for the wealthiest harm everyone as they force rich people to emigrate.'

- **Vary the types of questions in starters across lessons.** Often starters involve factual recall, for example, what is Pythagoras' theorem? Explore a range of questioning approaches in starters, including divergent and higher-order questions.

- **When you plan a question, consider alternative versions at different levels of challenge.** For example, what do Buddhists believe about life after death? How are Buddhist beliefs different from Christian beliefs? Why might Buddhist beliefs provide comfort to a mourner? The questions access similar knowledge but set slightly different types of challenge (see Chapter 8).

- **Ask questions that elicit a misconception.** It might seem counterintuitive to encourage students to give an incorrect answer. However, this can serve as a powerful learning experience. For example, in citizenship, students are shown iconic 'British' images, such as fish and chips or a pint of beer and asked if they feel they are British. This activity can challenge a perception of what it means to be British in a unit on immigration.

Slow burners

- **Plan the purpose of your questions**. When I carry out observations, it sometimes feels as if a teacher is asking questions simply because they believe it is expected of them. In such cases, the questioning appears automatic and unresponsive to the students' answers. It appears as if the teacher wants the students to guess what is in their head, and any differences or difficulties in understanding are ignored. To avoid this style of questioning, reflect on when and why you will use questions in a lesson. For example, questioning may be used to assess the current level of student understanding, but if that is the reason for your questions, ensure you are responsive to the information. If you are questioning to assess understanding, is this best done to an individual student or using an approach that involves the whole class? If there is evidence of gaps in understanding, plan for opportunities to bridge the gaps in knowledge (see hinge point questions above). Alternatively, you may be using questioning as a tool to stimulate thinking and in that case think about indicators you might use to show that students are genuinely engaging with a question, rather than regurgitating memorised knowledge. Try to make the purpose of your question clear to the students in the class - are they being asked this question so they can show their factual knowledge or is this prompt more about making a strong argument? Questions should arise from a clear pedagogical need which should be transparent to the teacher, the students and anyone watching the lesson.

- **Plan for a sequence of questions.** It is rare for teachers to ask a single question on its own. Rather than planning questions in isolation, think about the sequence of questions you will ask over the course of a lesson and plan a meaningful progression. Break down the final learning goal into underlying assumptions and necessary knowledge elements and set your questions appropriately. Questions can be useful for priming certain pieces of knowledge that will be brought together to answer a more complex question. It can be useful to anticipate the kind of answers students will give to your questions. Experienced teachers build an awareness of common misconceptions students hold that can interfere with learning. Questioning can be a powerful technique for addressing and challenging these misconceptions. For example, when teaching Newton's second law, it would be appropriate to probe students' knowledge of the nature of resultant forces and how they affect the motion of objects. A teacher might anticipate that some students would possess the misconception that an object moving at constant velocity must have a resultant force acting on it and plan questions to probe and attempt to alter this idea. In history, students might see primary sources as a 'window into the past' – that is, they believe that primary sources are a true and factual account of historical events. In this case, a teacher would use questions to highlight the motives of the author, which might challenge the perception of the source as an unproblematic record of the past.

- **Ensure an appropriate spread of questioning**. While planning a lesson, explicitly decide on the questions you will ask at various points. Think about the learning aims of the lesson and the kind of students in the class. In general, you might want to aim for a balance of questions at different cognitive levels, and of convergent and divergent types. However, you may find you need a greater number of lower-level questions in order to assess whether factual knowledge is in place and then use higher-level questions as spurs to further thinking. You could ask an observer to tally the number of questions of different types you asked during the lesson and reflect on the spread and aims of those questions. It is more likely that you will have too few high-level questions than a lack of low-level questions. Picture a graph in your head and imagine what the distribution of questions over time in your lessons would look like (see figure 5.2).

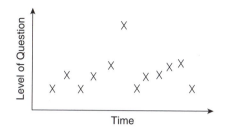

Figure 5.2: A example representation of the level of questions asked in a lesson over time.

There is no single correct distribution of questioning: the questions should match the aims of the lesson. However, picturing the distribution of questioning may be useful for understanding the shape of the lesson. Does the lesson consist of a period of factual questioning moving towards a single, complex open-ended question? Is the lesson set up around a few high-level questions and moves on to a series of more detailed closed questions in order to develop a knowledge base to address the big questions? Questioning that is frequently at too high a level may be exhausting and too demanding for students; questioning at only the lowest levels is repetitive, authoritative and is likely to be demotivating and dull.

Use questions to encourage higher-order thinking in students

- **Use verbs from the upper levels of Bloom's taxonomy.** For planning higher-level questions, base your prompts around verbs and phrases such as: evaluate, why does?, to what extent?, justify, predict, contrast, explain, criticise.
- **Do not answer your own questions**. If no student is able to answer a higher-order question, ensure you support students to reach the answer, rather than simply revealing the answer.
- **Decide on whether you will select a student before or after asking the question.** In some cases, you may wish to choose a student before you state the question. This places the focus on the individual and encourages them to think deeply. However, if you ask the question, allow an appropriate wait time to elapse and then select a respondent. The whole class is encouraged to engage with the question.
- **Attempt to ask authentic questions.** Questioning in class can sometimes seem like a meaningless activity to students. A teacher's questions may be seen as inauthentic as the teacher already knows the answer. Asking questions that express a shared uncertainty about the answer can be powerful learning experiences. For example, 'I've always wondered why the last line *Of Mice and Men* is 'Now what the hell do you suppose is eatin' them two guys?'
- **Probe a student's ability to transfer ideas between contexts.** An indicator that a student understands a concept may be that they can transfer the learning to new contexts. Follow up your first question with a test of the same principles in a novel situation. For example, in mathematics, students are often introduced to the idea of fractions by looking at divided circular cakes. A way to probe their higher-order understanding is to examine if they can apply this learning to rectangular or triangular cakes.

- **Get an observer to record the wait time you use for different questions**. Ensure that higher questions have sufficient wait time. The question 'Why does Hamlet struggle to decide to avenge his father?' is a complex question and will require a much longer wait time. Most likely it will also require some scaffolding for students to rehearse and develop their answers before they give a reply.

- **Count in your head after asking a question** to resist the temptation to follow up too early. Try repeating a phrase such as 'one elephant, two elephant, three elephant' to ensure you leave an appropriate wait time after each question.

- **In planning lessons, write out the questions you intend to ask and write a wait time in seconds in a circle next to the question**. For example, given the question 'How would you translate *chien*?', it may be assumed that with a simple recall question a short wait time will be appropriate. However, other factors, such as how long ago the information was taught and the level of the student targeted, will influence the choice of interval.

Slow burners

- **Plan for the most effective kind of student-teacher interaction during questioning**. A range of different student-teacher interaction patterns are possible and are appropriate for different kinds of questions and contexts. When you are planning your questioning approach, consider the possible responses a student may give and decide in different circumstances whether you will simply evaluate the answer, present further probes of the student's response or open the question to other members of the class. These ideas are discussed in the clip below.

Quick link

Watch Dylan Wiliam discussing effective questioning styles.

www.youtube.com/watch?v=O29fSeOaGio&feature=youtu.be

If your aim is for your students to acquire some factual knowledge - for example, some new vocabulary in a foreign language - a rapid, back-and-forth, table-tennis style of teacher-student interaction involving a single student response followed by a teacher evaluation may be an appropriate style. However, for more complex information, you may want to anticipate the most likely student responses and your reactions to them. If the student gives an incomplete or underdeveloped answer, will you ask them to enlarge or pass it to another member of the class? Even if a student gives a very good answer, how can you extend their thinking? What kind of evaluation will be most effective in the circumstances? Resist the temptation to feel that you must assess each answer as being correct or incorrect: you may wish to give more nuanced evaluations such as: 'There are some good elements to that answer. Can you restructure it in a different way?' or 'That is one interpretation. Let's hear some others.' The responsibility for evaluation does not have to rest solely with you and it may be beneficial if students come to learn how to assess the validity of different arguments.

Quick click

A powerful questioning technique is the so-called 'Pose – Pause – Pounce – Bounce' strategy. The approach recommends teachers wait after asking a question, then select a student to provide a response, before asking a second student to comment on the first answer. There are some useful resources on the technique on Ross Morrison McGill's excellent Te@cher Toolkit blog.

www.teachertoolkit.me/2011/11/04/pose-pause-bounce-pounce/

- **Make use of Socratic questioning.** Student thinking will not change if they are merely asked to recall facts they have already memorised. However, probing of assumptions, highlighting contradictions in thinking and asking for justifications can drive learning. Socratic questioning is an approach that makes students evaluate the assumptions that support their beliefs (Elder and Paul, 1998). The approach suggests that no idea a student holds should be considered completely developed and teachers should respond to students' answers with additional questions that attempt to understand their underlying beliefs. Consider the following scenario.

Real life scenario

Teacher: What is science?

Student: Science is about finding proof about what is true in what happens in the world around us.

Teacher: How can you find proof about the world?

Student: By doing experiments and collecting data.

Teacher: Is data collected from experiments always 'true'?

Student: If you repeat the experiment many times, it becomes true.

Teacher: How many times would you have to repeat an experiment till the knowledge becomes 'true'? Ten times? A hundred times?

Student: I don't know. Many times. It depends.

The Socratic approach is a useful technique when you are encouraging students to consider the premises of their thinking. However, it is worth noting that the technique can initially be frustrating for students. Students tend to assume that the classroom is about being taught facts and may initially feel uncomfortable with an approach in which the teacher adopts the role of the questioner. In certain contexts, however, it may be a powerful approach for encouraging students to think critically. It has been argued that the use of Socratic questioning can lead to students internalising a critical thinking approach.

- **Use a wide range of responses to students' answers**. It is tempting to respond to students' answers with either a 'yes' or 'no' and then move on. However, a more stimulating approach is to engage in more detail with student responses. If their answer is correct, you could reply with 'Yes, but is that the case in all circumstances?' or 'Could you provide some evidence to convince the class that your answer is correct?' If an answer is incorrect, rather than simply acting as a judge of knowledge, you could support the student to see why their answer is incorrect and give them extra information to find a better response. You could say: 'I see why you might think that, but . . . '. Keep in mind that questioning is an opportunity to encourage further learning, rather than simply an opportunity for summative assessment. When a student offers an answer, think of it not as a finished and final response but a work in progress. How could the student be supported to develop their answer?

In summary

You should think of questioning not only as a means to find out what your students know, but also as a tool to encourage learning. Ensure you plan for an appropriate variety of questioning, and try to maximise opportunities for questions that go beyond simply asking students to recall a piece of knowledge.

Before the lesson

- **Plan for a range of types of questions.** Ensure the questions you have chosen match the aims of the lesson and consider whether there are enough opportunities for higher-order questions.

- **Plan higher-order questions.** Open-ended questions can be challenging to create in the moment, so consider the exact phrasing of critical questions before the lesson.

- **Plan for your responses to questions**. Especially for higher-order questions, be prepared for common answers and plan your follow-up questioning strategy in advance.

During the lesson

- **Allow sufficient wait time after questions,** particularly for higher-order questions.

- **Ensure that all students are engaged in questioning.**

- **Target your questions appropriately.** Ensure the level of your questions match the ability of the student targeted.

- **Listen to students' responses.** Don't move on too quickly but value and engage with the nuance of students' answers.

After the lesson

- **Use responses to questioning to inform your planning**. Consider in which areas students require additional support.

- **Reflect on individual student performance**. Consider how individuals dealt with different types of questions and consider the best approach to take in the future.

Further reading

Elder, L and Paul, R (1998) The role of Socratic questioning in thinking, teaching, and learning. *The Clearing House*, 71(5): 297–301.

A brief but good introduction to Socratic questioning in the classroom can be found in this article.

Marzano, RJ and Simms, JA (2013) *Questioning Sequences in the Classroom*. Bloomington, IN: Marzano Research Laboratory.

This book focuses particularly on structuring the sequences of questions but also presents a good and detailed review of research.

Pope, G (2013) *Questioning Technique Pocketbook*. Alresford, Hampshire: Teachers' Pocket Books.

This *Pocketbook* is an easy-to-dip-into guide to different approaches to questioning.

Walsh, JA and Sattes, BD (2011) *Thinking Through Quality Questioning*. Thousand Oaks, CA: Corwin.

If you are interested in research evidence from cognitive science and a focus on the relationship between questioning and thinking, this book is a good place to start.

Wragg, EC and Brown, G (2001) *Questioning in the Secondary School*. London: Routledge.

A thorough and extensive survey of the theory and research behind different forms of questioning.

References

Bloom, BS, Engelhart, MD, Furst, FJ, Hill, WH and Krathwohl, DR (1956) *Taxonomy of Educational Objectives: Cognitive Domain*. New York: McKay.

Brock, R (2007) Differentiation by alternative conception: Tailoring teaching to students' thinking. *School Science Review, 88*(325): 97–104.

Elder, L and Paul, R (1998) The role of Socratic questioning in thinking, teaching, and learning. *The Clearing House, 71*(5): 297–301.

Hastings, S (2006) *The Complete Classroom*. Abingdon: Routledge.

Krathwohl, DR (2002) A revision of Bloom's taxonomy: An overview. *Theory into Practice, 41*(4): 212–218.

Jones, J and Wiliam, D (2008). *Modern Foreign Languages Inside the Black Box*. London: GL Assessment.

Mehan, H (1979) *Learning Lessons*. Cambridge, MA: Harvard University Press.

Petty, G (2009) *Teaching Today. A Practical Guide* (4th edn). Cheltenham: Nelson Thornes Ltd.

Pring, R (1971) Bloom's taxonomy: A philosophical critique (2). *Cambridge Journal of Education, 1*(2): 83–91.

Rowe, MB (1986) Wait time: Slowing down may be a way of speeding up! *Journal of Teacher Education, 37*(1): 43–50.

Thelen, JN (1984) *Improving Reading in Science*. Newark, DE: International Reading Association.

Tobin, K (1987) The role of wait time in higher cognitive level learning. *Review of Educational Research, 57*(1): 69–95.

van Zee, EH and Minstrell, J (1997) Reflective discourse: Developing shared understandings in a physics classroom. *International Journal of Science Education, 19*(2): 209–28.

Wittmer, DS and Honig, AS (1991) Convergent or divergent? Teacher questions to three-year-old children in day care. *Early Child Development and Care, 68*(1): 141–7.

Wragg, EC and Brown, G (2001) *Questioning in the Secondary School*. London: Routledge.

6
Assessment

Teachers' Standard 6 – Make accurate and productive use of assessment

This section looks to support you with strategies that will enable you to develop your summative and formative methods of assessment, to help you both measure and support pupil progress. However, assessment overlaps with many other aspects of the standards, including the following.

- Setting appropriate goals to challenge pupils (TS1).
- Being accountable for pupil progress and attainment (TS2).
- Being aware of assessment arrangements and approaches for your subject (TS3).
- Using assessment to discern learners' strengths and needs, to appropriately support and challenge pupils (TS5).

Introduction

You might equate assessment with marking, testing or examinations. Assessment is so much more than that.

Using assessment effectively is rather like undertaking a building project – whereas your 'cowboy practitioners' will use it to cover up any cracks in understanding, or to paint the impression of a thin veneer of learning over the classroom (that students have met success criteria), the 'master practitioner' will use it to gain a genuine insight into the inner workings of their classroom, which carries both the risk and reward of identifying serious structural faults in learning. Too often assessment is viewed by both teachers and students negatively, in that it leads to increased marking and is only seen as a means to determine performance. Yet this is a narrow view of assessment, as a summative process, which is conflated with testing and checking performance.

Assessment is undoubtedly difficult. On the one hand, it is a vital tool for teachers, students and parents, to guide learning. How can you possibly help students to improve if you have no idea what they know or have learnt? On the other hand, the mere mention of the word assessment can strike fear into the heart of many students, because of the highly charged and emotional strain that comes from feeling as if you are being judged. Assessment is both a pedagogical challenge in trying to design assessments that give you a genuine picture of students' learning, or that help learners to make progress, and also a professional challenge in trying to create a classroom environment in which assessment is seen positively.

You should therefore see assessment as a fundamental tool for uncovering learning, or the lack of learning. Hopefully, you will see this constructively as a way to gain an insight into the learning that is taking place. However, it may well present you with some uncomfortable truths – that your students are not learning and that your teaching wasn't a success. Therefore, it is important that you embrace assessment as a tool to help you lift the veil covering the learning in your classroom, so that it becomes 'visible' (Hattie and Yates, 2014). Rather than being fearful of assessment, and the findings it presents, you should (like your students) celebrate any failures that you uncover, and see them as learning opportunities for you and your class. Just because students are able to regurgitate the lesson objectives or answer low-level questions in a plenary does not mean that genuine learning has taken place. If assessment is not done correctly, you might get the impression that you have created a veneer of learning. However, cracks may soon reappear because deeper misconceptions lie undetected and unaddressed within the foundations of students' learning.

With this in mind, you should not see this chapter as offering sticking-plaster solutions to the assessment problems you will no doubt face. The range of quick wins presented in this chapter will help to get your teaching on the right track; the slow burners will ensure that you embed formative assessment into your day-to-day teaching practice. This will help you create a positive classroom environment in which assessment is embraced, by both you and your students, and is at the heart of your planning and teaching.

Targets

What targets does this chapter cover?

- Ensure you consistently clarify and share learning objectives and success criteria with students.
- Include a range of AfL strategies to effectively monitor progress and inform your teaching and planning.
- Widen your use of formative assessment, to encourage students to be more aware of their own progress and learning needs.
- Develop a secure understanding of how to accurately and effectively assess pupils' attainment and progress.

The purpose of assessment

Assessment underpins all aspects of planning for learning, because it is impossible to plan for an effective learning journey if you don't know where students need to be picked up from at the start. Without effective assessment, lessons run the risk of being directionless and unproductive. Assessments should therefore be a fundamental part of your planning, and should be designed to support your students on their learning journey. It gives you both a map with which to plan the learning route and signposts along the way to ensure that students don't take a wrong turn. At the end of the journey, assessment helps you to see if the final destination has been reached. It thereby provides a vital signal for the destination of the students' next learning journey.

Real life scenario

The teacher is halfway through a lesson and knows this is a good point to ask students to traffic light their understanding.

Scenario A

Teacher: Raise green if you are totally clear, amber if you are a little unsure and red if you are not sure at all.

[Half the class signal that they are red or amber.]

Teacher: OK, great, so let's move on to the next activity.

Scenario B

Teacher: Place your cards on your desk: green if you are totally clear, amber if you are a little unsure and red if you are not sure at all.

[Half the class signal that they are red or amber.]

Teacher: OK, I want to go through this with anyone who showed red. So come forward to these two tables. I want those displaying amber to move to these two tables and work together on these questions. Everyone else can move on to the challenge activity. In 8 minutes, I will be getting feedback from all groups.

Too often assessment is seen as a tick-box activity. In Scenario A, the teacher might feel they have 'done' assessment for learning, but the activity is a waste of time if the information gained is not acted upon. Both teachers have carried out assessment, but in the former it seems more like a performance rather than a genuine technique to engender learning. The teacher in Scenario B has established an environment where students feel as if they can be honest, have the self-awareness to accurately judge their own learning, and are well versed in the routines of assessment (see the section below on assessing pupils' attainment and progress).

Given the messy nature of learning, and that what you teach is not always the same as what students learn, assessment provides a torch that can shine a light on the learning in a classroom. I, too, often observe trainees attempting to check understanding by asking the whole class 'Is everyone clear on that?' or even nodding their head vigorously as they ask the loaded question of 'You all understand that don't you?' Although this might appear to be a way to check understanding, it usually only produces unenthusiastic nods or the odd murmur of agreement. If you have not fostered a learning environment that allows students to admit they are unclear or misunderstand, you are unlikely to get an accurate picture of student learning.

Forms of assessment

You should be aware of three forms of assessment, which each serve a different purpose (McTighe and O'Connor, 2005).

- **Diagnostic assessment** is used to identify learning needs prior to or at the early stages of teaching. It provides you with information to help guide your planning and teaching and ensures your teaching is appropriately challenging and doesn't repeat unnecessarily.

- **Formative assessment,** sometimes referred to as Assessment *for* Learning (AfL), is concurrent and takes place while learning occurs. This will be used, by you and your learners, to inform and shape the learning process. This is a form of on-going diagnostic assessment allowing you to identify needs and act upon them as you are teaching.

- **Summative assessment,** sometimes referred to as Assessment *of* Learning, is designed to assess what a student has achieved, understands or can do – for example, public examinations or end-of-unit tests.

The first two approaches are designed to use assessment *for* learning, to modify and differentiate learning activities, or by using assessment *as* learning, to make students more independent so they are able to regulate their own learning (Earl and Katz, 2006). In contrast, the purpose of summative assessment is to undertake assessment *of* learning, as a means of reviewing what students know, understand or can do.

Too often schools and teachers have been overly focused on the summative aspects of assessment, to monitor and grade students, at the expense of using it formatively, to support learning. It is clearly too simplistic to state that summative assessment is less valuable than formative assessment. However, it has come to dominate the UK education system, which has created an imbalance of assessment methods, with too much weight being given to the assessment *of* learning and too little to assessment *for* learning (Black and Wiliam, 2005). You should recognise that all assessment has its place, and summative assessments are useful markers of progress and attainment. Indeed, summative assessments can provide you and your learners with information, which can be used to shape and improve learning (see Chapter 7). However, if summative assessment, purely as a means of awarding and accumulating grades, comes to dominate, it can create a negative atmosphere which will not help you with your teaching, or your students with their learning (Butler, 1988).

Keep in mind the old adage that 'Just weighing a pig doesn't make it fatter' when you are considering your use of classroom assessment. If you are constantly 'weighing the pig', without considering or adapting its diet, it's unlikely to get 'fatter'. Too often I have seen lessons in which the trainee has moved from one review activity to another, without actually doing anything with the assessment data this has generated. It is important that you get the right mix of assessment methods so you can constantly adapt your teaching and organise learning opportunities to suit the needs of your pupils. Any trip to the doctor might start with a diagnosis, but without the relevant treatment you are unlikely to get better. It is the same in your classroom.

Key learning point

Assessment should enable you to both diagnose the problems in your classroom and develop an appropriate treatment.

Therefore, when you are looking at how to develop your own assessment practices, it is not simply a choice between using either summative or formative approaches. What is more important is how you employ the range of methods available to you. This may require you to rethink your own views of assessment and how you share this with pupils. Move away from seeing it in purely negative terms as a means of 'catching out' students, and instead see it as a constructive way to support learning and encourage greater independence. When I was a student (many years ago) assessments were often something that were 'done to me' by the teacher, rather than something I would 'do myself' to help my learning. In order to get the most out of assessments, you need a shift of mentality that values learning over testing, and gives precedence to the process of learning rather than the final outcome. You need to emphasise and articulate to students in your classroom the importance of assessment *as* and *for* learning as opposed to focusing purely on assessment *of* learning. You should therefore look to widen your repertoire of formative approaches to assessment, which give support during the learning journey. This will ensure that you are using assessment when it is most needed – when students are actually learning.

Formative assessment

Formative assessment is a useful tool for checking understanding and for identifying any underlying misconceptions, and addressing these to support students in their learning. I often ask those I have observed 'How can you be sure they have all learnt what you intended?' or 'How did you adapt the lesson in the light of the responses to the formative assessments you planned?' Some respond with oblivious looks, while others offer little more than vague assertions. Therefore, it is important that in planning your lessons you consider fully how you will integrate a range of methods of formative assessment.

There is certainly considerable evidence that formative assessment *is an essential component of classroom work and that its development can raise standards of achievement* (Black and Wiliam, 1998, p12). Yet, the concept and practice of formative assessment, from an educational perspective, is not clearly defined and has been seen as a *work in progress* (Bennett, 2011, p.21). Indeed, there is considerable overlap with the wide body of literature on Assessment *for* learning, which has sprung up since Black and Wiliam's seminal work (1998). When you plan to carry out assessment, always consider its purpose and what you will do with the information it generates. In this way, any assessment can be formative as long as it is used to inform the next steps in teaching and learning (Wiliam, 2011).

Leahy *et al.* (2005) identified five broad approaches which are the bedrock of formative assessment.

- Clarifying and sharing learning intentions and criteria for success.
- Engineering effective classroom discussions, questions and leaming tasks.
- Activating students as the owners of their own learning.
- Providing feedback that moves learners forward.
- Activating students as instructional resources for one another.

These are a useful guide when you are looking to improve your own methods of formative assessment. However, in essence, formative assessment strategies can be broken down into two main areas. First, there are those that are designed to support you in your teaching. These strategies will effectively help you to use assessment as a classroom thermometer in order to judge the 'temperature' of your class or the individuals within it, so that you can make necessary adjustments to keep learning on track. They can help you to keep learning within the 'Goldilocks spot', which is neither too hot nor too cold. Second, there are those strategies that are designed to support learners by encouraging them to take ownership of their learning and more effectively self-regulate it. You will no doubt find this a more difficult task, as such approaches are much more tangential and less within your own control. Using formative assessment to develop students as learners is difficult because of the emotional as well as the cognitive challenges of assessment. These can be deeply ingrained issues related to motivation, mind-set and self-esteem (Jones and Tanner, 2006, pp76–9). Yet, if you are to make the most out of formative assessment, it is this aspect which is the most vital, and without it all the other strategies and measures are doubtless doomed to fail.

Sharing learning aims

Always ensure that assessment is underpinned by a clear understanding among pupils of 'What is being assessed?', 'How it is being assessed' and 'Why it is being assessed'. In this way, assessment is about ensuring that students 'know the rules of the game', otherwise it is viewed as a rather secret affair in which many of your less able students will feel they are doomed to fail. Although some students have an innate ability to understand what is expected of them and to get inside a teacher's head, most pupils need to be given the 'rules of the game'. Sharing success criteria (see strategies below) is an important part of your teaching, and these can be externally imposed by examining bodies or restrictive schemes of work.

During one whole staff INSET, I was asked to draw a house. Despite lacking any understanding of why I was being asked to do this, I enthusiastically begun to sketch a basic house design, before changing tack and drawing a wigwam. When we were asked to review each other's creation, around a very strict and narrow set of assessment criteria (such as having a square structure, a chimney exuding smoke and a picket fence surrounding the house), there was a groan of understanding among the audience. We had all been set up to fail. Once I had seen the assessment criteria, I drew a house which secured maximum marks. I was delighted. However, on reflection, I considered the potential restrictions imposed by sharing such a narrow set of assessment criteria. Although I had achieved full marks for my 'house', I felt that my creativity had been stifled and my beautiful, artistic wigwam was unfairly penalised for not satisfying the narrow success criteria laid down for the task. Do we want all our students to become mindless automatons, merely producing identical and uncreative pieces of work? As a teacher, you will find there is a difficult balance to be struck between enabling students to meet success criteria, which might be imposed by external bodies, and the desire to foster their originality and verve.

 **Key learning point**

Sharing success criteria is vitally important, especially for achieving examination success. However, you need to ensure that this does not come at the expense of creativity and enthusiasm for your subject.

The same principle applies to sharing learning objectives because, although there will be some students who will willingly undertake a voyage of discovery and go on a learning journey to an unknown and mysterious destination, many students will need, and want, to know where they are going. By clarifying and sharing learning intentions and success criteria, you are mapping out the learning journey for students and allowing them to take greater ownership of that learning. Along the way you will thereby look to build in opportunities for assessment, so that students can review and reflect on their progress.

Creating a positive culture of assessment

Given the issues that arise from undertaking formative assessment, you will need to put significant input into creating a safe and supportive learning environment, where it is acceptable to make mistakes. You will need to use a range of strategies to help you overcome the social difficulties of assessment to ensure that you truly gain an insight into student learning and understanding. There are obvious things you can do, such as maintaining a positive view of assessment which you articulate to your class. If you see assessment as a boring but necessary evil, your students are unlikely to be enthralled at the prospect of being assessed.

- Ensure you use positive language when talking about assessments with your classes. Focus on how they can learn from assessments rather than how they do in assessments.

- Avoid comparing students, which can contribute to feelings of inadequacy.

- Celebrate individual improvement rather than just attainment.

As you can see in scenario B below, the teacher is not comparing students and is more obviously celebrating Amanda's improvement, rather than purely focusing on her attainment.

Real life scenario

A teacher is returning a writing assessment on the causes of the Peasants' Revolt.

Scenario A

Teacher: Ahmed, well done, you are top of the class again. Another fantastic and well-focused evaluation of the causes.

Teacher: Amanda, you still need to work on explaining each cause like Ahmed does.

Scenario B

Teacher: Excellent Ahmed, you are really starting to show how the different causes interrelate.

Teacher: Amanda, well done. You really took on board my last feedback and have identified a number of different causes this time. Now work on developing your explanations of some of these causes in the places identified.

Overall, although assessment can feel onerous, you should see it as a celebration of student success. It is not just a way of working out what students don't know, but of making them aware of how much they have achieved or progressed.

There is clearly a danger of adopting formative assessment practices in a superficial way and seeing assessment *as* and *for* learning strategies as a quick panacea for the difficulties you face as a trainee teacher. You should realise that it is not just a case of trying out different strategies, but really committing yourself to embedding formative assessment into your day-to-day teaching. You must clearly articulate this philosophy to your students and act upon the information that formative assessment gives you to adapt your teaching, or encourage students to act upon this same information to maximise their own learning.

Strategies themselves are a starting point, but it boils down to two questions.

- Do I genuinely know where my students are with their learning?

- Am I responding to the information I receive about student learning?

Careful thought and professional decisions need to be made by you in employing the following strategies effectively and deciding which will work best with a particular class at a given time. You should thus look to explore the range of techniques and strategies outlined below to embed effective assessment into your classroom practice, and recognise that what works now may not always meet the needs of all your students all of the time. Be prepared to reflect and change your approach as your own teaching develops.

Targets

Ensure you consistently clarify and share learning objectives and success criteria with students

Quick wins

- **Make sure lesson objectives are easy for students to understand** and use appropriate learner language. If they can't understand them, it is highly unlikely they will be able to track their own progress towards meeting them.

- **Try phrasing your learning objectives as key enquiry questions**, which students will be able to answer by the end of the lesson. For example, a Geography lesson might be based around the key questions 'What are the key features of life in Nairobi?' and 'To what extent does life in Nairobi differ from your own?' Not only does this help to make the objectives more understandable to students, giving them a clear focus across the lesson, but it will also allow you to undertake a quick and effective plenary to review these questions.

- **Relate key activities to the learning objective** so students can see the link between what they are doing and the objectives. This will signpost how the task is going to help them meet the objectives, although you need to be careful not to overdo this. Very simply you might state: 'This activity will help you to . . .'.

- **Share assessment criteria with students**, so they are clear on what you are looking for. This needs to be more than just reading out a pupil-friendly mark scheme, but should help them understand the assessment criteria and ensure they are clear on any abstract or unfamiliar terms, which will form the basis of assessments. One way I used to do this was to share small extracts of work with the class so they could be more confident about the difference between descriptions, explanations and arguments.

- **Use exemplars** to demonstrate what you are looking for. Share a concrete example of a completed response so that students know what to aim for.

- **Give students an overview of the learning objectives** before you start a scheme of work, so they are able to see the long-term learning journey.

- **Display learning objectives and success criteria around the classroom,** so they can be viewed at any point in the lesson.

- **Differentiate your success criteria** so students of different abilities know what they are aiming to achieve.

 Slow burners

- **Be clear on what success will look like** in your lesson and what this will look like for different students in your lesson. Ask yourself these two questions when you are planning: What is successful learning in this lesson? How will I know when different students have achieved this? For example, a business studies lesson might have the objective of learning the advantages and disadvantages of being a public limited company. The teacher will need to consider what successful learning will look like for different ability students in their class. In very broad terms, the least able might be expected to complete a table with at least two advantages and two disadvantages; middle ability pupils might be expected to outline multiple advantages and disadvantages, and make use of some examples; for the more able pupils, it might be expected that they can use their knowledge to evaluate a case study and recommend an appropriate course of action for a private limited company, about whether or not to go public.

Trainees are sometimes satisfied with the same learning outcomes for all their students and might be delighted with a highly able student who has produced a table full of advantages and disadvantages. Although this shows engagement in the task, I am always keen to ask the trainee if this represents success for that individual. If the trainee had started with a clear set of success criteria in mind, arising out of the learning objectives, they would have known that this was not a sufficiently challenging outcome for the more able pupils in their class.

- **Avoid 'wallpaper' objectives and outcomes** which are pasted on to the board at the start and ignored for the rest of the lesson. You should look to explore ways to engage students with the objectives, without just reading them out or getting students to copy them into their books. You must encourage students to engage with the learning objectives, think about them, and ultimately understand them.

You could review progress towards learning outcomes across the lesson, allowing students to track their own progress and confidence as the lesson develops. This is not just an opportunity to assess progress but a time to celebrate the success of individual students regardless of ability. In an MFL lesson I observed, the trainee displayed the outcomes on the back wall. When students felt they had met an objective they could stick a post-it note with their name next to the relevant outcome. This kept the outcomes fresh in students' minds and gave the teacher an overview of progress, so they could target interventions to support or challenge pupils appropriately.

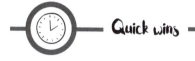

Quick click

David Didau has a very useful website which looks at issues in education. In particular, his review of different approaches to introduce learning objectives is a good source of ideas.

http://bit.ly/2d5GXVe

- **Use students to create success criteria**, rather than just supplying these to students yourself. Essentially, this will help your students to engage with discussions about how to successfully provide evidence that they have met the learning objectives or how they will be able to demonstrate their learning. One particularly successful D&T lesson I observed started by giving students an example logo design board from a previous year, which the teacher had identified as being particularly strong. Groups were then asked to discuss why it was such a good design board and use this to compile a set of success criteria. The result of this was a clear set of student-generated success criteria, which students understood and were able to refer to as they began to develop their own design boards. This activity gives students ownership of the assessment criteria, rather than having them imposed. However, sometimes this is not possible, especially where success criteria are dictated by examination bodies.

Include a range of AfL strategies to effectively monitor progress and inform your teaching and planning

Quick wins

- **Plan for regular mini-plenaries** (see Chapter 1) to review progress and consolidate learning across the lesson.
- **Use targeted questioning** (see Chapter 5) to review students' starting points; this will enable you to adapt learning and teaching activities based on their needs.
- **Use whiteboards to quickly gauge knowledge and understanding** across a class. This works particularly well in helping you to identify pockets of misunderstanding, so you can adapt your lesson. For example, you could use this information to organise the class into groups, allowing some to continue working on more challenging work independently or with the support of a TA while you work with those who need extra support.
- **Use RAG rating (Red, Amber or Green) and traffic lighting** to allow students to share their understanding. You could simply ask students to traffic light keywords, or the level of confidence that they have met the objectives. Alternatively, get students to signal their understanding throughout the lesson by using the colour-coded pages of the planner on their desk.
- **Use number cards** to engage the whole class in discussions or to check understanding. Use cards, numbered from 1 to 5 or from A to E, so students can respond to multiple choice, or true

or false questions. They can also be used to generate discussion around a topic. I would use them to let students articulate their judgement on the lesson theme, such as 'What was the most important cause of the English Civil War?' (with different causes being allocated a number) or to indicate how far they might agree with a statement, such as 'Dunkirk was the most important turning point of WW2' (with responses scaled from strongly agree to strongly disagree).

- **Use hot seating,** where students are asked to prepare a brief summary of the learning in the lesson before facing questions from the class. Although this might make students anxious, with preparation time and a positive classroom environment (where mistakes are expected or at least accepted), this strategy can help reinforce the process of checking the learning in a lesson. Alternatively, and less threateningly, you could ask pairs to hot seat each other, while you circulate and listen.

- **Apply the hands-down rule during question-and-answer sessions**, whereby you target your questioning at students as a means to assess understanding. Hands-up questioning will only tell you who knows the answer, will generally be dominated by a few pupils and runs the risk of reinforcing your own delusions that everyone has got it. Hands-down questioning is certainly more challenging, as it requires a positive classroom environment in which it is safe to make mistakes, and also runs the risk that you might find pockets of misunderstanding or serious misconceptions among pupils. However, it should give you a way to more genuinely assess understanding, and allow you to adapt the lesson appropriately, to deal with any misunderstanding or to address particular misconceptions. When you use this strategy, always make sure you provide students with plenty of thinking time or 'talk partners' (see below) so that they can process and think about their response first.

- **Give students a 'passport to leave'** which needs to be completed before they can leave the lesson. Place questions on a small card for students to answer at the end of the lesson. These will allow you to be clear on the knowledge, understanding or skills they have taken from a lesson. Alternatively, this might be targeted to measure existing knowledge, such as 'Note down the most important things you know about energy'. This will give you an insight into what they already know so you can plan appropriately for the next lesson.

- **Take time to talk to students**, either informally or by creating time in the lesson where you can arrange targeted discussions with particular students. Such time might be used to discuss general progress, set targets or to address any misconceptions and misunderstanding.

- **Focus on the wrong answers**, which can be explored in order to gain a deeper insight into students' understanding of a concept, or to identify and address any misconceptions. In maths – for example, asking students to explain how they arrived at an answer might provide you with a better understanding of where they have misunderstood a concept you are trying to teach.

- **Use random name generators** to avoid the temptation of allowing a few enthusiastic and engaged pupils to dominate the lesson, while others in the class remain passive onlookers. When doing this, you must avoid the student trying to opt out of responding with a stock response of 'I don't know', by returning to the student later to re-emphasise that everyone must be involved in the learning journey. Alternatively, you could allow the student to 'phone a friend' or 'ask the audience', while being careful not to allow this to be overused by students who are just reluctant to think and engage in the lesson.

- **Plan to observe particular students within your lesson** to assess how well they are doing and to support their learning. Keep a track of these interactions and observations over time. This will be especially important during practical subjects, such as PE or drama, where assessment comes from these observations of students.

- **Review your own assessment methods** by creating a table of all the different forms of formative and summative assessments you have used in your lessons, over a week or a term. Consider how far there is a balance to the different forms of assessment you are using, and what you might do to readdress any imbalance.

Quick click

Russel Tarr has collated a range of useful online games, quizzes, activities and diagrams, including some engaging and easy-to-use random name generators, on his website.

www.classtools.net/

Slow burners

- **Use a range of whole-class assessment tools (see above)** to regularly take the 'temperature' of the class and measure whole-class understanding, rather than being reliant on a few students with their hands up or general nods to the question 'Has everyone got that?'. In its simplest form, this might be by undertaking a traffic lighting review or a self-checking 'Heads-down, thumbs-up' exercise, in which you ask the class to put their heads down (to minimise the embarrassment of not knowing) and indicate their level of understanding or confidence with their thumb. Alternatively, you could gauge understanding by using whiteboards or by asking the class to choose from a series of options, provided on the board, by holding up the requisite number of fingers. More recently, I have seen a number of trainees using interactive learning games as a way to both generate enthusiasm and review knowledge and understanding (as an alternative to holding up numbered cards, in response to multiple choice questions). A host of quiz generators (see quick click below) will allow you to design your own mini assessments. Although many of these might be focused on checking knowledge, a carefully worded question could help you to identify any potential misunderstanding or lingering misconceptions. In this way, asking students to assess the accuracy of a range of statements, such as whether a heavier ball will fall faster than a lighter ball, might elicit formative information about their understanding so you can adapt your teaching accordingly.

Quick click

There are a range of education-based quiz generators available on the Internet as freeware, which can be used to undertake formative whole-class assessments. Kahoot is one, which allows students to respond to questions using their own electronic devices, with the results collated and displayed on a shared screen, so you can quickly review how the class responded.

https://getkahoot.com/

In particular, you should look to widen your use of 'straw polls' to check understanding or uncover misconceptions in the class. Rather than responding yourself to a student's answer, ask the class to individually indicate, perhaps with their thumbs, if they agree or disagree with the response. If necessary this will allow you to ask students to elaborate on their reasons, or share where they disagree. I have seen this work particularly well in a number of classes, such as maths, where students were asked whether they agreed with the working out of a peer, or in languages where students where asked if a particular sentence was grammatically correct. In both cases it allowed the teacher to gauge who had a genuine understanding of the processes and rules being taught, and who would need further intervention to develop or solidify their understanding.

All of these strategies for whole-class assessment are useful at giving you a relatively 'rough and ready' insight into learning. However, you must use these with a range of other strategies, such as deeper questioning, which can give a more nuanced view of individual learning and written responses, which give students more time to develop considered responses. Assessment requires a balanced approach. When you are travelling, while a large-scale map will show you the ultimate destination with which to plot your route, a smaller-scale map will be effective to help you identify possible short cuts or hazards.

Key learning point

Whole-class assessment provides you with a general picture of learning but this must be utilised alongside other forms of assessment to track individual progress and learning needs.

- **Undertake diagnostic assessments with your class at the start of a lesson or a new unit of work**. You should design these assessments so they give you an insight into the initial knowledge, skills or understanding of your class, or to uncover any potential misconceptions which will act as a block to future learning. Additionally, they can give students a clear idea of their particular strengths and areas to develop, which will help focus their learning. Obviously, you should be aware that these can exacerbate student feelings of inadequacy and failure, which are likely to occur when students feel they are being tested for what they don't know. However, one way to overcome this is by not sharing the complete results with the class, but instead using these to identify two or three particular targets that each student will work on.

Alternatively, you could use a multiple choice diagnostic quiz, which can be designed to help you gauge if students hold any subject misconceptions, which you can then look to address over the course of subsequent lessons. In this way, a science lesson on forces might begin with a series of hypotheses, such as the incorrect claim that 'A ball remains stationary on a table because no forces are acting upon it'. Student responses (such as True/False/Unsure) to these hypotheses should help the teacher to judge the level of understanding that students currently hold about the concept of forces. Similarly, a series of history lessons on using evidence might ask students to decide how far they agree with a series of statements, designed to give the teacher an insight into their evidential reasoning, such as by asking whether 'A person from the time is more likely to know what occurred' or 'Because people lie some sources are not useful, as they cannot be trusted'.

These diagnostic assessments have the final advantage of allowing you to revisit them at a later point in the lesson, or unit of work, to see how far pupils have come. It can give students a tangible sense of progress and allow you to be more confident that the lessons you taught had an impact on the learning of the class. In one Year 7 English class, students were given a shampoo advertisement in their very first lesson on persuasive writing. They were allocated 15 minutes to respond to the question: 'How does this advert persuade you to buy their product?' All students were able to access and respond to this question regardless of ability (an important element of any diagnostic assessment); this acted as a basis for comparison when students were asked to complete the same activity later on in the unit of work. This served as motivation for both students, who could see how far they had progressed, and for the teacher, who could see the impact of their teaching on student written responses.

Diagnostic assessment is challenging: although its purpose is to inform you of the current state of student learning, you don't want to waste 20 minutes of the lesson on an assessment which you might expect that the vast majority of students will score zero. Finding out that a class of Year 8 students have very little knowledge of the French Revolution is both unsurprising and not very informative to the teacher. It is important to use your professional judgement when undertaking diagnostic assessments. Diagnostic assessments should be as follows.

- Accessible to all students in the class.
- Designed to produce a range of responses.
- Planned to give you an insight into misconceptions or misunderstanding.
- Presented in a positive light, so students do not feel they are 'failures' if they do not do well.
- Undertaken purposefully to inform you of starting points so you can adapt future lessons.

- **In formative assessment, distinguish between *Discussion Questions and Diagnostic Questions* (Wiliam, 2011, p93).** Whereas discussion questions are designed to encourage dialogue by identifying and challenging potential misconceptions, diagnostic questioning is designed to gain concrete evidence of what students have learnt, without the need for further discussion.

In this way, diagnostic questions are those you will use to check if students have the ability to apply Pythagoras' rule or are able to distinguish between nouns and pronouns. You should design these so that they give you a genuine indication of student understanding and minimise the chance that students can get to the right answer for the wrong reason. Contrastingly, discussion questions are those that are designed to encourage debate and uncover possible misconceptions. They do not provide straightforward answers and will inevitably require follow-up discussions, in which you will be looking to check the reasons why pupils gave certain responses. This might be by asking students to look at a picture of a boat floating on water, and deciding which set of statements best describes the forces acting upon it, or by exploring different interpretations which might exist about when the Cold War began. These might lead to a variety of responses from your students and cannot be used as quick diagnostic checking tools, as they will require a deeper level of discussion, in order to help you grasp the exact nature of your students' understanding and uncover any particular misconceptions. Dylan Wiliam (2011, pp 93-104) exemplifies a number of examples of these diagnostic and discussion questions, which will be well worth exploring so that you can begin to identify appropriate questions within your subject.

Widen your use of formative assessment, to encourage students to be more aware of their own progress and learning needs

 Quick wins

- **Build in opportunities for students to reflect** by varying the pace of the lesson and allow moments where students are able to reflect on their learning. This is most obviously possible in a plenary where you could simply encourage them to consider 'The most important thing they have learnt in the lesson'.

- **Undertake periodic self-reviews** to allow students to articulate how they are feeling about their learning. I often used the *Big Book of Blob Trees* (Wilson and Long, 2009) to ask students to review their learning at the end of the lesson. This always elicited some interesting answers, such as one student's comment that they felt like 'the Blob who has fallen off the tree, because I thought I got it, but now I'm not so sure . . . '.

- **Use thinking time or 'talk partners'** to ensure that all students are engaged in your lessons. As well as 'Think-Pair-Share', you could create 'talk partners', which will usually be their neighbour, so they can articulate their thoughts first, in a small and safe environment, before you undertake a whole-class discussion. Even making sure you are taking time between asking questions and targeting pupils to respond will help. I have always had a tendency to fill silences in a lesson, so I would often count to five in my head before asking for a response.

- **Create opportunities for student questions**, so they can ask questions about what they have learnt, or share ideas for what they would like to learn. Very simply, you could ask them to note down one thing they are still unclear on or would like to learn about the topic covered. This could be undertaken at the start of the lesson and used to guide the lesson, or as a plenary activity to plan future lessons. Alternatively, you could set up a question box in the class to allow students to post questions.

- **Organise group plenaries**, where students are asked to work collaboratively to reflect on, and reinforce their learning. Get each group to collectively write out a question, or questions, that they are still unsure about. You can then review these as a whole class, or draw out themes relating to pockets of misunderstanding. Alternatively, you could ask each group to compile a list of things that they have learnt in the lesson.

- **Get students to develop 'top tips' for future classes** as a useful way to draw together learning for a topic. Ask your students to reflect on their learning so they can draw out Key learning points from a topic, and identify what future students should look to avoid.

- **Establish student help forums**, which could be a board in the room or a section of the VLE in which individuals can post questions or ask for help from their peers. Others can be encouraged to respond to the posts or track down the pupils and help them. These can be tracked by the teacher, who can check and intercede themselves if no one has helped them.

—⏱— *Slow burners* —————————————————————

- **Create a collaborative culture in which students support each other with their learning**. Those who have completed their work, or quickly show a well-developed understanding, can be used as student teaching assistants to support others in the class. First, this will benefit the 'student TA', who will deepen their own learning by having to articulate processes or concepts to their peers. Second, it will help those being supported, who will be provided with one-to-one peer tutoring. This could be combined with traffic lighting, such as the use of colour-coded pages in student planners, so the 'student TA' can identify which of their peers might need support. I also used to give my 'student TAs' a medal to wear, which signalled that they were able to move around the class to support other students. This also worked as a real motivator for students to keep them focused and on task, with the hope that they might be rewarded with a plastic medal (cheap but effective). Care must be given to ensure that the 'student TA' provides explanations, rather than just answers. In addition, you should always be confident that the 'student TA' has been sufficiently challenged by the tasks set before they can support others (you must still meet their needs, especially if they are a particularly able student). You might also look to vary which students are allowed to become TAs, so all students can aspire towards this.

The main way to create a collaborative learning environment is to encourage your students to see others in the class as a valuable learning resource. I would often remind my class that there were '33 teachers in our class', and that we all had a responsibility to help each other to learn. To further develop this, you should look to have clearly established procedures for encouraging greater independence and minimising the reliance on you as the teacher for quick answers. The most obvious way is by bouncing questions back to the class, rather than giving the answer yourself. Therefore, you might say, 'What an interesting question. Does anyone else in the class know the answer?' I was aware of some teachers who would never directly answer a question and any unanswered questions were put on to a question wall, with students being given credits if they could independently find out the answer and share their findings with the class.

Similarly, you should also introduce clear procedures so that pupils are aware that asking the teacher is the final, rather than the first, port of call. In this way I would use the 5Bs, in which students were encouraged to seek answers in their brain, on the board, in their books, or with their buddies before they were allowed to ask the boss. Others use the rule of 'C3B4ME' (see three before me), in which students must ask three peers before they can ask the teacher.

- **Train your students to use a range of learning strategies to support their performance**. Do not assume that your students will have the skills to revise, take notes or prepare for summative assessments. Instead, look to regularly introduce such strategies to students, such as by asking them to highlight key information, generate exam-style questions, or produce a mind map to summarise the key learning from across a topic.

One strategy could be to ask students to keep a 'learning book', which could be used to set structured revision activities for homework. Therefore, you can easily track and support students in revising, by asking them to complete a one-page synopsis of their class notes, produce a mind map, or generate a series of possible exam questions, without just asking them 'to revise'. I was aware of one trainee who asked students to generate an A3 learning mat, for a topic, which they had laminated and asked students to use as a place mat on their breakfast table. Whatever strategies you employ, you must be sure to emphasise that the focus is on helping them to learn, rather than on their performance in an exam.

Develop a secure understanding of how to accurately and effectively assess pupils' attainment and progress

 Quick wins

- **Discuss and review marking by other members of the department**. Look at particular assessments by students with a range of abilities, and discuss the different performances and attainment they exhibit. You should also discuss colleagues approaches to marking and assessment, to identify any strategies they employ to make the workload manageable.

- **Use a Think Aloud Protocol** to see the processes involved in assessment. Ask an experienced teacher to think aloud and explain their thought processes as they mark and assess work.

- **Moderate work with your mentor,** either by getting them to review and discuss your marking to see how far they are in agreement, or by simultaneously marking a few sample responses before comparing the results.

- **Use a marking schedule** to plan ahead with your marking and assessment of books or written work. This will enable you to avoid marking overload, where a backlog of marking builds up, but also ensure that you have time to review any common errors or misconceptions, and to guide children on how they can improve and progress.

- **Conduct quick recall reviews** to check knowledge and assess understanding. This will allow you to undertake a quick fact check, or review their understanding of a key concept.

- **Rethink when you assess students**, so it is best used to support their learning. Undertake an initial diagnostic assessment (see above) before you begin a unit of work, to give you a starting point for their learning. Help students to see the value of such assessments, not in producing a grade but for establishing a baseline of what they already know or can do, in order to help them progress and measure their achievement. Similarly, you could introduce mid-unit assessments allowing you to support learners and help them improve their work along the way, rather than just waiting to judge their performance in an end-of-unit assessment.

- **Keep the end in mind** by sharing the main methods of assessment and key success criteria at the start of a unit of work. If you are clear on this, it will help keep you focused on the end goal, and if your students are clear on how they will eventually be assessed, they should be able to more easily regulate their own learning and understand what they are trying to learn over a series of lessons.

 Slow burners

- **Before developing assessments, you must be clear on what you want to assess and widen your understanding of progression in your subject.** First, you must be clear on what you are trying to assess, as this will determine the type of assessment you will undertake, and help you to understand the different levels of response you might expect from pupils.

  If your aim is to review the learning objectives, and the level of understanding gained in a lesson, or a series of lessons, you might have very narrow assessment criteria, which use explicit and concrete success criteria. This will enable you to confidently assess if the students have learnt what you have taught. In history, for example, you might be looking to assess knowledge and understanding of a topic, such as the development of the Cold War. In this case, you would explicitly look to outline in the success criteria that students are able to 'Describe at least two key events in the development of the Cold War' and that they are 'Able to use a range of appropriate historical terms (such as communism or capitalism)'. This would give clear direction and clarity on what is expected, which will ensure both you and the students get the most out of the assessment.

Alternatively, you might be looking to assess the more abstract conceptual understanding of your students, relevant to your subject. This will require a broader and more general set of assessment criteria, underpinned by an understanding of progression in your subject.

Therefore, to continue the example above, if the purpose of the assessment is to assess a student's conceptual understanding of causation and the reasons why the Cold War developed, you need to have in mind a model of progression that can be used to underpin the assessment. In this case, a narrow and tightly defined set of assessment criteria will not work and might give an artificial or inflated view of student understanding. Instead, you need to consider models of progression in causal reasoning to develop a more generalisable set of assessment criteria (which will be transferable to other historical contexts). This will enable you to assess how far students have a simplistic and deterministic view of the past, through to those who are able to grasp the multicausal and interconnected nature of the past.

- **Design assessments to uncover misconceptions in order to tackle the root causes of student misunderstanding**. Your students might be able to articulate if they are unclear or misunderstand something which you have taught, because this is usually about whether they have grasped knowledge. However, *it is in the nature of a misconception that you believe that you understand completely* (Jones and Tanner, 2006, p27), meaning that your students will not be able to identify when they have a misconception. Therefore, it is important that you develop your subject pedagogical knowledge to consider what possible misconceptions might lie at the heart of any student misunderstandings.

One approach is to assess their understanding of concepts, through deep questioning (see Chapter 5). For example, I observe many maths lessons in which trainees review answers without any deeper probing of how students arrive at their responses. This would not only deepen student understanding, but would also act as a useful tool to uncover possible misconceptions, which might be missed if a student provides the correct answer. Remember that a broken clock is always right twice a day, so don't always assume that providing the right answer means they are clear on the process for arriving at that answer. Dylan Wiliam (2011) uses a useful example to illustrate the important role of using assessment to uncover misconceptions. He points out that when students are asked if 3/7 or 3/11 is larger, it is generally not answered correctly in KS3, and seen as a bit of a trick question. However, the point is made that although it might not be suitable for a summative test, it is a question which will help you to formatively identify possible misconceptions and generate healthy discussion in a class which will allow you to address any misunderstandings. He refers to these as *questions which provide a window into students' thinking* (Wiliam, 2011, p77).

Another way to address misconceptions, especially in science, is to get students to develop their own hypothesis at the start of a lesson, perhaps by nudging them with 'What might . . . ?' or 'Why does . . . ?' questions. These hypotheses can then be tested and revisited across a lesson, or series of lessons, to see if they still hold true. Alternatively, you could look to deliberately build up a misconception perhaps at the beginning of the lesson, in order to overturn it in pupils' minds as the lesson progresses. I used to teach a particularly successful introductory lesson to a topic focused on migration to Britain, which began with a series of images which students assumed were quintessentially 'British' (such as fish and chips or the monarchy). Once students were praised for 'spotting the link' and writing their definition of Britishness, it was revealed that they were all, in fact, a product of migration to Britain (by Jewish settlers and the German royal family, respectively). It always created a buzz of discussion and incredulity in the class, and allowed us to revisit their definitions and concepts of Britishness, and migration, as subsequent lessons developed.

In summary

Assessment can seem daunting when you first begin teaching, but it is fundamental to all aspects of teaching and learning. You should look to develop both summative and formative approaches to assessment, ensuring that you and your students are confident about where they are and what they need to do to improve.

Before the lesson

- **Know the starting point of your students.** Access prior attainment data and discuss prior progress with appropriate members of staff.

- **Review external assessments.** Look at GCSE and A2 assessment criteria to consider how students will ultimately be assessed in your subject.

- **Undertake double or joint marking** with your mentor, or another experienced colleague. This will allow you to become confident in your marking and grading of students.

During the lesson

- **Experiment with diagnostic assessments** so you can gain an understanding of starting points. This can also act as a benchmark to make comparisons about progress across a lesson or series of lessons.

- **Use a range of formative assessment strategies** to regularly check understanding or to review progress.

- **Ensure you listen and respond to the information gained from formative assessments.** Assessment for learning can only be effective if you are prepared to adapt and change the lesson, especially when you identify pockets of misunderstanding or confusion in the class.

- **Don't be afraid to change the plan** or change direction. If it isn't working, you will need to develop the confidence to alter the plan during the lesson.

- **Ensure you use positive language when talking about assessments.** Articulate the benefits of assessment and reiterate that it is about supporting learning, rather than just measuring attainment.

After the lesson

- **Track progress and assessment data.** Recording the data, even if it is only for your benefit, will allow you to develop a picture of individual progress over time, or identify the particular areas of strengths and weaknesses of the students you teach.

- **Review the outcomes of assessments.** Reflect on the lessons learnt from any assessments you undertake. Consider the adaptions you will need to make to future lessons.

- **Use assessment data to identify particular students or groups of students who need further support.** Ensure you plan for how you will help these students in future lessons.

Further reading

Arguably, Black and Wiliam's (1998) *Inside the Black Box: Raising Standards Through Classroom Assessment,* is an essential starting point for you in establishing the main principles and research base for formative assessment. In addition, the *Inside the Black Box* series, which followed on from this, includes a range of subject-specific guidance on how to translate the findings into effective formative assessment, with subjects ranging from D&T to Geography.

An easy-to-read book, though targeted at an American audience, which has an excellent balance between theoretical and practical strategies, is Dylan Wiliam's book (2011) *Embedded Formative Assessment.* Similarly, Jones and Tanner (2006) also present a concise book, *Assessment,* which provides a balance between the practice and theory underpinning assessment in the classroom.

There are a host of other books which give more practical guidance on assessment and specifically formative assessment. Perhaps the most useful of these is David Spendlove's (2009) *Putting Assessment for Learning into Practice.*

Lastly, if you are looking for a deeper understanding of the research and theory underpinning classroom assessment, this is extensively covered in the *SAGE Handbook of Research on Classroom Assessment* (McMillan, 2013).

References

Bennett, R (2011) Formative assessment: A critical review. *Assessment in Education: Principles, Policy & Practice, 18*(1): 5–25.

Black, P and Wiliam, D (1998) *Inside the black box: Raising standards through classroom assessment.* London: King's College London School of Education.

Black, P and Wiliam, D (2005) Lessons from around the world: How policies, politics and cultures constrain and afford assessment practices. *The Curriculum Journal, 16*(2): 249–61.

Butler, R (1988) Enhancing and undermining intrinsic motivation: The effects of task-involving and ego-involving evaluation on interest and performance. *British Journal of Educational Psychology, 58*(1): 1–14.

Earl, L and Katz, S (2006) *Rethinking Classroom Assessment with Purpose in Mind.* Winnipeg: Manitoba Education, Citizenship and Youth.

Jones, S and Tanner, H (2006) *Assessment,* 2nd edn. London: Continuum International.

Leahy, S, Lyon, C, Thompson, M and Wiliam, D (2005) Classroom assessment: Minute by minute; day by day. *Educational Leadership, 63*(3): 19–24.

McMillan, J (ed.) (2013) *SAGE Handbook of Research on Classroom Assessment.* Thousand Oaks, CA: SAGE Publications.

McTighe, J and O'Connor, K (2005) Seven practices for effective learning. *Educational Leadership, 63*(2): 10–17.

Spendlove, D (2009) *Putting Assessment for Learning into Practice.* London: Continuum Books.

Thompson, M and Wiliam, D (2007) *Tight but Loose: A Conceptual Framework for Scaling Up School Reforms.* Chicago, IL: American Educational Research Association.

Wiggins, G and McTighe, J (2005) *Understanding by Design,* 2nd edn. Alexandria: ASCD.

Wiliam, D (2011) *Embedded Formative Assessment.* Bloomington, IN: Solution Tree Press.

Wilson, P and Long, I (2009) *Big Book of Blob Trees.* Milton Keynes: Speechmark Publishing.

7

Feedback

Teachers' Standard 6 – Make accurate and productive use of assessment

This section continues from the previous chapter and is designed to help you give pupils effective feedback, which can accurately target further improvement and secure rapid progress. However, like assessment, feedback overlaps with many other aspects of the standards, including the following.

- Appropriately challenging pupils, to promote their resilience, confidence and independence (TS1).
- Guiding pupils to reflect on the progress they have made and their emerging needs (TS2).
- Using subject knowledge to address common errors, misconceptions and misunderstandings among pupils (TS3).
- Understanding how a range of factors can inhibit pupils' ability to learn, and knowing how best to overcome these (TS5).

Introduction

Imagine if you went to see a doctor who used their medical expertise to undertake a thorough assessment of the symptoms you were exhibiting before proclaiming they knew exactly what was wrong with you and how to treat your condition, before showing you to the door without feeding back their diagnosis or the cure. Alternatively, imagine going to see a doctor about stomach cramps, only to be told to take a headache tablet three times a day.

These scenarios have some parallels with your own teaching practice – how often have you planned formative assessments, but done nothing with the information generated? How often have you marked work without giving clear feedback on how it can improve? How often have you given feedback which does not relate to the outcomes you were trying to assess? All teachers will be guilty of these practices at some point in their career, which is understandable because teaching is a hugely demanding profession. The thought of spending a precious evening marking a set of Year 8 books, after a five-period day, with detailed and formative feedback will probably not be top of anyone's wish list. However, marking smarter is not about marking more; providing effective feedback is time well spent in supporting learning, and can ensure that the hours you will inevitably spend giving feedback are not fruitless hours, which have no educational value.

Effective feedback has a huge impact on learning (Hattie and Yates, 2014; Shute, 2008; Hattie and Timperley, 2007), but poor feedback can be detrimental to progress (Wiliam, 2013; Hattie, 2012). It is not simply the case that all feedback is good, as some feedback is better than others. When done well, feedback provides a bridge between teaching, assessment and learning. However, I have seen many lessons where the teacher is teaching but the students aren't learning. The teacher's failure to implement any strategies to gain feedback on student understanding means they are oblivious to the lack of progress of their class. In other lessons, although the teacher makes use of a wide array of 'formative' assessment strategies, none of these are used by either the teacher or the students to support learning (see Chapter 6). Therefore, while it is true that 'just because you have taught it doesn't mean they have learnt it', it is similarly the case that, without feedback, 'you might know what they haven't learnt but you won't be able to support them in ensuring they do learn it'. Feedback is thus a vital ingredient in the learning mix, in that it serves to bind together teaching and assessment to foster learning – without it, the cake won't rise or will at least taste awful.

This chapter is designed to support you in giving effective feedback. It provides you with a range of practical strategies and ideas to ensure that you are providing feedback which has an impact on learning. It will also help you to ensure you are maximising the chances that students will receive and act upon the feedback they are given.

Targets

What targets does this chapter cover?

- Ensure you give pupils high-quality feedback to accurately target further improvement and support them in their learning.

- Allow time for students to process and engage with feedback, so they know how well they have done and what they need to do to improve.
- Widen your use of peer and self-assessment, to help students be more autonomous and engaged in their own learning.

What is effective feedback?

Giving effective feedback is not an exact science and there is no 'one size fits all' approach to delivering oral or written feedback. However, this does not support a *carte-blanche* approach to giving feedback. Instead, you should recognise that effective feedback is underpinned by a number of guiding principles.

First, you should remember that feedback is a medical assessment rather than a post-mortem in that you are trying to establish a treatment to make things better, rather than trying to dissect the reasons for death. You need to ensure that feedback is forward- rather than backward-looking. It should support students by outlining how to improve rather than only offering a critique of what went wrong. Second, feedback needs to be pitched at the right level so it is neither too challenging nor too easy for the student. It should provide stepping stones for crossing a learning gap, rather than a precarious tight-rope across a deep, wide chasm.

Lastly, be careful with praise and try to avoid grades. While overuse of the former can dilute the feedback messages you want your students to receive (Hattie, 2012), the latter is almost certain to lead your students to ignore your carefully crafted comments (Butler, 1988). Although it is difficult to overcome the 'cult of grading' which has gripped our education system, there is something to be said for avoiding grading while learning is taking place, because *as soon as students get a grade, the learning stops* (Wiliam 2011, p123).

Ensuring feedback is clear

As a child, I am sure you will all remember those balloons which were released at school fairs in the hope they would travel to far-flung destinations and find recipients who would take the time to reply. Alternatively, you might have journeyed down to the local seaside to throw a message in a bottle out to sea and waited expectantly for a response. Too often I have observed trainees taking such a scatter-gun approach to giving feedback, which is delivered in a rather haphazard and random way, in the hope that some of the nuggets of advice might hit home and lead to improvement. Therefore, it is important to understand that feedback is most successful when students are clear on what they need to do to narrow the gap to achieve a desired outcome. You should therefore look to provide targeted and precise feedback which allows learners to make specific adjustments, in order to achieve an appropriately challenging outcome.

Your students need to be clear on where they are, where they need to be and what they need to do to get there. Feedback is always underpinned by a clear outcome or set of success criteria, which allows everyone to be clear on the end goal. Your planning, especially in the long term, should therefore look to have clearly established end goals, and help you to clarify how students might be guided towards those goals (see Chapter 1). However, along the way, you should also plan to use a range of diagnostic assessments, which will help you identify the exact nature of any gaps and give direction to your feedback. Assessment and feedback are thus hand-in-glove; a combination of the two approaches allows you to go beyond measuring if students have or haven't 'got it' and do something with the information gained.

If nothing else, feedback must be clear and understandable to students, both in the sense of them being able to hear or read the feedback being given, but also in the more abstract sense of them being able to grasp the meaning of feedback, so they can use it to improve. Nothing brought this home to me more clearly than my own first attempt to introduce a review activity, following feedback on a piece of homework. At the start of the lesson, I gave students the opportunity to redraft their work, in the light of the detailed comments I had given to each of them. After a clear explanation of the task, I allowed students time to read and reflect on the comments given. However, this soon led to a growing number of bemused looks and a flurry of raised hands. With hindsight, it became clear to me (having spent the majority of my time going around the room and answering questions like 'What does this say?' or 'How do I do this?') that I had not ensured that my own handwriting was legible to students or that the feedback clearly outlined the next steps they needed to take in order to improve their work.

This was an epiphany for me, which I hope doesn't take you as long to work out: how many times had I spent hours marking books and writing comments to students which were either wholly unreadable or unusable in the eyes of the receiver? No wonder I felt like I was trapped in my very own *Groundhog Day* in that every time I assessed work, I very often found myself saying the same old things to the same old pupils.

 **Key learning point**

Feedback, of any kind, is only useful if it is clear, understandable and allows students to process it, so they recognise what they must do to improve. As Hattie (2012, p20) stated: *Teachers and leaders often give a lot of feedback, but much of this feedback isn't received.*

Ensuring feedback is sufficiently challenging

Giving good feedback is rather like being a baseball pitcher: if it is pitched too high, it is likely to go straight over a student's head; however, pitching it too low gives them no real chance of connecting with it. Therefore, feedback must be pitched at the right level and, wherever possible, personalised to suit the task, the context of the learning and the particular needs of the student. In its broadest sense, there are *Three Levels of Feedback* (Hattie, 2012).

- **Feedback for novice learners** is about how to improve in a given task, and is related to a specific set of success criteria.

- **Process feedback for intermediate learners** gives advice on the strategies a student might employ, or the process they might go through to improve. In this way students might be asked to sound out an unfamiliar word or try to infer meaning from the other words in a sentence.

- **Self-regulating feedback for advanced learners** looks to encourage students' ability to identify their own strategies and develop more independent approaches to improve their work, or which gives conceptual feedback which encourages mastery of conceptual understanding.

Key learning point

Feedback must be pitched at the right level so you can be sure that students are able to hit the learning 'sweet spot'.

Ensuring feedback is suitably positive and thought provoking

You must make sure you achieve a balance between the positive and negative elements of the feedback you give and err on the side of positivity. This is not to say that your feedback should be an endless stream of praise, which is in itself neither helpful nor conducive to learning. Instead, load the feedback scales so they are weighted towards positive aspects of the current state. In this way, you should always look to identify specific achievements related to the work or performance, as with the scenario below.

Real life scenario

Students in Year 8 are learning to serve in tennis.

Scenario A

Teacher: Well done, Suzie, a great serve. Russell, your turn. Okay, good effort, but you need to work on that.

Scenario B

Teacher: Well done, Suzie, it was good how you got more height on your throw so you got more power into your serve. Now try to work on consistency with this; I want to see you consistently get your next five serves into the service court and as an extra challenge try to hit the service line. Russell, your turn. Okay, good effort but take your time when you throw the ball into the air and keep your eye on the ball as you strike through it.

In scenario B, the teacher has given specific feedback to both students rather than the general and vague comments in scenario A. In addition, the feedback in scenario B gives clear direction to both students about what they need to do to improve their performance. In order to further support the students, the teacher might also look to model or demonstrate how to implement the feedback.

It is important for you to realise that praise alone will not assist learning, and you must not conflate feedback with rewards or praise because they are different – feedback is focused on learning while rewards and praise are about extrinsic motivation and classroom management. This doesn't mean that you should never use praise when providing feedback, but you need to make sure that the focus is on the particular elements of the work or performance and what can be done to improve. Fundamental to formative feedback is that it leads to action by the recipient (see student receptivity to feedback, below). Thus it is crucial that your feedback is specific, helpful and thought provoking by being clear what learners must do to improve. When considering the role of praise in providing feedback, it is about being judicious. The most important factor is the degree of *mindfulness* (Bangert-Drowns *et al.*, 1991) and thought it generates in your students. This should always guide your comments, so you can ensure they provoke thought in your students. Without generating this thoughtfulness, you cannot be sure that the well-crafted feedback messages you generate will reach a recipient or encourage them to respond to it (remember those balloons and bottles).

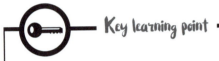

Key learning point

Focus on being positive rather than providing empty platitudes; identify what went well and how a student can move on.

Ensuring time is given to process and act on feedback

All the advice above will be of little use if students are not given time to engage with, make sense of, and thereby act upon your feedback. This was a point which was made very clear to me early in my own teaching career. My observer was quick to point out how great and formative my written comments were, leaving me with a warm, if brief, sense of self-satisfaction. However, this bubble was quickly burst when they continued: 'If only you had given them time to read and process your comments, before rushing into your starter.'

It was a point well made and still sticks with me today. You will no doubt have the same experience of spending hours labouring over your marking and assessment, only to return work before quickly moving on with the lesson, or frustratingly seeing that students are more concerned about how they did than the lovingly crafted comments you have added to their work (see DIRT, described in Slow burners, p154).

Teacher receptivity to feedback

Feedback is about giving and receiving. You should see it as a reciprocal process – with feedback both given to students and received from them. Indeed, feedback is neither binary nor one way, and works best when it is approached as a two-way channel of communication. The more channels you open up between yourself and students, the more likely you are to find the answers to the key questions assessment and feedback are designed to address: Where are my students now? Where do they need to be? How do they get there?

You should be receptive to the overt feedback signals given by student comments, or by the information generated from formative assessment strategies (see Chapter 6) in a lesson. You should see feedback opportunities in the tacit signals given by the body language of your students or by judging the atmosphere in your class. These all provide you with different forms of feedback, which you can use to adapt your teaching, change a lesson or to shape and give direction to your own feedback to students in your class. You should therefore embrace and be receptive to a range of diagnostic and formative assessment strategies.

Student receptivity to feedback

There is some truth to the old joke that schools are places that students come to watch teachers work, and this is certainly the case with a number of trainee teachers who feel they have to 'put on a show' in lessons. Feedback should be designed to put the onus on students to take greater responsibility for their own learning and allows them a greater degree of independence and autonomy. Therefore, feedback should always be more work for your pupils than it is for you. In general, the time you spend giving feedback should be exceeded by the time it takes students to process and respond to this feedback.

If nothing else, you should always remember that assessment is a collaborative learning partnership and the student must be a proactive participant. Students need to see assessment and feedback as something which guides them, not something which is just done to them. You therefore need to work on changing students' mindsets, from seeing feedback as an invasive dissection of their work to one in which it is viewed as a positive part of the learning process. This should ensure they are receptive to the feedback they receive, and increasingly seek it out, as a means of controlling their own learning so that they can improve. Similarly, students need to be encouraged to give feedback and develop their own confidence in being able to discuss specific attributes of their own work or the work of their peers. This will create a classroom environment where learning is more important than achievement, and where rich discussions can be facilitated about how work or performances can be improved.

A word of warning here. The skills of peer and self-assessment do not come easily to most students, as it is both cognitively and emotionally challenging. Therefore, you will need to develop these skills through training; a collective understanding that the focus is on improving learning and not allocating grades; and the establishment of a positive learning environment which encourages rich discussions about how to improve (Jones and Tanner, 2006; Sadler, 1998). I recall one trainee who was quick to dismiss peer assessment as a pointless activity after asking students to undertake it, with little more guidance than being asked to 'mark each other's work' with a two-page, and rather complex, mark scheme (lifted straight from the exam board website). Therefore, remember that students, like trainee teachers, need to be taught how to provide effective feedback. They need to be supported in developing the right mindset to help them effectively assess their own learning and engage with the feedback they receive.

Developing a growth mindset

Classroom climate is vital in ensuring that students are receptive to feedback. Feedback is powerful when mistakes are made, students don't know, or they don't understand. Yet these are the times when student self-esteem and confidence are most at danger of being damaged. Therefore, you need to encourage a climate in which mistakes are seen as learning opportunities, and feedback is embraced as a way to move forward. You should encourage your students to hold a positive view of assessment and feedback, and should actively promote the *language of learning* (Hattie and Yates, 2014) by sharing learning outcomes and success criteria with students to move them from where they are to where they want to be.

Real life scenario

A teacher is returning pieces of work in an art class which focused on shading.

Scenario A

Teacher: Joyce, is this the best you can do? You needed to develop shading in your pictures as yours are just dull and flat. We have been doing this for three weeks now and you are still not getting it.

Scenario B

Teacher: Joyce, I see you have tried hard with completing this task but the shading still needs some work. What did you find difficult?

Joyce: I don't know. I'm just rubbish at art.

Teacher: No, no – that's not true, the image itself is clear and defined but we just need to work on your shading.

Joyce: But I just can't do it.

Teacher: Joyce, we all find some things a challenge, but we are not talking about all of art – just working on shading – which you can improve. I am sure that we can work on improving that, can't we?

Joyce: I suppose.

Teacher: Good, we all make mistakes but it is what we learn from them which is important. Right, let's start by . . .

Developing a growth mindset in your pupils is a way of turning the vicious circles, in which failure to achieve leads students to fail to achieve, into virtuous circles, in which failures are seen as fundamental to the learning process (Jones and Tanner, 2006). As seen in scenario A above, the student's beliefs about themselves were left unchallenged by the teacher, whereas in scenario B Joyce was encouraged to change her assumption that she 'can't do it'. This is not a quick win and it takes time to develop a positive environment where students come to accept that talent is not innate. You could try to talk about how you overcame your own challenges, or make reference to others who have learnt from failure, such as Thomas Edison ('I have not failed. I've just found 10,000 ways that won't work'), or

Mark Haddon ('I'm not a terribly good writer, but I'm a persistent editor') (Haddon, 2016). The student in the scenario above appears to have a fixed mindset (Dweck, 2006) in which attainment is directly linked to 'uncontrollable factors' (like innate ability or poor memory). She should be encouraged to develop a growth mindset which would encourage her to see achievement as based on 'controllable factors' (like effort or revision). Therefore, you should look to ensure that feedback does not merely give affirmation to students that they are talented or talentless, and that there is nothing they can do about this, but should guide them to see feedback as a way to improve regardless of whether they have done well or not.

Developing reflective skills

Fundamental to feedback is that it encourages *mindfulness* (Bangert-Drowns *et al.*, 1991) in your students. It is therefore important that you build in regular reflection time to allow students to process and internalise the feedback they receive. Students therefore need time and support to juggle all the feedback messages they receive. If you have ever tried juggling, I am sure you are aware that your brain cannot initially process all the information needed to keep all the balls in the air at the same time. In the same way, bombarding students with feedback is no guarantee they will be able to process and act upon it. Therefore, you need to make sure you allow time for students to make sense of the feedback received and make a decision about when it is best to introduce further feedback (or more balls, in the juggling analogy).

Perhaps one of the biggest stumbling blocks towards students being encouraged to reflect on feedback is the focus on grading work. Feedback which merely provides a grade or compares students leads to emotional rather than thought-provoking responses from students and is detrimental to their learning. You therefore need to ensure that the focus of your teaching is on the process of learning and not just on the grading of learning.

Overall feedback is a vital ingredient in the learning mix and though a challenge is essential to ensure that the time taken in planning lessons and in assessing students' work leads to real impact on their learning. The following strategies therefore present ways in which you can develop the feedback you give to your students to ensure that it is effective.

Targets

Ensure you give pupils high-quality feedback to accurately target further improvement and support them in their learning

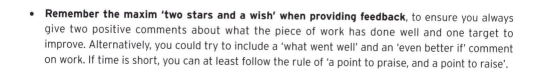 Quick wins

- **Remember the maxim 'two stars and a wish' when providing feedback**, to ensure you always give two positive comments about what the piece of work has done well and one target to improve. Alternatively, you could try to include a 'what went well' and an 'even better if' comment on work. If time is short, you can at least follow the rule of 'a point to praise, and a point to raise'.

- **Undertake comment-only marking** which doesn't give grades or levels, even if you record them yourself. Try to build a culture where the student is encouraged to value and reflect on your comments, rather than be drawn into a competitive environment where students are quick to compare grades, shouting out 'what did you get?' every time a piece of work is returned.

- **Give whole-class feedback on marking**, especially where you have identified common errors or misconceptions. This could be part of a general focus for the class, which is linked to a starter, or a task in the subsequent lesson. Make sure you signpost why they are doing this in the next lesson: 'It was good that you all . . . but I noticed you struggled with . . . so we are going to . . .'. Alternatively, you could group students, or refer to groups in the class, who might have similar targets to focus on.

- **Use student-generated assessment criteria** to act as a focus for class discussion and feedback. Demonstrate what you are looking for in a finished article by modelling this to the class or showing them an example of your own work. You can then use this to generate a set of criteria for successfully completing the task. In this way, a PE lesson might begin with a demonstration of a cricket shot in which the pupils are asked to dissect the constituent parts, or an Art lesson might begin with the teacher quickly sketching a self-portrait in order to identify the techniques or key features that you might look for when drawing the human face.

- **Don't mark individual responses as right or wrong**. Rather than ticking or crossing pupil answers and asking them to redo those which are incorrect, keep your own tally and ask students themselves to find the relevant incorrect responses. In this way, rather than giving a score of 8/10, you might say, 'Find and correct the two responses which you have got wrong'.

- **Use margin marking,** rather than identifying individual mistakes in a piece of work. Merely place a mark in the margin, such as that indicating that they have made a grammatical or spelling mistake, and ask students to find and correct the mistake.

- **Focus on the learning objective** rather than trying to give feedback on too many criteria. It is not always helpful, or possible, to comment on spelling, presentation, the quantity or the effort expended with every piece of work. Try instead to focus some of your marking on how far it meets the learning objective and related success criteria.

- **Avoid over-marking**, in which work is peppered with detailed comments and advice. Not only is this time-consuming, but it can water down the effect of feedback, as students are overwhelmed by it or unable to process exactly what needs to be done to improve.

- **Offer disconfirming feedback**, when you identify a clear misconception among students. You should address the misconception by working through an example of why it cannot be true. For example, in History, students often conflate the idea of reliability and usefulness – because it is not reliable it cannot be useful. Hitler's personal letters might not give a reliable view of Jews in 1930s Germany, but they might be useful at giving historians an insight into Nazi attitudes to Jews in this period.

- **Follow the four stages of marking, which focus on success and improvement against the learning objective.** The first stage is to identify success, by simply highlighting, circling or underlining a couple of places where they have best met the objective or success criteria. The second stage is to signal one place or a section of the work which could be improved, perhaps with an arrow or different colour highlighter. This should be followed by the addition of a specific comment so the student knows how they can improve that section of work. Lastly, they need to be given time in class to review the feedback and make the necessary improvements (see DIRT below).

Slow burners

- **Avoid grade comparing, which will inevitably lead to emotional rather than thought-provoking responses to feedback.** If you must provide a grade, then ensure your marking includes a thought-provoking question which students must respond to. You could ask them to extend their thinking by asking 'What is the alternative viewpoint?' or 'Explain which is the most important factor'. Alternatively, you might challenge them to 'Answer the following . . .' or undertake some independent research to 'Find out . . .'.

  Another approach is to provide comments alongside a +, = or - symbol, depending on whether the work was better than, the same as, or worse than the previous piece of work produced by the student. In this way, you reward individual progress (+ sign) rather than actual attainment. This serves to maintain motivation, as even the most able student is challenged to maintain their high standards, while the least able pupils will be encouraged to see they are making progress, without feeling that they are being compared to others in the class. You could compare their performance to a target grade, rather than comparing students against each other or ranking them.

- **Introduce formative grading as a means of weaning students (and parents) off an addiction to grades**. Ultimately, you might wish to work towards comment-only marking and the removal of grades altogether (but you might be constrained by departmental or school policies to provide grades on each piece of work). You could introduce comment-only marking for the first draft of a piece of work and record the grade yourself without sharing this with pupils. Once work is returned, students can be given some time to improve their work, based on your feedback, before you remark it. This time give them a grade, which is an average of the mark they received for the first and the second piece of work produced (for example, two As would remain an A grade, but a C grade and an A grade would become a B grade). You are thus rewarding those who try hard with the first attempt and those who engage with and respond to feedback.

  Another approach to formative grading is presented by Clymer and Wiliams (2006, pp124-7). They suggest that individual units of work can be broken down to identify a range of different learning intentions, and the potential evidence that these have been met, for a topic or across a term. Students are then graded on the evidence of mastery (2-strong, 1-partial, 0-no evidence). These can be recorded and regularly reviewed with students over the period, allowing them time to focus on improving and presenting further evidence of achievement against the separate learning intentions, before they undertake an end-of-topic summative assessment, to review overall learning. This can be formatively reviewed, with the student, to evaluate any disconnect between the summative achievement and evidence of formative progress over the period.

  Allow **time for students to process and engage with feedback,** so they know how well they have done and what they need to do to improve.

Quick wins

- **Give classroom time** to read feedback and, more importantly, to allow your students to use it to set themselves targets or improve their work. Ensure you have included this time in your lesson plan.

- **Encourage your students to see marking as a two-way dialogue.** Encourage them to write you a comment after a piece of homework – for example, explaining what they struggled with or didn't understand. Similarly, you can pose additional questions to them when you are marking their work: 'Why do you think . . . ?', 'What might be the counter argument to . . . ?' or 'How else could you have arrived at this answer?' Students can then respond to these questions in subsequent homework or during DIRT (see below).

- **Get students to respond to comments with a target.** This could be by simply asking them to complete the sentence 'Next time I will . . . ' Or 'In order to improve I must . . . '.

- **Always undertake a quick review of test papers** by getting students to review any questions they got wrong and traffic light whether they are clear on why they got them wrong. This will allow you to individually intervene or put in place peer-to-peer support to help them understand where they went wrong.

- **Track student responses** by using feedback sheets. These can be divided so the upper section allows you to give them feedback, while they respond to this feedback in the lower section. Alternatively, ask them to respond using a different colour pen, so it is easy to distinguish their responses.

- **Encourage redrafting**, so students become familiar with improving their own work. For example, you could ask students to peer or self-assess a first draft and then redraft it before presenting you with a final version. Similarly, you could ask students to redo a piece of work following your own comments on how to improve.

- **Get students to keep a learning log** as a means of reflecting on their learning at the end of each lesson or across a unit of work. You could keep these as separate reflective diaries, or merely get them to record this at the back of their books, so that you can track their reflections and respond to any issues they raise. In order to avoid this becoming a repetitive and boring task, you should look to vary the questions you are asking students to reflect on, or give them some choice about what they record in their reflections. For example, you could give them a list of questions and ask them to respond to any two, such as: 'What is the most important thing you have learnt today?'; 'What advice would you give someone who has not been taught this topic?'; 'What was the most difficult part of the lesson?'; or 'What questions do you still have about today's lesson?'

- **Carry targets forward.** When you set a task, if appropriate, get students to copy the target from their previous assessed piece of work to the top of the page. This acts as a reminder to them to act upon the previous feedback they have been given.

 **Slow burners**

- **Build into lessons Dedicated Improvement and Reflection Time (DIRT),** so that students have the opportunity to redraft or improve a piece of work for which they have received feedback. At the very least, allow some time for students to read your comments and process them.

  Dylan Wiliam (2011) argues that you should only give feedback when you have planned lesson time for students to respond to it. More interestingly, he argues that you should treat marking and assessment time as planning time. In this way, you should look to build in structured lesson time so students can process feedback, which will prevent them from completely ignoring, or giving scant attention to, your carefully crafted feedback.

In many ways, more practical subjects often have a virtuous feedback loop, which more academic subjects could benefit from (introduce – practice – feedback – practice again). Approach your lesson planning in a similar way, so that students have time to act on advice. After you mark the books, allow lesson time for your students to reflect on your comments and act on the advice given, perhaps in a different coloured pen so it is easier for you to see how they have improved their work as a result of your feedback. However, to ensure that DIRT is effective, it needs to be well structured and planned in advance, and not seen as a mere filler activity for the first 15 minutes of a lesson. In addition, you should incorporate DIRT into your long-term planning to ensure there is a balance between providing lesson time for actual learning and chances for students to reflect on their learning. Undertaking DIRT once a week might seem appealing, but this will undoubtedly eat into the time available to actually learn, and will become stale and repetitive.

Quick click

UKEdChat has posted an interesting article entitled 'Using DIRT as a Learning Journey' on its website. It provides links to other discussions about how to use it in practice and outlines how it can be used alongside other AfL strategies to improve learning.

http://ukedchat.com/2014/01/07/dirt/

- **Open up more lines of communication between you and your pupils,** because a wider range of communication channels can only serve to help you know individual needs and adapt your teaching accordingly. In particular, think about the ways you can capture student voice and how you will use the information it gives you. Don't be afraid of student feedback on your teaching or your lessons. Although student voice doesn't necessarily give you a 'true' insight into the reality of your lessons, it does give you an indication of how students perceive your lessons. Although an obvious way to undertake this is by carrying out interviews with students, they are time-consuming and do not always provide the immediate feedback needed. You should thus look to develop strategies to encourage your students to communicate with you as they are learning.

One method is to make use of props so that students can communicate when a lesson is going too fast or where they are confused. I have seen some teachers use coloured cards or discs on the desk to communicate with the teacher as the lesson is taking place. This can give a clear indication of whether the pace of the lesson needs to be changed, instructions and explanations need to be given more clearly, or to identify which students need additional support during independent activities. With homework, students should also be encouraged to add a post-it note, or brief comment at the end of their work, to share with you what they did not understand or what they would like more help with.

- **Look to change attitudes to assessment by building resilience in your pupils** and helping them to respond positively to advice and feedback. Remember the well-known phrase: 'A person who never made a mistake never tried anything new.' Indeed, attitudes towards assessment very often come from the tone and language used by the teacher in the classroom. I have often seen the look of dread on some students' faces, or at least heard a groan of despair, when the word 'test' is used. This carries with it all the negative baggage in pupils' minds which surround assessment. Pupils fear being found wanting or worry about being compared to their peers.

Instead, try to build a positive culture and attitude towards assessment in your classroom. A small change you could make would be to refer to assessments as 'learning reviews' or 'progress checkers'. However, the real change of culture comes from how you talk about assessment on a day-to-day basis. Encourage students to see assessments as an opportunity to identify where they are at and what they need to do to improve. Be prepared to share your own experiences of failure and how you learnt from this. Ultimately, you need to articulate to students that it is not the results that are important but how they use them. Even with summative tests, you should reinforce the message that their performance is secondary to the learning targets it generates. Be clear that these do not mark the end of a learning journey, but the beginning of a new one.

Use language to encourage resilience in your students, so that when they meet a challenge, fail to do well in an assessment or make a mistake, you give them clear messages that this is part of the learning process. Look at the table below for ideas about how your language can be changed to promote positive attitudes to learning and nurture a growth mindset, rather than feeding their sense of helplessness or fear of failure:

Alternative statements: to promote a growth mindset
Mistakes are expected and valuable - we all learn from them.
I am so glad you made that mistake, because you learned . . .
Okay, you didn't do as well as you wanted to. Let's look at this as an opportunity to learn.
If Plan A isn't working, how else can you try to learn it? What have you done which worked in the past?
Start by thinking about the parts you do well in and then consider what parts were difficult for you. How would you do things differently next time?
Congratulations, it was good to see you using a different strategy to help you learn . . .

Widen your use of peer and self-assessment, to help students be more autonomous and engaged in their own learning

Quick wins

- **Get students to undertake a 'pre-flight checklist'** (Thompson and Wiliam, 2007, p10) before they hand in a piece of work. Assessments which have a clear set of criteria should allow you to pair students up so they can undertake a brief check of each other's work. This is about ensuring that the work meets a minimum standard in terms of structure or composition, rather than assessing the quality of the work. For example, science students may be asked to produce a report which includes a title, abstract, introduction, method, results and a conclusion. These can be easily checked by a peer, using the 'pre-flight checklist'.

- **Help students to improve peer assessment.** Get students to review each other's work, but ask them to write their comments on to a post-it note, so that you can collect them at the end of the activity. You can then look at some anonymous examples of feedback and discuss which feedback is most helpful or how other feedback could be improved. Over time, this should help to train students in providing specific and helpful feedback.

Quick click

Tom Sherrington, author of headguruteacher.com, has posted an article about the power of improving peer-to-peer critique. Read it and watch the imbedded video to consider how you can help your students give more effective feedback.

https://headguruteacher.com/2013/11/05/lesson-from-berger-austins-butterfly-and-not-accepting-mediocrity/

- **Use blind marking to encourage students to review each other's work.** This involves providing feedback on separate strips of paper. You can then get students into groups of four and ask them to read each other's work and try to match your comments to each piece of work. This helps them to re-engage with the objectives and also gives them an insight into how to provide effective feedback.

- **Use oral frameworks to support students in discussing each other's work.** Break down and share the key questions which students might ask of each other's work to give structure to peer-to-peer conversations.

- **Let students take the role of an assessor** by giving them an example piece of work which includes common mistakes or misconceptions. You can undertake this as a quick starter activity to allow you to share and discuss possible misunderstandings. However, you could also share a misconception with the class and ask them to try to work out what is wrong with the response. In one science lesson I observed, the trainee gave out an exemplified response to a question which was littered with misconceptions, such as the interchangeable use of the terms 'force' and 'energy'. This facilitated a rich discussion about what the misconceptions were and how the student might be given appropriate feedback to assist them in tackling this misconception.

- **Get students to share and compare responses** to build a positive discussion around the reasoning behind certain answers or judgements. This could be through a debating activity in which students with different interpretations are asked to present their judgements to the class. The class can be given opportunities to probe or question these students before undertaking a vote on the strongest argument. Alternatively, I have seen students asked to present different approaches to answering a question on the class whiteboard, allowing the whole class to engage in discussing and positively critiquing the different approaches.

- **Get students to design questions in order to assess each other.** This is not an easy task, as it is both cognitively challenging and requires a deeper understanding of the subject matter. However, you will find this easier if you snowball the task allowing individuals, pairs and then groups to redraft and present their top question. These can be used in a range of ways, such as forming the basis of challenge tasks, plenaries, future starters, homeworks or just as a valuable revision source for the whole class.

- **Experiment with groups to explore the best dynamic to enable peer-to-peer support.** Use the information gained from traffic lighting to decide on groupings. In this way those students who are green might be grouped to support those who are amber, while you work with students who have signalled that they are red. Alternatively, you might get them into mixed groups and ask those who are green to support and lead the group, while you work your way around the classroom and support all groups.

- **Get students involved in peer teaching.** Homework or classroom activities can be designed so that students are given time to learn about a topic and prepare a feedback sheet to share with a partner or group. The partner or other group members can then discuss how clear the explanation was and ways to improve the response. This worked well in my own 'flipped classrooms' (see Chapter 1) – for example, when students were given research tasks for homework, their findings were then disseminated through a classroom carousel or a speed dating activity.

 **Slow burners**

- **Engage students in peer assessment** so they have an opportunity to become familiar with assessment criteria and reflect on how their peers can improve. However, this does need to be well planned and prepared in advance. I have seen this done well, but too often I have seen it done poorly. Indeed, a common mistake is simply asking students to swap books to mark each other's work, without any guidance on what they should be looking for, or how it should be assessed. Similarly, I have seen lessons where a detailed mark scheme has been shared with students who have been left to negotiate this and mark a peer's work, without any support in understanding the assessment criteria or what it might look like in practice. Feeding back on these lessons, I ask the trainee: 'How would you feel if you were asked to undertake examiner marking without a mark scheme?' 'Could you be confident you were marking the work accurately without a standardisation event?' 'Could you ensure you were being fair and consistent in your marking?'

Given that it would be almost impossible to guarantee these things, it stands to reason that students need time, and training, to become better at peer and self-assessment, and it cannot be approached as a quick-fix activity to impress an observer. You should therefore take time to consider how you will set up peer assessment. Look to the assessment criteria and consider how accessible it is or whether it needs to be adapted. In designing a pupil-friendly mark scheme, you should be able to consider what skills or understanding pupils will need in order to access the mark scheme. For example, when looking at extended writing, pupils often need support to identify the difference between description, explanation, argument and judgement. A good way to help students access the mark scheme would be to allow them to review some sample extracts, or undertake a whole-class standardisation of an example response first. Indeed, by modelling this as a whole class, you are also ensuring that they understand the process and procedures for peer assessment, which will help you to reinforce the rules and expectations when assessing someone else's work. Furthermore, take time to consider groupings when peer assessing, as it might be practical but not always best to just swap books with the person they are sitting next to.

I remember a lesson where this was done particularly well, with students being put into roughly similar ability groups. They were given a short time to look at and comment on each other's work within the group; asked to swap books with another group; and then given slightly longer to mark a book from that group in more detail.

What is most important when undertaking peer assessment is to emphasise the rationale for peer assessment and deal with the anxiety it creates among students. Make sure students are encouraged to see the value of this activity and that you set out the rules and expectations for undertaking it. It is also worthwhile reiterating that you will be looking at how well they are assessing each other's work, as well as the work itself. This in itself often gets them to focus their efforts on providing detailed and appropriate feedback.

- **Use summative assessment data formatively.** Rather than seeing summative tests or end-of-unit exams in a negative light, encourage students to see them as important milestones so that you can redirect their learning and adapt your teaching. You should use summative data to get a picture of your class needs and identify how you might adapt future lessons or units of work to support students. Students should use summative data to reflect on their results and use it to set appropriate targets for the future, whether these are developmental (relating to key understanding, skills or concepts), attitudinal (such as their motivation) or logistical (such as timing or reading instructions). The key point is to emphasise to your students the importance of learning from the process, rather than merely focusing on the performance. They are a good opportunity to set transferable targets which students can use to improve future summative assessments, such as asking them to 'highlight the command words in the question' or 'only spend one minute per mark on the exam paper'.

A simple approach to using summative assessments formatively is to review exam papers with a class and go through particular questions after they have been marked. Alternatively, you could try to build in time, before you mark assessments, for students to undertake a self or peer review activity. I would often return assessments to a group of students, along with a blank exam paper. They are then set the objective of working together to design a model exam script, discussing and reviewing the answers they originally provided to collectively agree the best possible response. Whole-class feedback after this activity then allowed everyone to review and evaluate the assessment, providing a much richer opportunity for individual students to reflect on where they went wrong and what they needed to do to improve. In addition, when marks were eventually returned, there were no surprises and the result was more than a meaningless score on a test paper.

In summary

Feedback is integral to assessment and essential to learning. Although you may be concerned about whether you are giving the right type of feedback, or whether that feedback is being received, this is perfectly natural. All teachers are constantly looking to improve their approaches to giving feedback and, because it is so important, increase student receptivity to feedback. Therefore, keep this in mind and ensure you develop your own ability to listen to the feedback messages from your class as well as your ability to provide effective feedback to support learning.

Before the lesson

- **Explore the written feedback given by colleagues.** Review current or previous books for the classes you teach. Consider the feedback given, and how they are structured to support students with their learning.

- **Observe other teachers with a focus on verbal feedback.** Assess the types of verbal feedback which students regularly receive in a lesson. Consider how the teacher identifies the ways in which a student can improve.

- **Plan opportunities for students to respond to and action feedback.** This might be by planning DIRT time (see above).

- **Ensure you have marked books (especially if you have said you will) with clear feedback on how to improve.**

During the lesson

- **Provide time for students to reflect on or respond to feedback.**

- **Train students to give and receive feedback.**

- **Support students in assessing the work of peers** and encourage them to engage positively with the feedback they receive.

- **Make sure you are receptive to the formal and informal feedback information given by students.** This should act as a barometer, allowing you to identify when you might need to change the pace of the lesson, redirect learning or completely change course.

- **Ensure verbal feedback is clear and specific.** When praising students, be clear about what they have done well. When giving advice, make sure that students understand exactly what they need to do to improve.

After the lesson

- **Ensure you review student responses or actions arising from your feedback.** This will not only ensure reluctant students are encouraged to improve their work, but will also encourage keen students to see the value you place on improving and redrafting work.

- **Experiment with a range of ways of providing feedback,** to identify what works well with different individuals or different classes.

Further reading

Many of the books recommended in the assessment section have chapters which pertain to feedback, and in particular Dylan Wiliam's (2011) book, *Embedded Formative Assessment*, is very useful in this regard. Also Shirley Clarke's (2014) book, *Outstanding Formative Assessment*, although targeted at both Secondary and Primary teachers, has a useful section on feedback, which includes exemplars and links to 'Video Clip Tasters' that you may find useful from a practical point of view.

Hattie's (2012) article 'Know thy impact' in *Educational Leadership*, provides a good overview of the key methods to give powerful feedback which students can use. This is a more practical synopsis of the findings outlined in *The Power of Feedback* (Hattie and Timperley, 2007) which is a very good starting point for exploring the evidence base around the impact of feedback on learning and achievement.

However, a summary of all the literature and research relating to feedback is extensively covered by Dylan Wiliam (2013) through his chapter on *Feedback and Instructional Correctives*, which is in the *SAGE Handbook of Research on Classroom Assessment*. Certainly, this will point you towards further reading and specific research into classroom feedback.

References

Bangert-Drowns, R, Kulik, C-L, Kulik, J and Morgan, M (1991) The instructional effect of feedback in test-like events. *Review of Educational Research, 61*(2): 213–38.

Butler, R (1988) Enhancing and undermining Intrinsic Motivation: The effects of task-involving and ego-involving evaluation on interest and performance. *British Journal of Educational Psychology*, 58(1): 1–14.

Clarke, S (2014) *Outstanding Formative Assessment: Culture and Practice.* London: Hodder Education.

Clymer, J and Wiliam, D (2006) Improving the way we grade science. *Educational Leadership, 64*(4): 36–42.

Dweck, C (2006) *Mindset: How You Can Fulfil Your Potential.* New York: Ballantine Books.

Haddon, M (2016) 'My Writing Day'. *The Guardian*, 23 July. Available at: **www.theguardian.com/ books/2016/jul/23/my-writing-day-mark-haddon** (accessed 2 December 2016).

Hattie, J (2012) Know thy impact. *Educational Leadership, 70*(1): 18–23.

Hattie, J and Timperley, H (2007) The power of feedback. *Review of Educational Research, 77*(1): 81–112.

Hattie, J and Yates, J (2014) *Visible Learning and the Science of How We Learn.* Abingdon: Routledge.

Jones, S and Tanner, H (2006) *Assessment*, 2nd edn. London: Continuum International.

Sadler, R (1998) Formative assessment: Revisiting the territory. *Assessment in Education, 5*(1): 77–84.

Shute, V (2008) Focus on formative feedback. *Review of Educational Research, 78*(1): 153–89.

Wiliam, D (2011) *Embedded Formative Assessment.* Bloomington, IN: Solution Tree Press.

Wiliam, D (2013) Feedback and instructional correctives, in J McMillan (ed.) *SAGE Handbook of Research on Classroom Assessment.* London: SAGE Publications, pp. 197–214.

8

Differentiation

This chapter aims to introduce the concept of differentiation and to present a number of strategies to implement effective differentiation in the classroom. As such it addresses the following teachers' standards.

- Know when and how to differentiate appropriately, using approaches which enable pupils to be taught effectively (TS5).
- Have a clear understanding of the needs of all pupils, including those with special educational needs (SEN); those of high ability; those with English as an additional language (EAL); those with disabilities; and be able to use and evaluate distinctive teaching approaches to engage and support them (TS5).

Introduction

Imagine you are to attend a cookery class for adults. You are not a bad cook if you're being honest and you are keen to improve. You can boil an egg, make a mean spaghetti bolognaise and your steak, accompanied with hasselback potatoes and asparagus is, quite honestly, a tour de force, if you don't say so yourself.

When you get to the class, you are teamed up with Graham and John. Graham has never cooked in his life and has reluctantly been dragged to the session by his flat-mate, Simone. John, on the other hand, is an experimental chef and really wants to push himself in all aspects of food.

You are being taught how to make moussaka. You have made lasagne once so have an idea what the process and end outcome might be. You're relatively pleased – it seems about right for where you are in your culinary odyssey. Graham shakes his head and looks a little daunted. What's moussaka? Didn't he play right wing for Newcastle United? John is disappointed. He's well past moussaka. That's like a Tuesday dish for him and he was keen for something more challenging.

Now unpick this scenario in terms of learning. The teacher wants all the students to learn how to prepare and then make moussaka in an hour. There is, even in this group of three students, a range of abilities, confidence and enthusiasm for the lesson.

- How is the teacher going to ensure that the inexperienced Graham is supported and made to feel confident in tackling something that seems daunting?

- Is the teacher going to use your prior knowledge about lasagne to support you in making moussaka?

- How are John's cookery skills going to be developed if he has already mastered moussaka?

These are the questions that differentiation addresses. A typical classroom contains a range of different abilities, different attitudes, different confidences. If the teacher does not do anything different and teaches to your standard – roughly the middle – what is going to happen to Graham and John? You and other competent cooks might prosper, but what about the lower and higher ability? Graham might give up if he's not explicitly shown the steps to take or made to feel comfortable in something he is not confident about. Worse, he might start throwing aubergines at John's head as John seems to be doing it effortlessly. John might simply not bother if he's not had the challenge modelled to him or he's not stretched by the task. He might start throwing aubergines at Graham's head as he seems to be trying really hard at what he feels is an easy dish to make.

In summary, the teacher in this scenario needs to be aware of the following.

- Know their students – their strengths and areas for development; their resilience and emotional competencies.

- Know what success is for all students and how they can ensure that students are able to meet these targets.

- Explore different ways to approach the teaching of moussaka.

- Support and challenge *all* students. The next week it might be steak, which John is not as good at and you excel at. He might need more support in this lesson where you might need to be challenged.

This chapter will examine the process of differentiation – that is, the changes a teacher can make to adapt lessons to the needs and interests of their students. While the idea sounds wonderful in theory, the implementation can feel like a burden and teachers often believe they have fulfilled the differentiation requirement by producing a single alternative worksheet, which is given to some selected less able students. This chapter will hopefully suggest some differentiation strategies that are not too onerous but will allow you to support all students to access work that is both achievable and sufficiently challenging.

Targets

What targets does this chapter cover?

- Ensure the less able can access your lessons.
- Ensure the most able are sufficiently stretched.
- Pitch your lessons at an appropriately challenging level.
- Make better use of support staff.
- Support learners who have English as an additional language (EAL).
- Support students with special educational needs and disabilities (SEND).

Types of differentiation

In 1898 a physicist and inventor, Amos Dolbear, wrote an allegory in an educational journal under the pen name of Aesop Jr. He described a school for animals that has decided that all its creature-students should be equally able at all skills. Therefore, the eagle was forced to learn to climb trees and the eel was made to run. This story might prompt you to reflect on the meaningfulness of the activities you set in your classroom. I can remember many 'eels' in my classroom and the frustration both they and I felt when they struggled with the 'running' tasks I set them. Not all students are the same: they will vary across a large number of traits: motivation, background knowledge, ability in literacy and numeracy, physical and cognitive abilities, size of working memory and ability to focus, among others. Therefore, you cannot expect all your students to reach the same final level of achievement. However, you should aspire to give all your students an equal opportunity to achieve their potential. In order to manage this difficult task, you need to set students activities and expectations that are appropriate for their abilities, and so provide both sufficient support and achievable challenge.

Differentiation is the process by which the type, level or pace of instruction is altered to match a learner's needs or interests (Heacox, 2002, p5). There are at least six different approaches to differentiation (Farrell, 1999, pp50–2).

1. **By outcome**. Students complete the same task but the teacher has different expectations of the level and/or the extent of progress for different students. For example, you might give all students the same set of questions to complete in a set time but set different expectations as to the number of questions completed or the depths of answers. Alternatively, you might set the whole class an open-ended task, such as an extended written assignment, but outline what achievement at different levels might look like and set individual targets. The cookery teacher might expect Graham to create a dish which has all the components of moussaka. You might be expected to create a well-seasoned, well-cooked moussaka. John might be expected to add a twist to the normal moussaka recipe.

2. **By task**. Different students are set different tasks that cover the same content area. The tasks might differ in the demands they place on the student or in the mode in which students express their answers. Graham might not make moussaka in the first lesson. He might start with an easier dish and build up to moussaka. John might be tasked to deconstruct moussaka for fine dining.

3. **By support**. A teacher can vary the assistance students receive from teachers, teaching assistants, peers or additional material resources such as computers or dictionaries. Graham might have peer or teacher support. John might have an independent task.

4. **By organisation**. Students work in groups that are structured to best support their needs. This might mean students of similar abilities working together or more and less able students collaborating on a task. You and Graham could work together and you could take the role of the expert.

5. **By resources**. Students are given access to resources such as word processors, dictionaries or extra worksheets to support their learning. There might be support and challenge tasks for all students in the class; as learning is messy and transient, some students might need to be supported or challenged more than the teacher thought. Despite not being the best cook, your experience of lasagne making might mean you need to be challenged further.

6. **By extension**. Some students may be set additional tasks beyond those set to other members of the class. John might have a challenge sheet, so when he is making the moussaka, he has to adapt the dish while still ensuring he uses the main ingredients that make up a moussaka.

 Key learning point

> Differentiation need not just relate to the outcome of a task or type of task set. There are many ways to vary the challenge for students.

Knowing your students and finding the 'sweet spot'

At the heart of successful differentiation lies an understanding of students' individual strengths, interests and needs. Imagine planning as a process in which you develop learning objectives into activities which are suitable for the abilities of a particular group of students. The process of targeting teaching to individual students' needs and abilities is known as personalised learning and is seen as central to successful teaching and learning (DCSF, 2008). When writing a lesson plan, you might imagine different members of the class attempting the task: how will a student with ADHD approach this practical task? Which students will find this worksheet difficult? Will the most able students really be challenged to think by the extension material or is it just more work?

In order to be able to carry out this kind of analysis, it is important to build a body of data about your students: the level they are working at; their numeracy and literacy abilities; and their preference for types of task. Some of this knowledge will exist in the formal data you have on students, but some of it will be implicit and gleaned from your relationships with your students. With experience, you will come to develop a sense of the kinds of activities that will work well with particular classes.

One approach to learning about your classes is to give students a questionnaire which allows them to express their strengths and weaknesses, and to describe topics that interest them and their particular skills. For example, as I got to know the students in a class, I developed a lesson on forces based around the martial art a student practised. I asked the student to bring in some of their equipment which helped to turn a potentially abstract topic into one in which students engaged with ideas about forces in a genuine way.

Your task in differentiating work is to pitch it at a level that should be sufficiently challenging to stimulate learning, but not beyond the reach of the student. Vygotsky (1978) argued that learning occurs most successfully when work is targeted at a learner's zone of proximal development (ZPD). The ZPD is the group of activities which the learner would struggle to complete individually but could complete with support from peers or adults. A similar concept that illustrates the difficult balancing act of differentiation is Csikszentmihalyi's (1991) notion of flow. Flow is the optimal experience you feel when the level of challenge is neither too high nor too low. You might describe it as 'being in the zone' and have the experience of time passing rapidly due to your high level of focus – for example, when playing a musical instrument or a sport. You should aim to pitch your activities towards this experience in your students. Consider the extreme examples in the box below.

Real life scenario

Scenario A

Maria: [Looking at worksheet] This is too hard. I can't do it I don't know what any of this means. I really hate science.

Scenario B

Eyram: Miss, I've finished the questions.

Teacher: Well, try the extension questions at the bottom of the page.

Eyram: I've already done them. They were really easy.

Teacher: Okay, then you can get out a reading book and read quietly.

In scenario A, the work set is too challenging for Maria and insufficient support has been provided to help her to engage with the activity (there may also be a motivational issue, but let's put that aside for the moment). In scenario B, Eyram has completed all the work rapidly, without being challenged and he is allowed to move on to a different task. No teacher can target work to precisely meet the needs of their students at all times, but through the thoughtful use of assessment you will gain the ability to pitch work at an appropriate level.

As you gain experience you will develop a sensitivity, almost a sixth sense, to your class's engagement with a task. An increased level of chatter might mean the task is too easy and the students have become distracted. Bemused looks and raised hands are a clear sign that the work is too hard. Teaching involves a constant feedback cycle of increasing and decreasing the level of challenge to find the 'sweet spot' at which a class is adequately but not overly challenged.

You might find that the learning outcomes expected of your students are beyond the current abilities of some members of a group. In that case you can try to provide scaffolding to differentiate the challenge. Scaffolding was originally described by Wood *et al.* (1978) and refers to a kind of cognitive support that anticipates the difficulties a student may encounter when attempting a task (Mercer, 1994, p96). You may find it helpful to break down a learning aim at the planning stage into specific skills necessary to the aim, and ensuring that those abilities are fluent and practised before attempting the more challenging task.

Consider the example in the scenario box below.

Real life scenario

Scenario A

Teacher: Now that we have talked about some different ideas, I want you to spend the next 30 minutes writing a response to the statement: 'Global warming is a natural process and it is futile to act to slow it down.'

Scenario B

Teacher: In a few minutes I am going to ask you to write a response to the statement: 'Global warming is a natural process and it is futile to act to slow it down.' Before you do that, I want you to consider how to structure your response. What sections should be included? [Takes response from class]. Good, I would like to see an introduction, sections arguing for and against the statement, and a conclusion. Let's brainstorm some points to include in each section.

In the first scenario the teacher presents the students with a complex task that requires them to carry out several steps in order to produce a suitable response. This is cognitively challenging and some students may require extra support. In scenario B, the teacher has provided additional scaffolding – that is, support that enables students to complete the task. Notice that the teacher hasn't given the students any additional information related to the task, but has helped them by breaking down a complex task into simpler steps: first write an introduction, then write three points in favour of the argument, etc. When you are planning tasks, consider where challenges will arise for your students and what scaffolding you can put in place to help them reach the learning goal by themselves. You may wish to consider different levels of scaffolding for different students. In the example above, some students may have been able to produce a structured response without support.

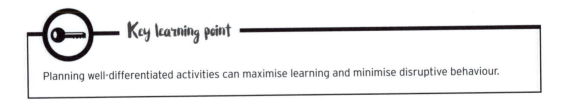

Key learning point

Know your students' abilities so you can set work that is sufficiently challenging without being too difficult.

The rewards of differentiation

Differentiation can seem like a daunting task (McGarvey *et al.*, 1996). Rather than planning a single lesson, you may feel that you have to plan a different activity for each of your students. This is not the case. Though some students, might, at some times, receive additional tasks, there are many other appropriate ways of differentiating that do not require the production of additional tasks. While some support for individuals needs to be set up before the lesson, part of successful differentiation is responding flexibly to needs in the moment in the classroom (Weston *et al.*, 1998, p82). I once observed a lesson in which a student teacher abandoned a well-prepared plan to teach adjectives in French when it became clear that the students did not understand what an adjective was in English. Had the teacher not altered the lesson to match the needs of her students, a form of in the moment differentiation, the lesson could have led to only limited learning.

Differentiation is an essential part of any lesson plan as poorly differentiated activities can cause students to feel alienated from the classroom and lead to poor behaviour (DES, 1989). A well-differentiated lesson is likely to both increase the potential for learning and minimise opportunities for students to become bored or disengaged. It is well worth the added time taken to ensure that all the members of the class you are planning for will be able to engage with the material and be appropriately stretched.

Key learning point

Planning well-differentiated activities can maximise learning and minimise disruptive behaviour.

Differentiation for all

We all learn in different ways. One person might be able to learn songs with little effort but might struggle to recall a telephone number. A different person might be quick to pick up dance moves but find it difficult to learn how to do calculations. This variety of ways of approaching learning has been described as neurodiversity (Silberman, 2015). One might imagine that students belong to two groups: those with special educational needs and disabilities (SEND) and those without. Around 15 per cent of students in schools in the UK were identified as having special educational needs (DfE, 2015). A more useful categorisation might be to consider the neurodiversity that exists in your classroom. While diagnoses such as dyslexia or dyspraxia might be useful for grouping together students with some common traits, there will also be significant differences between students within a diagnosed group. While it is important that you develop knowledge of the general traits of common SEND and strategies to support students with that SEND (see strategies below), keep in mind that a diagnosis does not define a student. Recent reports suggest that a British intelligence agency has sought to recruit dyspraxic and dyslexic individuals because of their talents at code breaking (Wright, 2014). All your students have individual learning needs. You need to find ways to make your subject accessible and motivating for all the members of your class.

Language plays a major role in learning. Therefore, it is important to remember that there may be a variety of different levels of language ability in your classroom. Some students may struggle with language due to SENDs such as dyslexia, but others may be taking on the same learning challenges as other students, but in a second language. Such students are described as having English as an additional language (EAL) and it is reported that the percentage of students with EAL in primary and secondary schools in England has risen from 8 per cent in 1997 to 16 per cent in 2003 (Strand *et al.*, 2015, p5). If you have ever attempted simple acts of communication in a foreign language, such as buying a train ticket, you will appreciate the frustrations of working in a language that is not your own. Imagine the much greater challenge of learning about complex concepts such as harmony or cause and effect in a second language. Even the apparently simple classroom commands can be confusing – for example, 'taking the register' is an idiom that can easily be misunderstood. The strategies section, below, introduces a number of approaches that will help you support students with EAL.

Although many teachers associate differentiation with the less able, highly able students also need appropriate differentiation to ensure they are fully stretched. A recent Ofsted Report (2015) reported that a large proportion of the most able students did not reach their expected level of achievement. A consideration in planning should therefore be, as well as supporting the less able, to set the most able students tasks that will offer a genuine challenge. For example, when teaching Year 7 students about floating and sinking, a few of the most able students were already aware of the concepts I was teaching the rest of the class, so I set them the challenge of creating a poster answering the question: 'Will a glass of water, filled exactly to the brim, with an ice cube floating in it, overflow as the ice melts?' This question provoked some interesting discussion and thought about the nature of floating.

Social and emotional aspects of a learner's experience in school are increasingly seen as part of teachers' responsibilities (Humphrey *et al.*, 2010) and may have a significant impact on learning. Psychological variables may therefore be another factor that teachers consider when differentiating work. For example, Jane Kise (2007) has suggested that preferences for extroversion and introversion, or logical versus emotive decision-making, should be responded to in the classroom.

While differentiation is, in general, a powerful approach for supporting students' learning, it is important to reflect on the potential negative effects of differentiation. It has been reported that children who see the goal of school as entirely performance focused can avoid challenges, as they fear failure (Dweck, 1986). It may be that some students, of both high and low ability, prefer lower challenge tasks as they have less potential for stimulating difficult feelings of failure. If a task is not sufficiently challenging, some students may develop learned helplessness – a failure to attempt challenging tasks or activities due to a perception that failure is inevitable (Jarvis, 2015, p161). One student I taught would demand, in a loud voice, the 'thicko sheet' and would complain that he was not allowed to do any writing because of his special educational needs. It took many weeks of work, with an excellent teaching assistant, to encourage the student to attempt tasks that appeared challenging and overcome their fear of failure.

Teachers should be sensitive to feelings of shame or embarrassment that some students may attach to receiving additional support (Fraser and Meadows, 2008, p357). By definition, differentiation highlights differences between individual learners, which can be a difficult process for some students. Differentiation should be managed so that it does not make students feel isolated from their peers – the purpose of differentiation is to create a sense of equality of opportunity not division. Although differentiation has many challenges for the teacher, when carried out effectively, it can allow all students to achieve their potential. The next section explores a series of strategies you may find useful in progressing towards the targets listed above.

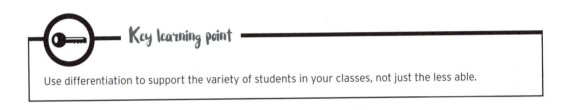

Key learning point

Use differentiation to support the variety of students in your classes, not just the less able.

Targets

Ensure the less able can access your lessons

Quick wins

- **Use Bloom's taxonomy.** Initially structure activities around the lower levels of Bloom's taxonomy, which include skills such as describing, recalling, labelling, grouping and locating. This can apply to questions, learning outcomes and worksheets.

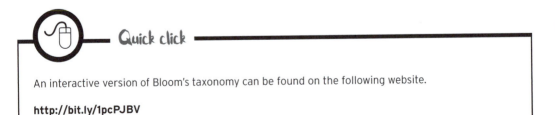

Quick click

An interactive version of Bloom's taxonomy can be found on the following website.

http://bit.ly/1pcPJBV

- **Jigsaw tasks.** Divide the cognitive load of a task between different students. For example, when learning about the British empire, some students may be assigned to study some written sources on trade and answer some questions, others may watch a video about military campaigns and complete a spider diagram, while a third group uses online resources to study how religion was introduced. Groups would then be formed that included one member who had carried out each activity to complete a final task that drew on the learning of each participant. This approach has the advantage that each student completes a task appropriate to their strengths but can still cooperate with and learn from their peers.

- **Breakdown multi-stage process.** Think about all the steps that are involved in the task you have set a student. Imagine the task from a particular student's point of view and pre-empt the difficulties that could arise at each step – for example, not understanding a word, having forgotten some of the taught material, struggling with written expression. By breaking down the process into steps, different support can be provided for students who are likely to have difficulties at different stages.

- **Grouping.** Think about which of a student's peers may be best able to support them to reach their potential. It may be that working with another student of similar ability is supportive for some tasks, but for other activities, a paring of high- and low-ability students may be beneficial to both. When forming groups, it may be useful to define roles for members of the group or to define rules for the way that students should interact. For example, one student could think of advantages related to a proposal and another disadvantages. Alternatively, students might be assigned different sections of an experimental write-up such as describing the method or drawing a graph.

- **Give support sheets rather than extra sheets.** Differentiation doesn't have to mean that students do different tasks. Students of different abilities may be able to carry out the same task if they are given extra information or support. This approach can be more inclusive than setting alternative activities as students will feel that they are engaging in the same tasks as their peers. For example, where a task calls for a longer piece of prose, some students could be given a sheet that outlines a structure to follow in their writing. Alternatively, students working on mathematical problems may be given a series of hints to break a multi-step process into manageable chunks.

- **Offer a menu of tasks to the whole class.** In some contexts, you might offer a class a choice between different types of task addressing a single aim. The tasks might differ in various aspects: level, medium of expression, whether they are completed alone or in a group. Rather than offering a free choice, you could set differentiated outcomes for individuals. For example, students with a particular target grade are expected to complete a certain number and type of tasks, ensuring that the activities are appropriately targeted. The sense of agency generated by being offered a choice can be highly motivating.

 **Quick Click**

Mike Gershon is a well-known writer and educationalist whose website contains a large number of excellent resources. The link below will open a PowerPoint containing 80 strategies for differentiation in the classroom.

http://mikegershon.com/resources/download-info/the-differentiation-deviser/

- **Shadow a pupil**. The foundation of good differentiation is understanding your students' abilities and needs. One way of finding out a student's strengths, weaknesses and interests is to take the opportunity to shadow them in other lessons (do seek permission from the teacher of the other classes). Observe what kinds of activities the student engages well with and notice what difficulties they encounter. This information can be used to develop tasks appropriate to that particular student. Although this may seem like a time-consuming task, a difference in the engagement of a single disengaged student can change the attitude of a whole class.

- **Find out your students' strengths and weaknesses.** Take time to talk to individual students. Find out what kind of tasks they enjoy and where their skills lie. It is not practical to adapt the classroom entirely to the interests of your students. However, if there are learners who enjoy music or drawing, for example, setting at least some work in these media may provide a motivational boost for other activities. Relatability is an important aspect of teaching but there is a health warning attached here. If you only target what students find interesting, you are in danger of creating a narrow focus which might affect their development of cultural capital. Sometimes students don't know what they will find engaging or interesting until they experience it for themselves. Would students be interested in an itinerant worker scratching around for a job, talking endlessly about rabbits set against the backdrop of the Great Depression? Not on the face of it, but they mostly enjoy *Of Mice and Men* when they experience it. You need to balance things that they like and find interesting with things that they never considered in the first place. For example, I was working with some drama PGCE trainees as they were designing an activity for a Year 10 lesson and observed them as they were choosing a topic. Bullying, one said. Social media, another trainee proposed. Gangs, another offered. All of these topics were fair and appropriate, but sometimes we need to expand our students' experience. I suggested how older people were treated and a trainee argued that students wouldn't be interested in that topic. Perhaps, I replied, but they should be. The question is how we can engage them with respecting the older generation. So, get to know what they like, but remember, don't eschew other topics just because they haven't identified them as of an interest or importance.

  Ask students which steps in lessons they find most difficult and how they would most like to be supported by teaching assistants. As discussed above, reflections on one's own weaknesses can be difficult, so these kinds of conversations may not be appropriate for all students and need to be handled sensitively, perhaps with the involvement of members of the learning support department, parents or form teachers. This information can be collected either through a brief conversation or by giving a questionnaire to the group. The following questions might provide useful information to guide your teaching.

  - What topic do you find hardest in this subject?
  - What kinds of activities do you learn most in?
  - What do teachers do that helps you learn?
  - Are there any topics in this subject you would like to know more about?
  - What's the best lesson you've ever had and why?

- **Reflect on the nature of assessment.** It may be the case that particular features of the assessments your students undertake prevent them from demonstrating their full potential. For example, some students may struggle with expressing their ideas in extended written passages or find certain quantitative skills challenging. Try to anticipate such issues and build scaffolding into class tasks to prepare students for future assessments. You should think of scaffolding as support that you put in place when a student's understanding or abilities are developing and then gradually remove as the learner develops confidence. For example, for the student who struggles with writing, allow them to initially use writing frames or bullet point responses and gradually remove layers of support to move the student closer to being able to fully express their potential on assessments. A different approach is to model how to deconstruct extended assessment questions. There may be few students who can attempt a question such as 'With reference to case studies describe how different factors affect human migration' without support. You can scaffold a student's ability to answer this question by modelling how to break apart the question. First list the case studies you have studied related to migration and then brainstorm factors that caused migration, etc.

- **Feedback as a form of differentiation.** The formative comments a teacher adds to assessed pieces of work can be thought of as a form of differentiation. Although marking can be an onerous task, it is an opportunity to tailor comments to the particular needs of a learner. Rather than a general comment, setting a student a specific task to carry out in response to a previous piece of work will encourage active engagement. It may be helpful to structure lessons such that, when work is returned, the students spend some time engaging with your comments and carrying out a set of individualised tasks based on their last piece of work. Students could keep an on-going list of the feedback comments on their recent work in the front of their books, which will act as a set of targets to focus their achievement. The teacher and student can jointly edit this list of targets as they are completed and different aims become appropriate (see formative assessment strategies in Chapter 7).

Ensure the highly able are sufficiently stretched

- **Use Bloom's taxonomy.** Ensure that your most able students are not just using processes on the lower levels of the taxonomy such as recall or carrying out tasks involving repeated procedures. Able students should be engaged with the skills of critiquing, evaluating, synthesising, justifying and interpreting.

- **Set open-ended tasks.** Highly able students should be allowed to engage with open-ended tasks where there is not a clearly defined right or wrong answer. For example, rather than simply knowing facts about sources of power, a highly able student might be asked to present a case for a suitable balance of different types of electricity generation for the UK in the future.

- **Extension resources.** Devote an area of your classroom to a set of resources, perhaps grouped by level, which students who have finished a task early can engage with. These may be books, articles or other artefacts. It is important that clear guidelines are set for students being able to access these resources (Do they need to show permission to access the resources or can they go as soon as they have judged they are finished?). Encourage the students who use these resources to present evidence of their learning in some form.

- **Use able students as peer supporters.** It may, in some classrooms, be appropriate to use the most able to support other students. This can be in the form of circulating when they have finished a task, preparing a topic to teach the whole class or acting as an expert within a group. Careful management of this approach is required to ensure that peer teachers also benefit from the experience.

- **Trust able learners to jump ahead.** It may be that some able learners need to spend less time on drill-like practice than their peers. You may be able to design a system in which once students have displayed competence at a certain skill they can move on to a more challenging task, while others continue to practise.

Slow burners

- **Encourage independence.** A valuable skill to foster in your most able students is an ability to be self-directed. Arrange a meeting with your highly able students and discuss with them procedures for what they should do if they find the work too easy or run out of tasks to do. Discuss strategies they might use to read around the subject or to find reliable information online. Highly able students can sometimes become bored in the classroom as they understand topics more quickly than their peers. This can lead to disengagement and alienation from learning. Discuss with highly able students strategies they might use if they feel insufficiently challenged. You could make available a list of challenging open-ended questions or puzzles they could address. They might work on an on-going, open-ended project. It is easy to assume that able students will necessarily be diligent and engaged learners. However, those with particularly active minds can find it difficult to engage in a classroom environment which they find repetitive and easy. Take the time to talk to your highly able students and find out if they feel they are being sufficiently challenged. One of the privileges of being a teacher is working with highly able students, but you have a duty to ensure that their talent and enthusiasm is fostered in your class (see Chapter 6).

- **Set open-ended projects.** Highly able students are likely to have a drive to learn more about your subject than just the material on the curriculum. They are likely to thrive when engaging with projects that allow them independence of thought and creativity. You may, therefore, wish to set those students an on-going project they can work on in their own time. The project should be open-ended and focus on higher-level skills. For example, they could create a piece of art in a medium they don't use in class, design an app to meet a particular need, or write an essay about an author they love. If you set students such tasks, it is vital that the students feel that the outputs of their work are valued and engaged with. Don't just set the task and then glance at the output. In order for the work to feel valuable, and so the students can progress, the projects they carry out should receive some form of formative feedback. Do allow the students to be involved in choosing the project and give them plenty of freedom in choosing which direction to take the work. Students of all abilities rarely have the opportunity to genuinely direct their own learning and follow their interests. It can be an incredibly powerful experience for students to feel in control of their learning. Take the time to research if there are any national or local competitions related to your subject area, for example the following.

Young scientists can enter the CREST awards.

www.britishscienceassociation.org/crest-awards

Budding poets can enter the Poetry society's Young Poet award.

http://poetrysociety.org.uk/competitions/foyle-young-poets-of-the-year-award/

Artists might enter the Young Art competition, organised by the Royal College of Art.

www.young-art.org.uk

Pitch your lesson at an appropriately challenging level

 Quick wins

- **Differentiate learning objectives**. Students should be aware of their targets, therefore different learning objectives can be set for students with different targets. For example, level 4 students will be able to . . . . As students work on the tasks, a sensitive teacher can circulate round the class and personally adjust students' learning aims for that lesson.

- **Colour-coding your seating plan.** Colour-code your seating plan to show students' target levels. This will enable the teacher to target support and questioning appropriately.

- **Target questions.** Stick students' names and levels on to cards and place them into a bag. When asking questions, draw a name from the bag and do not replace it. This approach ensures that you question evenly and that you can target questions of the appropriate level to each student.

- **Plan activities with increasing levels of difficulty.** If you are unsure of how challenging students will find a particular lesson, produce a range of questions of increasing challenge. If some students find the lowest level questions easy, they can easily be moved on to more challenging work.

- **Ensure you use assessment**. It is important to know the current levels of students in order to set work of an appropriate level. Therefore, include plenty of opportunities for discovering students' level of understanding in lessons to ensure that tasks match students' needs as closely as possible.

- **Keep notes on students' engagement.** Try to notice what kinds of activities have engaged individuals in your lessons and what kinds of tasks they found most challenging. Try to discern patterns, perhaps related to time of day, and target work accordingly. For example, you may find that you need to set different kinds of tasks for successful lessons in the afternoons for certain students, while others may prefer faster paced work in the mornings.

- **Think through all the hitches on a worksheet.** When preparing a worksheet, imagine the different kinds of difficulties a student could encounter at each point. Develop support to overcome these issues such as including a word bank, swapping an open response for a fill-in-the-gaps activity.

- **Remove distracting information.** Be clear about the aim of the activity and remove all information that is not entirely essential that could act as a distraction or complication.

- **Determine the prior knowledge required for a task.** Write a list of the knowledge and skills a student will require to complete an activity and ensure these are acquired before attempting the task.

- **Check the readability.** Use online readability tests to monitor the level of language used in an activity and try to reduce its complexity (for example: **https://readability-score.com**).

- **Modify existing worksheets.** Use post-it notes, highlighting the information printed on the reverse of a sheet, to allow students to complete the same tasks with additional support or challenge.

- **Change the output medium of a task.** If a particular student struggles to express themselves in writing, change the main outcome of the task to a different form, such as a diagram, mind map or song, and include a few short answer questions to scaffold their developing writing skills.

- **Get student feedback.** Leave space on your resources for students to comment on which areas of the worksheet they found easy or difficult to complete. Use this information to design future resources.
- **Modify resources to match students' interests.** If there is a particular context that motivates an individual, design resources around that context, if possible. For example, a set of abstract mathematical calculations related to calculating areas could use data about the size of various objects in a local football team's stadium. An activity to practise punctuation could use text from a recent film.

 **Slow burners**

- **Teach subgroups separately.** It may be the case that you divide the class into subgroups and spend time with each group, targeting teaching and the types of activities set, to the level of the group. Teaching assistants could be used to facilitate the teaching of some of these groups. This can be a powerful way to allow different sections of the class to focus on learning tasks that are appropriate for their needs. The division of the groups does not have to be only by ability. You might ask students for their views on a particular topic – for example, their interpretation of a play. These groups could work together to develop their argument. An alternative is to divide the students into groups that share a similar misconception and then set each group an activity that starts from their initial beliefs. For example, students might be grouped by their ideas about electricity, with each group carrying out a practical activity that addresses misconceptions in their understanding (see Brock, 2007).
- **Differentiate the classroom.** Design your classroom so students in certain areas have access to resources that provide additional support. For example, one area of seats could be close to a set of posters that remind students of key information, or laptops may be available to assist with word processing. This process doesn't have to involve large changes. It could be as simple as placing a laminated card with key words on a particular student's desk at the start of the lesson, or allowing your most able student to sit next to a collection of books with a card giving instructions for an open-ended research treasure hunt. Think about where students with particular needs should sit to maximise their access to learning. One student may find a seat in front of the teacher's desk distracting as there are objects they can fiddle with; another may feel calmer if they are sat near the door.
- **Plan for independent progression through a series of graded activities.** Computer programs which present students with different activities depending on their answers to previous questions, known as adaptive learning environments, are becoming increasingly popular. You can model this task by devoting a lesson or series of lessons to a series of graded tasks that students work through at their own pace. The first task should be a diagnostic task which will enable you to assign students to a number of different tasks depending on how they have performed. In this way students can progress independently on different activities and at different rates while you can target support to those needing help or extra challenge. This kind of activity will require some preparation and it is important you are confident that your students can work independently and you set graded expectations for their outcomes. Also, ensure that as students complete tasks they are given formative feedback that assists them in completing the next task. For example, a science teacher might set students an initial set of calculation problems and ask them to come to the front desk when they are complete. The teacher would rapidly mark students' work as they came to the front: those who had completed the questions with no mistakes would be given a

set of extension problems; those who had made mistakes in converting units, would be given a sheet practising that skill. Other students, who needed support with the mathematical techniques themselves, could be given a different sheet to work on.

Make better use of teaching assistants (TAs)

Quick wins

- **Set up a routine for contacting TAs**. Choose a time, possibly after you have done your weekly plan, to contact the TA and inform them, briefly, of your plans for the lesson and any particular information relating to individual students. This might be as simple as having a quick chat at one break-time each week, or before assembly starts.

- **Seek feedback from TAs.** Take the opportunity to talk to TAs at the end of a lesson, or during your weekly briefing session. They are likely to have useful information about the progress of individual students.

- **Design a lesson information note.** Create a template for a short note you can fill in before a lesson and pass to a TA to communicate information about the lesson without having a conversation in front of the students. This might include topics you think will be most challenging or expectations for individual students.

- **Encourage TAs to focus on learning, not task completion.** Teachers sometimes direct TAs to act as enforcers who simply tell students to get on with it. A more appropriate role is for them to focus on students' learning. Therefore, you might encourage your TAs to replace: 'Come on, you haven't started' with 'I notice you haven't started. What don't you understand?'

- **Ensure that all students still have contact time with you.** You might assume that because a TA is working with the least able students, you no longer need to spend time with these individuals. This is not the case. You are the teacher and all the students in your class need and deserve your attention.

- **Deploy a TA to deliver a particular targeted session with an individual or small group** - for example, working on a particular skill such as graph drawing or punctuation. It would be your responsibility, as the teacher, to find or prepare resources to structure this interaction.

- **Encourage TAs to support learners of all abilities.** Remember, highly able, socially anxious and middle-ability learners need support too.

- **Talk to your TAs about subject knowledge**. It may be that your TA is unclear on the subject knowledge of a lesson, but does not have the time or the confidence to raise the issue with you. Take the time to ensure they are comfortable with the learning aims of a lesson and would be confident in addressing and correcting students' mistakes.

Slow burners

- **Create time for an on-going conversation.** TAs are professionals who will have opinions and insights into your classroom. Make use of this information. Take the time to engage in a continuing conversation about how individual students are working and discuss which strategies can best be employed to support their learning. It is important to remember that TAs are skilled professional colleagues and you should treat them with respect by including them in discussions about the learning that occurs in your classroom. It can be easy to fall into the habit of not speaking to your TA. They arrive at the lesson, spend all their time focused on a handful of students and then leave without feeding back. This pattern is understandable as both TAs and teachers are often busy. However, the additional adult you may have in your classes is one of the most valuable resources you have to assist you. The TA may well support a student you find challenging in other lessons and have insights into strategies that have worked well. Don't be afraid to hear critiques of your practice. I was initially disheartened when I asked a TA about one of my most challenging student's behaviour in other lessons and they replied that they were making excellent progress in Maths and English. However, the discussion lead to the implementation of some new strategies, moving the student and reducing the complexity of texts they were presented with, which lead to great improvements in the student's achievement. By fostering a collegiate relationship with your TAs, you will gain insights into the learning of your students which can be used to better target your teaching.

- **Develop support plans for lessons.** Differentiation by support is a powerful way to facilitate learning but it benefits from careful design. Think, and discuss with the TA, which students might need the most support at different times of the lessons. Predict moments - for example, transitions between tasks or towards the end of an activity, when students will benefit from extra support and plan for the TA to pre-empt any difficulties that may arise at these points. Try to predict the kind of learning difficulties students will face at different points in the lesson and support them in those moments with additional resources or extra support. The plan does not need to be formally written out and might occur in the five minutes before a lesson. You might suggest the TA positions themselves in a certain location at the start of the lesson and support students who find it difficult to settle. However, you might then ask them to work with highly able students in the main activity and suggest a couple of challenge questions they could pose. This would enable you to work with students who were struggling. Remember to listen to the ideas of your TA in this conversation.

- **Encourage TAs to foster student independence.** Although TAs can be invaluable in providing support to students, their presence may impact on students' ability to work independently. If a student knows that whenever they find a piece of work challenging, an adult will appear and tell them the answer, they will be conditioned into not trying. Work with your TAs to foster a culture in which students develop the skill of working independently. This requires that the tasks set for the students are appropriately challenging, but also that you discuss with your TAs how they engage with students who are stuck. Consider the following recommendations for best practice.

  - Rather than telling the correct answer, support students to get there themselves.

  - Ask open questions as well as closed questions.

  - Allow students sufficient time to think about work or their responses before requiring an answer or offering help.

  - Avoid spoon-feeding; rather, encourage students to develop strategies they can use when they are stuck.

Quick click

The Education Endowment Foundation report on the use of teaching assistants contains many useful insights and strategies.

https://v1.educationendowmentfoundation.org.uk/uploads/pdf/TA_Guidance_Report_Interactive.pdf

Support learners who have English as an additional language (EAL)

Quick wins

- **Create a buddy system**. Choose a student to support EAL students in your classroom. Reflect carefully on the student you choose; you may find someone who is eager to help and gets a lot out of the experience. Spend time introducing the new student to the buddy and give the supporting students guidance on how to support effectively. Be sensitive to the needs of both students – imagine how you would feel if you were assigned a buddy without any choice.

- **Use buddies to translate.** Where possible, use another student who speaks their language to orally translate commands in the formative months. However, there should not be an over-reliance on these students. As the student becomes more comfortable and picks up language, then this might be the time to move the student so they do not rely on the native speaker.

- **Use 'before reading' strategies.** Consider tasks to support students before they engage with a piece of text. You might introduce key vocabulary, break the text down into smaller sections, or play a video that gives the gist of the text first.

- **Create word banks, posters or tablemats.** Give students access to glossaries of key words on a laminated card or mat that they can access quickly when working.

- **Show an interest in the student's country or culture and make links, if possible, in your teaching.** Some students may be experiencing a sense of alienation or culture shock as they integrate into a new way of life. Try to learn about their background and highlight links in your teaching to make the work relevant to their experiences.

- **Don't judge ability on language - keep expectations high.** It is easy to assume, because a student is not verbally fluent, that they are not intelligent. Consider how you would perform in a foreign language classroom.

- **Teach to students' strengths.** As you get to know your students, you may find that while their written communication is developing, they can communicate effectively in spoken English. Choose activities that allow students to express their learning regardless of the medium. This will provide motivation to develop their skills in other forms of expression.

- **Ensure you communicate in non-linguistic ways.** Consider how you can include visual explanations to support your verbal explanations. Can you show a diagram or a series of pictures? Be careful, though, using confusing images might be counterproductive. I observed a music trainee once where they had a Big Ben image next to the learning objective. In the post-lesson discussion, I asked him why he had put this image on. He shrugged and said in a quizzical voice, 'For the EAL learners'. Consider: does this image bring the word to life?

- **Check that basic lesson survival English is clear.** It is easy to assume that new students will know the meaning of common school vocabulary such as credits or head of year. Think what the key phrases for your classroom are and take the time to check that students are comfortable with them.
- **Try not to over-correct.** Think of the purpose of the language a student is using. If communication is the main aim and they are achieving the goal, resist over-correcting as it can dampen enthusiasm.
- **Have dictionaries available** and, if possible, create lists of keywords translated into appropriate languages.
- **Be patient.** If you have learned a second language you will appreciate the additional cognitive demands of translating an academic question, processing the subject content and then developing an answer. Learning in another language is hard.
- **Smile!** This strategy applies to any student who enters your classroom but remember, these students are potentially in a brand new country let alone a brand new school, so they might feel particularly vulnerable.
- **Use positive body language** so students feel comfortable in your classroom **and make sure EAL students can see your facial expressions.**
- **Avoid colloquial phrases or slang as this might confuse a non-English speaker.**
- **Use teachers who speak the same language** to help you with worksheets where appropriate.
- **Translate key words for students** either on a sheet or on the board.
- **Find opportunities for role play or drama.**
- **Ensure that home languages are valued.**
- **Learn from the students.** Model lifelong learning. They may be in the process of learning English, but you might not be able to speak Urdu, French or Polish!. This forges relationships and shows to the student you are making an effort.

 **Slow burners**

- **Get to know your students and their abilities.** As with all forms of differentiation, knowing your students well is essential. This performs a number of useful functions. First, it makes the students feel valued and welcomed into your classroom. Knowing something about their background can help you structure your teaching and interactions with the student. See beyond their classification as EAL students and learn about their interests and talents. Second, students can have different fluencies in different aspects of language: they may be confident in written English but lack conversational skills.

Find out what kind of topics they have covered in your subject. Their prior knowledge may differ greatly from that of your other students. It may help if you research the common mistakes that learners of different languages make when speaking in English - for example, Japanese speakers commonly miss out articles. A comprehensive list of such mistakes for a number of languages can be found in Swan and Smith (2012). Third, do ask the student what support they need or what strategies they have found useful in other classes.

- **Set up an induction programme for your subject.** Your school will have an induction programme in place to support learners with English as an additional language. In addition, you might want to consider producing a pack of information that introduces students to your subject. Depending on the ability of the students you might prefer to produce a short presentation or a pamphlet with many visual prompts, giving key facts about your subject. It would be useful to provide information on the following topics.

  - Safety rules.

  - Classroom expectations.

  - Information about internal and external assessment.

  - The systems for grading work and homework expectations.

  - A guide to the curriculum areas that have been and will be covered.

It is easy to assume that students can seamlessly pick up the rules of your classroom, but put yourself in the position of going to a school in a different culture. There are all kinds of explicit and implicit rules that a new student will be working hard to assimilate. I recall, when I taught in Japan, that it took a long time to adapt to different cultural norms - for example, sleeping in class was acceptable as students may have been tired from going to extra classes at a private tuition centre. Many of the rules of the classroom are implicit and may be hard for a new student to pick up - for example, is it acceptable to talk during the time you are getting your books out? Try, as far as possible, to empathise with the difficult task of adapting to a novel culture.

- **Support early stage EAL students with appropriate activities.** There will be EAL students who you would have no idea that English is not their first language. EAL students, as any student in the world does, progress at different speeds. This can depend on many factors: how much English is spoken at home; their social interactions at school; their personal confidence and attitudes; their previous experience of learning English in their home country; their motivation to develop the language to name but a few. Therefore, the points below will focus on activities for early stage EAL students. It is important that EAL students are given the opportunities to access work and learning; there are a range of ways you can do this.

  - **Cloze exercises.** Students can fill in words to complete sentences using their dictionaries to help them. This helps them see words in context.

  - **Triangles.** Students can listen to a pair talk about the work or complete a task. This is where the teacher in you will be concerned that your expectations are not high enough. Do not worry. This is a starting point.

  - **Translation.** Students could be given five key words to do with the topic and they have to translate using their dictionaries. Students could write a sentence in their own language and then, for homework, translate it into English.

- **Card sort.** Students could be given images to match up with the corresponding words. Students could then sequence these to tell a story in their own language. There could be a challenge built into this with more words than pictures.
- **Language prompts.** Students could be given sentence starters to help scaffold their oral responses such as: I am . . . , I think . . . , It is . . . .

- **Think about how texts are presented.** It may be the case that some EAL students have greater fluency in spoken English than in writing and processing texts. As students adapt to life in the UK they will have many opportunities to practise speaking and listening, but may have limited exposure to written language. Handing out or projecting chunks of text is a norm in many classrooms, but such information can be intimidating when it is presented in a second language. Consider how you can provide support for EAL students to engage with large blocks of text. The strategies below may be useful.

  - Where possible break large chunks of texts into smaller units.
  - Explain key words in simpler terms before introducing the text.
  - Include visual stimuli to give a sense of the meaning of the text.
  - Read the text aloud.
  - Allow students to work on the text in pairs.
  - Ask a student in the class to summarise the key points of the text.

  All of these strategies may be helpful to other students in the class as well as EAL learners.

- **Structure group work to support learners' difficulties with language.** A major challenge of developing fluency in spoken English is that it can hamper students' ability to engage socially with their peers. It is not uncommon for EAL students to pass through a period when they prefer to remain silent (Krashen and Terrell, 1983). This may simply be a stage in the process of language acquisition and should not automatically be treated as a cause for concern. Remember that the students have the additional cognitive load of processing a new language on top of the academic demands of your subject. You should not be afraid to use group work in classes with EAL students. It can be a powerful tool for supporting language learning, but you will need to plan carefully to ensure that the students are included in the learning of the activity. Consider the following strategies.

  - Place EAL students with learners who are native speakers so they can learn from role models.
  - Ensure the student is aware of key vocabulary necessary for the task. For example, for a practical activity in science, do they know what a beaker and Bunsen burner are?
  - Assign roles and provide a structure that allows turn-taking. Rather than ask students to simply critique the language of a poem, set the expectation that, before discussion begins, each student contributes one feature they think is significant.
  - Prepare a sheet with useful phrases for the student to practise before the lesson. For example, in a debate, they might need phrases such as 'I disagree because . . . ' or 'What is your evidence for that?'.
  - Think of ways for students to engage with the activity in a non-verbal way. Can they match phrases, produce a model or draw something on a whiteboard?

Support students with special educational needs and disabilities (SEND)

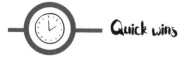

Quick wins

- **Break the lesson into chunks.** As you get to know your students, you will develop a sense for the length of time they can focus on an activity. You may need to plan lessons consisting of a number of short sections to keep the pace high and students focused on the task. Limit the number of concepts you present at one time.

- **Provide scaffolding for texts**. If students struggle with blocks of text, break them into chunks; introduce key vocabulary first; present a visual representation; read the text out loud; show a video with a similar meaning first.

- **Use multiple representations.** Present animations, videos, models, role plays, diagrams or other representations.

- **Simplify instructions**. Plan instructions so they are simple and as short as possible. Students may struggle to complete a series of instructions, so break down tasks into a series of short achievable instructions, which can be interspersed with a short explanation: 'First I am going to give you two minutes to . . .'; 'Okay, now I want you to . . . You have five minutes', etc.

- **Provide a set of bullet points on the board for complex tasks.** When you have asked students to write an extended piece, or carry out a complex task, provide a set of simple bullet points to support them. For example, write the steps of the activity on the board or on cards. Don't assume students can keep a number of steps in their working memory.

- **Teach study skills.** Teach students how to revise by drawing mind maps or making notes. Don't assume they will know how to do this.

- **Set realistic expectations for tasks**. What you assume is an adequate time for a task may be insufficient. As you get to know your students, you will become sensitive to what is a realistic time to complete a task. Talking to other teachers of the students and your TAs might help you decide.

- **Find alternatives to writing such as dictating to a TA or using laptops.**

- **Think about seating locations to minimise distractions.** Knowing your students will help you decide whether being seated next to the window or the heater at the back focuses or distracts a particular student. Experiment and talk to other teachers of the student about their arrangements.

- **Display a timer** so that students can manage their time in tasks efficiently. Some students may find long countdowns – for example, twenty minutes – difficult to respond to, so try to break tasks into relatively short chunks.

- **Reduce unstructured time.** Students may lose focus if they have nothing to do. Ensure that students have an appropriately levelled activity at all times.

- **Provide a clear model of the desired outcome of the task.** This could be your own construction or a previous student's work.

○— **Slow burners** ━━━━━━━━━━━━━━━━━━━━━━━━━

- **Get to know your students**. It may sound clichéd, but your students are individuals. Although a dyslexic student may share some traits with other dyslexic learners, they have their own individual strengths and weaknesses. Use all the information available to you: read the information your SEND department provides, talk to the students about their own views on their abilities, discuss their learning with a TA who knows them well, talk to other teachers and their parents. You may find it useful to shadow a student in a number of other lessons (though do ask permission from the relevant teachers). Observe the kinds of environments and approaches that allow the student to flourish and those that prompt disengagement. Even information about interests and achievements not directly related to school can be useful. I struggled teaching a demotivated student for many weeks before finding out her passion for ice-skating. Although I did include an occasional reference to the sport in my subsequent teaching, the change in our relationship that developed from her knowing that I didn't just see her through her disability was transformative.

- **Explore strategies to support students with specific SENDs.** A huge body of literature exists that detail specific strategies for different learning needs. As with the strategies in this book, it will not be the case that every strategy works for every learner with a particular need but it is worth looking up what has been suggested for particular learners. It is beyond the scope of this chapter to go into the detail of these strategies, but the quick click box below can act as a source of information on specific needs.

○— **Quick click** ━━━━━━━━━━━━━━━━━━━━━━━━━

The following links give useful guidance on how you can support students with common SENDs that you will come across in your classroom.

Asperger's spectrum disorders

www.autism.org.uk/teacherpack

Attention deficit disorder

http://livingwithadhd.co.uk/teacher/teacher-home

Behavioural, emotional and social difficulties

http://bit.ly/2d5GBxM

Dyslexia

http://bit.ly/2daHqBA

Dyspraxia

http://bit.ly/2cjV9c3

Dyscalculia

http://bit.ly/2cxX60B

Hearing impairments

http://bit.ly/2clhNYk

Physical disabilities

http://bit.ly/2coXkcJ

Speech and language impairments

http://bit.ly/2chK9qC

Visual impairment

http://bit.ly/1u9pPN6

- **Design appropriate tasks for your students.** Although it might seem obvious, one of the most challenging but powerful techniques is ensuring that you set students tasks they can achieve with an appropriate level of challenge. If you were presented with tasks that were difficult to understand and criticised for failing to perform, you would likely lose motivation and possibly become upset. Students who find academic work challenging may experience school as a round of activities they find confusing, mixed with punishments for failing to achieve those tasks. Good teaching begins with a thorough knowledge of your students' capabilities and a sufficient understanding of your subject to be able to develop learning activities that are appropriate for your students. This is a skill that takes time to develop, and even experienced teachers get the level of activities wrong sometimes.

Consider a learning objective that requires students to learn the function of the organs in the digestive system. An experienced teacher might run through a number of different options for teaching this aim, and reflect on how a particular class might respond.

- I could show the 3D model torso to give an idea of shape, but that might involve the students sitting and listening too long. Maybe I'll use it, but only for five minutes and turn it into a plenary quiz so the students are actively engaged.

- The questions in the textbook will be too challenging for most of the students in the class, I need to find a different activity.

- There is a worksheet where students cut out the organs and stick them on to a pre-printed diagram. This will take too long and the students will spend 30 minutes cutting and sticking and not learning.

- I could print large versions of the organs and run a whole-class activity in which the students stick the organ on to a life-size outline of the body. This would be nicely visual and would allow everyone to contribute. However, I'll have to keep it short so the students don't get distracted.

– I could create a worksheet which involves simply matching pictures of organs to a single sentence description of their function. All the students could complete this task. What extension could I add for the more able?

Perhaps one of the fundamental principles of good teaching, regardless of students' ability, is knowing your students and teaching accordingly. If your tasks are pitched at an appropriate level and stimulate learning in your students, you are a long way towards having a good lesson.

In summary

Your classes will contain learners with a variety of interests, strengths and weaknesses. To teach them most effectively you should target your teaching to match their needs. Not only will this support more successful learning, but it will likely also improve students' engagement and behaviour in your classes.

Before the lesson

- **Get to know your students** in order to ensure that the work you set your students is appropriate. You will need to use formal and informal assessment to develop an understanding of your students' abilities.

- **Choose or design activities that support and stretch**. Once you have a clear picture of your students' abilities, design tasks that fall into the 'Goldilocks zone' – not so hard that they discourage students, but not so easy that they can be completed without thinking.

- **Experiment with a range of differentiation strategies.** Differentiation doesn't mean you have to create three versions of every worksheet to support different abilities. The 'quick win' strategies above describe a number of ways in which you can plan for differentiation without the need to create new resources for each class.

During the lesson

- **Be sensitive to how your students are performing.** Differentiation doesn't finish with the planning stage. During every lesson you should be looking for signs that individual students are finding the work too easy or too difficult and acting to readjust their learning challenges.

- **Adjust the level of support students receive.** You can adjust the difficulty of tasks students face during the lesson without having to alter the activity. Consider altering the deployment of TAs, providing extra resources such as dictionaries and textbooks or changing grouping to provide or withdraw support.

After the lesson

- **Use feedback from one lesson to differentiate the next.** How students perform on one set of tasks can provide useful information for planning future activities.

- **Talk to your TAs.** Your TAs are likely to have information on how individual students engaged with particular tasks. Try to make time for a short debrief to gain information you can use to plan your next lessons.

Further reading

Sousa, DA and Tomlinson, CA (2011) *Differentiation and the Brain: How Neuroscience Supports the Learner-Friendly Classroom.* Bloomington, IN: Solution Tree Press.

A text that refers to research in neuroscience that underpins classroom approaches to differentiation.

Thompson, J (2010) *The Essential Guide to Understanding Special Educational Needs.* Harlow: Pearson Education.

A good place to start if you would like further information on specific special educational needs and information on how to support students with those needs in the classroom.

Tomlinson, CA (1999) *The Differentiated Classroom: Responding to the Needs of All Learners.* Alexandria, VA: Association for Supervision and Curriculum Development.

If you are interested in learning more about differentiation, this is a good book that discusses a wide range of issues related to differentiation while also listing a number of practical approaches.

Winebrenner, S (2012) *Teaching Gifted Kids in Today's Classroom.* Minneapolis, MN: Free Spirit Publishing.

A good resource that discusses the identification of, and strategies to support highly able students.

References

Aesop, Jr (1899) An educational allegory. *Journal of Education, 50*(14): 235.

Brock, R. (2007) Differentiation by alternative conception: Tailoring teaching to students' thinking. *School Science Review, 88*(325): 97–104.

Csikszentmihalyi, M (1991) *Flow: The Psychology of Optimal Experience.* New York: Harper Perennial.

Department for Education (DfE) (2015) Special educational needs in England: January 2015. London: DfE. Available at: **www.gov.uk/government/uploads/system/uploads/attachment_data/file/447917/SFR25-2015_Text.pdf** (accessed 10 August 2016).

Department of Education and Science (1989) *Discipline in Schools* (Elton Report). London: HMSO.

Department for Children, Schools and Families (DCSF) (2008) *Personalised Learning – A Practical Guide.* London: DCSF. Available at: **http://webarchive.nationalarchives.gov.uk/20130401151715/http://www.education.gov.uk/publications/eOrderingDownload/00844-2008DOM-EN.pdf** (accessed 23 October 2015).

Dweck, CS (1986) Motivational processes affecting learning. *American Psychologist, 41*(10), 1040–1048.

Farrell, M (1999) *Key Issues for Primary Schools.* London: Routledge.

Fraser, C and Meadows, S (2008) Children's views of Teaching Assistants in primary schools. *Education 3–13, 36*(4): 351–63.

Heacox, D (2002) *Differentiation Instruction in the Regular Classroom: How to Reach and Teach All Learners, Grades 3–12.* Thousand Oaks, CA: Corwin Press.

Humphrey, N, Lendrum, A and Wigelsworth, M (2010) *Secondary Social and Emotional Aspects of Learning (SEAL): National Evaluation*. Nottingham: Department for Education.

Jarvis, J (2015) Inclusive classrooms and differentiation, in Weatherby-Fell, N (ed.) *Learning to Teach in the Secondary Classroom* (pp154–71). Melborne: Cambridge University Press.

Kise, J (2007) *Differentiation through Personality Types*. Thousand Oaks, CA: SAGE.

Krashen, SD and Terrell, TD (1983) *The Natural Approach: Language Acquisition in the Classroom*. New York: Pergamon.

McGarvey, B, Morgan, V, Marriott, S and Abbott, L (1996) Differentiation and its problems: The views of primary teachers and curriculum support staff in Northern Ireland. *Educational Studies, 22*(1): 69–82.

Mercer, N (1994) Neo-Vygotskian theory and classroom education, in B Stierer and J Maybin (eds) *Language, Literacy and Learning in Educational Practice* (pp92–110). Clevedon: Multilingual Matters.

Ofsted (2015) The most able students: Are they doing as well as they should in our non-selective secondary schools? Available from: **www.gov.uk/government/uploads/system/uploads/attachment_data/file/405518/The_most_able_students.pdf** (accessed 23 October 2015).

Silberman, S (2015) *Neurotribes: The Legacy of Autism and the Future of Neurodiversity*. Crows Nest, Australia: Allen & Unwin.

Strand, S, Malmberg, L and Hall, J (2015) *English as an Additional Language (EAL) and Educational Achievement in England: An analysis of the National Pupil Database*. University of Oxford, Department of Education. Available from: **https://v1.educationendowmentfoundation.org.uk/uploads/pdf/EAL_and_educational_achievement2.pdf** (accessed 10 August 2016).

Swan, M and Smith, B (eds) (2001) *Learner English: A Teacher's Guide to Interference and other Problems*. Cambridge: Cambridge University Press.

Vygotsky, LS (1978) Interaction between learning and development (trans. M Lopez-Morillas), in M Cole, V John-Steiner, S Scribner and E Souberman (eds), *Mind in Society: The Development of Higher Psychological Processes* (pp79–91). Cambridge, MA: Harvard University Press.

Weston, P, Taylor, M, Lewis, G and MacDonald, A (1998) *Learning from Differentiation*. Slough: NFER.

Wood, D, Bruner, J and Ross, G (1976) The role of tutoring in problem solving. *Journal of Child Psychology and Psychiatry,* 17(2): 89–100.

Wright, O (2014) Dyslexic spies: There are benefits worth waiting for. *The Independent*. Available at: **www.independent.co.uk/life-style/health-and-families/features/dyslexia-there-are-benefits-worth-waiting-for-9749607.html** (accessed 10 August 2016).

Index

Added to a page number 'f' denotes a figure.